REGIONAL ENVIRONMENTAL HISTORY
Issues and Concepts in the Indian Subcontinent

Edited by
VULLI DHANARAJU

REGIONAL ENVIRONMENTAL HISTORY
Issues and Concepts in the Indian Subcontinent
Edited by Vulli Dhanaraju

First Published 2016

ISBN 978-93-5002-426-3

Published by
AAKAR BOOKS
28 E Pocket IV, Mayur Vihar Phase I, Delhi 110 091
Phones: 011 2279 5505, 2279 5641
aakarbooks@gmail.com

Laserset at
Arpit Printographers, Delhi 110 032

Printed at
Saurabh Printer, Greater Noida

Contents

Section III: Culture, Nature and Eco-Feminism

Section IV: Science & Technology and Medicine

Preface and Acknowledgements

The book is divided into four thematic sections covering 14 chapters and introduction by historians and scholars in order to understand the regional environmental history of the Indian subcontinent. Regional history has an importance of its own particularly in a vast country like India with its numerous historical/environmental regions. An appropriate study of the regional history with its historical background is essential to understand the unique features of that particular regional environment. Thus, the scholars will find this book dealing with regional concepts and issues in the study of environmental history in the Indian subcontinent.

For preparing of this edited book I am indebted to the contributors who presented their papers in the National Seminar on *Debating Environmental History: Reading from Regional Discourses* organized by the Department of History, Assam University (Central University), Diphu Campus, Assam, India during November 24-25, 2014 in collaboration with the Indian Council of Historical Research (ICHR), New Delhi. Without these contributors' cooperation and support this book would not have been realized in this form.

I wish to express my gratitude to the Indian Council of Historical Research (ICHR), New Delhi for collaboration and financial assistance in organizing of the National Seminar at the Department of History, Assam University (Central University), Diphu Campus, Assam, India. I also thank the entire faculty and staff of the Department of History, Assam University, Diphu Campus for all their academic and administrative support.

Words fail to express my gratitude to Prof. Y.A. Sudhakar Reddy, Centre for Folk Culture Studies, University of Hyderabad for his intellectual guidance and support. Interacting and engaging with him on various occasions has been a great learning experience and source of intellectual enrichment. Without his exceptional generosity and scholarly support, this book would not have been possible. I am deeply indebted to my teacher, Dr. J. Krishna Prasad Babu, Associate Professor and HoD, Jawahar Bharathi Degree College, Kavali, Nellore, Andhra Pradesh who took a keen interest in my career and gave valuable suggestions to pursue my higher education. He is the person who inspired me to read history during my graduation days at college.

I am thankful to my beloved brother Raju (late) who helped me in many ways, without his support I would not have succeeded in my life. His all round presence in my academic as well as personal life has strengthened my morale and bolstered my spirits to pursue academics in an uninterrupted way. Though he is not around, I still remember his memories which always give immense confidence to my life.

I owe an intellectual debt to Prof. Chinna Rao Yagati, JNU, New Delhi, Prof. B.C. Dash, Assam University, Diphu Campus and Dr. B. Eswara Rao, University of Hyderabad, for their encouragement and support in completing this book. I also extend my special thanks to the distinguished personality in my life, Dr. R.K. Bijeta, Assam University, Silchar for her support and encouragement in completion of this book. Like any other work this edited book is a collective endeavour. My students and friends have always inspired me to expand new ideas that constantly helped me in preparation of this book. I extend my heartfelt thanks to some of my friends, Lokesh, Prabhakar and Harbi Babu for their constant encouragement and support in completion of this book. I also extend thanks to my research scholars particularly, Rupali Rongpipi, Junmoini Hansepi Nukshirenla and Rashmi Engtipi for their assistance in proof reading of this book. This endeavour would not have come to fruition but for the support that I have received from my family members, especially my mother and sisters.

No words are left to express my gratitude to Aakar Books, New Delhi especially Mr. K.K. Saxena for his keen interest in the publication of this book.

Vulli Dhanaraju

Introduction

Ecology and environmental issues have been attracting modern scholars and historians since the 1980s by shaping the historical narratives of Indian history.[1] Human and nature interactions of the past are necessary to understand as it played an important role in changing discourses of regional environmental history of the Indian subcontinent. Environmental factors had an extensive impact on human civilisation and culture.[2] There are several evidences in history where environmental factors changed the course of history such as many foreign invasions and the consequent assimilation of migrant groups from other civilisations into the Indian society that have influenced and altered its approach towards the exploitation of its natural resources and its management in different historical regions.

I

In order to understand the roots of environmental history we need to study the concepts that have developed in the field of ecology and geography in the 19th century. These two subjects are the modern products of the Industrial Revolution. In environmental history, ecological concepts are used to analyse past environments and geographical concepts are used to study the ever-changing face of the earth. The surface of the earth is constantly changing and reshaping under geological, climatic, biological and human forces. At the beginning of the 20th century geographers stressed the influence of the physical environment on the development of human society. The idea of the impact of the physical environment on civilisations was first adapted by the Annales School[3] of Historians to describe the long-term developments that shape human history. Two other roots of environmental history are archaeology and anthropology of which the latter introduced ecology into the human sciences. The emergence of world history, with works by McNeill and Thomas[4] among others, introduced interdisciplinary and continental wide, even world scale studies into history. These were the foundations on which environmental history was founded as an academic field in the 1960s. Rodrick Nas[5] coined the term 'Environmental History' in his article 'American Environmental History: A New Teaching Frontier' that is published in the *Pacific Historical Review* in 1971. He has discussed the impact of past human societies on the environment.

Consciousness towards the environment has been a way of life in the Eastern world. In the West, concern for environment, known as 'Environmentalism', gained attention after the realisation of the consequences of industrialisation and its impact on nature and environment. But the initiation point of the environment concern here itself is in debate. In the conventional Western or, so-called modem social theory, this concern for environment is known as Environmentalism.[6] In 'Environmentalism and Cultural Theory', Kay Milton (1996) writes,

> Environmentalism appears to have grown, over the past thirty years, out of long-standing but relatively low-key minority interests, to become signficant, but far from dominant political influence at national and international level. Environmentalism is a feature of what we have chosen to call 'industrial' society. Within this context, because it is seen as a relatively new and growing phenomenon, analysts often describe it as a social movement. And because it has become an important and distinctive component of political discourse, it is often characterised as an ideology.

Environmental history is a kind of history about human interaction with the natural world or the interaction between culture and nature.[7] Environmental history is one of the emerging areas in the recent past and it has been attracting more research scholars in the recent decades. It is also a new historical trend in modern India. The main goal is to study the interaction between humans and the environment in the past and the relationships between humans and the surrounding world. Donald Worster's[8] definition states that "Environmental history is the interaction between human cultures and the environment in the past." It is the history of the mutual relations between humankind and the rest of nature". It investigates the interactions between society and its physical environment, on symbolic, material and organisational levels. It opens up new perspectives for deciphering contemporary issues related to modifications of landscape, for understanding reoccurring conflicts over the allocation and protection of natural resources, as well as for grasping the complexity and historicity of the social representations and uses of the environment. Man exploits nature for the sake of economic development. There is a growing conflict between economic and technological development on one side and the quality of the environment on the other.

We have hitherto been describing the nature-human interface in the context of human version to the limits determined through nature. Till the advent of agriculture[9] the connection flanked by man and nature was highly tilted in favour of nature, where man was mostly the recipient of the benevolence of nature. Apparatus of the pre-historic ages—Paleolithic, Mesolithic, or Neolithic were basically instruments of facilitation towards the benevolence of nature. Man had to manage with the survival offered through nature and could do little to power the procedures or patterns of nature. The survival pattern of this age was termed as hunters and gatherers and life-approach was itinerant. The civilisation was moving from an easy social structure to an intricate social structure slowly. A fully manifest intricate social structure appeared with the advent of agriculture that helped generate surplus and began the procedure of urbanisation. Up to this time the connection flanked by man and nature was to a considerable extent determined through the harshness/benevolence of nature to existing stages of technology. A qualitative and epoch-creation shift in the nature-human interface became apparent with the onset of the industrial age. The stage of technology of the industrial age liberated man from physical labour and introduced the use of biotic sources of energy that replaced human and animal energy. Since ancient past thermal energy had been used in direct applications, but throughout the industrial age it was used to mechanise apparatus. The industrial age introduced the conversion of thermal energy to mechanical energy, hence expanded the possibilities of its use. The ever rising demands also led to the search for newer shapes of energy and to the detection of hydrocarbons, i.e. coal, petroleum products, etc., as their principal source. Unlike earlier renewable sources of energy, though, hydrocarbons are non-renewable. The introduction of non-renewable sources of energy redefined the connection flanked by nature and man and the concept of the conservation of natural possessions came into subsistence.

Thus, environmental history is always about human interaction with the natural world or, to put it in another way, it studies the interaction between culture and nature. The principal goal of environmental history is to deepen our understanding of how humans have been affected by the natural environment in the past and also how they have affected that environment and with what results.

II

Environmental history is an interdisciplinary discipline[10]. It is necessary for historians to study the history beyond their discipline. Historians must be aware that they should adopt some concepts from other disciplines such as ecology, biology, economics, anthropology, geography and forestry, to understand the interdisciplinary nature of environmental history. However, the contemporary valuation of environmental criteria is different from those used in the past. According to K.J.W. Oosthoek, to analyse the impact of human action on the natural world in the past and the changes caused by this, a historian must use the modern principles of ecology and the environmental sciences.[11] John Opie[12] argues in his introductory article that the environmental historian needs to combine an understanding of the methodology of the general historian with knowledge of modern scientific ecology. He suggests an approach similar to that needed by the historian of science who must know both historical methods as well as a good deal about the content of the natural sciences. As Opie expresses it, environmental history deals not with mankind alone but with mankind in its ties to a natural setting. The science of ecology provides many generalisations and concepts about ecosystems and how they function that may be useful to the environmental historian.

When history became an academic discipline in the 19th century, its foremost inspirations were German philosophers who believed in the power of ideas and who regularly denigrated geography's influence.[13] The insistence on careful documentation, associated with the scientific history of Leopold von Ranke[14], drew historians' attention to the sorts of things that first got written down and then got preserved in libraries and archives, which guided researchers towards political and intellectual history. It almost ruled out consideration of forests, soils, fish, or air pollution as subjects for historical inquiry, or even commentary.

In the early and middle 20th century, members of the French Annales School, particularly Lucien Febvre[15], traced the reciprocal influences of human societies and the environment on a global scale[16] seeking to broaden the horizon of history; they emphasised the importance of geographical settings, thus providing a formative impulse for world environmental history. Annales historians had been writing on environmental issues although they never adopted the term, 'Environmental History' before 1974. Their general approach however proved inspirational for many who have become environmental historians in later periods.

An additional source of inspiration, mainly for US environmental historians, was and to some extent remains, the frontier history of Frederick Jackson Turner and Walter Prescott

Webb, and the explicitly ecological history of the Great Plains of James Malin.[17] These were historians fully alive to the environmental transformations of North America's grasslands that came with Euro-American and to some extent Afro-American settlement, and saw in the process of frontier transformation defining forces in American history. Equally inspirational to US environmental historians, if much less so elsewhere, was the book by the diplomat and polymath George Perkins Marsh, *Man and Nature*, first published in 1864. Marsh argued, as have many environmental historians since, that human action, mainly farming, degraded environments to the point where agricultural production was threatened. His evidence came mainly from his native Vermont and his travels in Italy and the Ottoman Empire, where he held diplomatic posts. Marsh came into vogue again in the 1960s, at least in scholarly circles, in part thanks to the republication of his work in an edition prepared by the geographer David Lowenthal.[18]

George Perkins Marsh's[19] work, *Man and Nature*, first published in 1864, was intended to be a worldwide survey of the ways in which humankind had disturbed nature's harmonies.[20] His familiarity with the Mediterranean countries, Europe, and North America led to an emphasis on those areas, however, and he said little, except in general, about the rest of the world.

Environmental history also profits from various disciplines from history, economic history, the history of science and technology, and some sub-fields within social history, notably agrarian history and urban history. The traffic back and forth across these borderlands is probably greater in African, European, or Chinese environmental history than it is in American, where the emphasis on wilderness and the West remains powerful (although not what it was two decades ago). In the US the border traffic with urban history and the history of technology has attracted some systematic notice.[23]

Environmental history has become an independent field increasingly institutionalised in academics from the 1970s onwards[21]. The first scientific society dedicated to this type of research, the *American Society for Environmental History*, was established in 1977. Jose Augusto Padua observes that the publication of substantively historical/environmental analyses, however, something quite different from the simple proposition of natural influences in human history, began taking shape in the first half of the 20th century and, to some extent, since the 19th century. Thus, to reflect on the genesis and evolution of this field of knowledge, we must bring to bear sociological and epistemological factors.

In academics the first college level course was introduced as 'Environmental History', in 1972 at the University of California at Santa Barbara, by cultural historian Roderick Nash[22], who had published *Wilderness and the American Mind* in 1967, a classic book on the presence of wildlife images in the construction of ideas on North American identity. Explaining the course's concept, which was presented as indicating a new frontier in history teaching, the author explicitly stated that he was also "responding to the cries for environmental responsibility which reached a crescendo in the first months of that year."[23]

The following works also reveal the interdisciplinary nature of environmental history. Richard White's *Land Use, Environment, and Social Change: The Shaping of Island County, Washington* (1980) is one of the foundational texts of the modern field of environmental history. White's research involved field observations of the island landscapes, his methodology borrowed heavily from ecosystem science, and his bibliography cited not only George Perkins Marsh, but the work of natural historians such as Marston Bates, Andrew Clark, John Curtis, Frank Fraser Darling, James Malin, and Carl Sauer, all of whom had contributed to *Man's Role in Changing the Face of the Earth*. White's paraphrase of Darling harked back to an older natural history while calling on a current generation of historians to participate in the interdisciplinary study of the biophysical world: "Frank Fraser Darling, a leading ecologist, has called social history, political history, and natural history the three horses pulling the chariot of the study of human sociology and its relationship with the natural world. But historians have been reluctant to acknowledge their horses, much less harness them."[24]

III

Colonialism was a watershed in the environmental history of India which marked an important landmark to theorise the colonial experience in the context of the colonial state that initiated agendas and policies on forests, agriculture, irrigation, topography, wildlife, flora and fauna. The colonial initiatives created a hegemonic order over nature and its people in colonies. It however, still remains a very significant area for historians to investigate the issues of ecology/environment of India as a region virtually continental in scale and in its degree of internal diversity with immense and varied ecosystems and its topography of landscape contains wide mountain ranges, major hydraulic water bodies, vast forests, deserts, etc. In this perspective, environmental history needs to broaden its research so that it may further advance our understanding of the way in which social-historical formations in the regions have been generated.

The following section deals with various writings about the study of regional environment and ecology that shape the environmental history of India.

Scholars from various perspectives have extensively contributed to the development of environmental history as an independent discipline in the study of pre-colonial India. Francis Zimmermann[25] has examined ancient texts to construct the ecology of the era. He has questioned the practice of equating the term jungle with the forest. Zimmerman has explored the suggestive ecological references from the ancient texts where animals are classified in two groups: *jungla* "those of the arid lands," and *anupa*, "those of the marshy lands" and pointed out that through closely examining such texts we can infer a great deal in relation to the ancient ecology. The recent work of Irfan Habib's *Man and Environment: The Ecological History of India* which shows in recent decades matters relating to ecology, especially under the influence of the debate on climate change.[26] He has briefly outlined the issue of environmental history from the Pleistocene period. Aloka Parasher Sen[27] has tried for the Mauryan era to understand how the state perceived the forest dwellers and sought to subordinate and assimilate them. Geography and the perceived subsistence of the hostile tribes defined the frontiers of the empire and both had to be mastered for the expansion and integration of the state. Ranabir Chakravarti[28] has highlighted the role of hydraulic management in the procedure of resolution in the ancient era. In a similar vein, Elizabeth Whitecombe[29] has argued that irrigation "works were financed through loan capital. Hence, in the sanctioning of constructions the emphasis was necessarily placed on the prospect of their remunerativeness." Mark Poffenberger and Betsy McGean's[30] edited book examines revolutionary changes occurring in the management of India's forests over the past two decades with growing realisation of scarcities of natural resources. It also explores the historical roots of deforestation, the alienation of tribes and their re-entry into resource management. The fourteen articles discuss the institutional, economic, ecological and political implications of this transition in forest control.[31] Chetan Singh[32] largely focuses on the way environment structured human activity over a sizeable period of time. He focuses on the entire Western Himalaya to show the manner in which different elements were integrated into an ecological and social whole.[33] Christopher V. Hill[34] looks at South Asian environment and ecological changes in the modern period. This work is a chronological study of South Asia that emphasises the effect on their environment, and in return the influence of nature on the evolution of human society. Mayank Kumar[35] also looks at the interaction flanked by environment and civilisation in medieval Rajasthan. He has questioned the notion that the traditional civilisations always practised the methods aimed at a prudent use of natural possessions and has cited many cases of use of nature through traditional civilisations in Rajasthan. He cautions that the magnitude of use of natural possessions did multiply manifold under the impact of the Industrial Revolution.

There are divergent ideological streams in Indian environmental history. The first stream of scholars have argued that colonialism is a watershed in the environmental history of India as it disturbed the state harmony in pre-colonial India between the communities and their lived environment.[36] Madhav Gadgil and Ramachandra Guha and others[37] argued that in pre-colonial India, resource utilisation was in harmony with nature and resource sharing in the middle of several strata of civilisation was extremely cordial. The caste civilisation with dissimilar claims on dissimilar possessions led to a state of equilibrium in turn providing stability to the resource demand and supply. Caste was seen as consisting of endogamous groupings that were each marked through a scrupulous economic action and a scrupulous ecological niche. They romanticised the image of the human-environment interaction in the context of Indian environmental history. They also argue that the colonial state advocated "conservation" for its economic and strategic needs and in the process trampled upon the traditional rights of local communities which in turn generated a series of peasant and tribal revolts. They argued that the local communities depended on the forest resources from times immemorial but the colonial government's regulations deprived them of their customary user rights on forest resources. The attention of the British towards the vast forestry of India from the early 19th century was primarily, because of the imperial demand for the oak and, timber needed for ship building for navy and huge demand of the rapid construction of railways in the mid-19th century.[38]

Ramachandra Guha's[39] study on colonial Forests Acts reveals that the Government Act of 1865 and the Indian Forest Act of 1878, established complete colonial monopoly over Indian forest lands. He says, "as the commercial use of forestry began and the construction of roads opened the hills to commercial penetration, traders and Sahukars from the plains came to the mountainous regions and gradually took hold of tribal lands by confiscating properties of the indebted peasants and

Muttadars."[40] David Arnold and Ramachandra Guha's edited work, *Nature, Culture, Imperialism: Essays on the Environmental History of South Asia*[41] outlines the complex relationship between various policies of the colonial state and their forest acts and their negative effect on the livelihood of local communities and, pastoralists, agrarian society and its economy, traditional forest practices by the local communities, colonial models of the hydraulic environment, irrigation systems and their unintended consequences. In this same volume, the articles of Neeladri Bhattacharya, Atluri Murali, Prabhakar and Gadgil deal with a particular combination of ecological features and markers of ecological change in Southern India. The articles of South Asian historians discuss the economic and cultural life, changes in the physical status of forests and pasture, as well as changes in the social institutions governing their use. This is a major area of research for environmental history in the forests of South Asia. They defined, in more than one cultural system, the 'primitive' from the civilised. Vandana Swami's article describes the theories of nature in modern Western social thought. The recently emerging genre of environmental history has covered a small but significant niche for itself in this direction.[42]

The above arguments show that the Indian landscape had altered with the beginning of the colonial era. India's biological diversity was scientifically documented through the colonial policies. It is not only the forest cover, which gives a glaring testimony to the alteration in the landscape of the region. Creation of canal networks in parts of upper India and eastern India led to drastic changes in the landscape of these regions. Rohan D'Souza has pointed out the changes in the Orissa delta due to construction of canals in the initial stage and later on railways to protect the imperial interests. He argues that due to the advance of colonial capitalism the water landscape of Orissa was dramatically transformed from the beginning of the 19th to the middle of the 20th century.

Secondly, David Hardiman's[43] approach is different from other environmental historians. He looks at different views with regard to early conservation measures. He calls it anachronistic to talk about the "conservationist" mentality among Indian forest dwellers for the pre-colonial period, because the idea of conservationism emerged out of the European reaction to the destruction brought by the Industrial Revolution. He criticised the Indian environmental history writings that were based on the assumption that the indigenous is rooted in an ancient wisdom, which is far superior to that of the West. After that research has been shifted from the disastrous effects of colonial rule to a more nuanced narrative emphasising the study of colonialism and pre-colonial India. David Hardiman[44] pointed out in his study on the small-scale water harvesting systems in Gujarat that commercialisation, indebtedness of peasants and agricultural change predated the colonial regime. He suggests that large dam projects of the colonial and the post-colonial state have transformed agriculture and the rural society to such an extent that a return to small-scale dams does not seem viable[45] In a similar way, David Mosse[46] argues in favour of continuous developments suggesting that the construction and maintenance of tanks in South India underwent phases of expansion and intensification as well as decline prior to colonial rule. Sivaramakrishnan[47] has also presented the same view in study of state-formation, commercialisation, agricultural transformation and environmental changes. Sivaramakrishnan's *Modern Forests: State Making and Environmental Change in Colonial Eastern India* examines forest management as a form of government rationality. For him, forest management has to be understood in the wider context of evolution of state power and its intervention in day-to-day life.[48] He also takes up the issue of forestry and environmental change in the eastern part of India. His work contains an important critique of both Guha and Grove, as well as of the dominant model of writing environmental history. According to him, their work derives from the Western, mostly American paradigm. Mainly, what he feels is that South Asian environmental history remains conceptually caught up in the nature-culture dualism, in addition to having a preoccupation with identifying colonialism as a watershed in ecological terms. The author also gives a fair warning about the need to be more careful about the deployment of categories like coloniser and colonised, because their shape and occupants are not always as readily apparent as they might seem. For example, in south-western Bengal, landlords are at times conservationist, and at other times, they exploit forests to their own detriment. Similar ambivalences characterise the peasantries, bureaucrats, and professional foresters. He therefore suggests that rather than simply juxtaposing "Third-World" environmental history against "First-World" environmental history, one should try to see how these are intermixed and interconnected.[49]

Thirdly, the generalisation of first stream assumption was contradicted by Richard Grove.[50] He argued that the colonial state policy first rose in the Island colonies and this ideology was imported to India by the company officials. For him, the British were the pioneers of scientific forestry in India. While, the early phase of British forestry was influenced by personnel belonging to professions like medicine and botany, who were genuinely concerned about the conservation of forests, the environmental degradation that followed in the later years coupled with fear of rebellions, drove the colonial state towards conservation. Several instances of ecologically destructive activities were carried out by pre-colonial regimes as well. Richard Grove has particularly argued against the "golden-ageist" view, rejecting Guha and Gadgil's dismissal of the efforts of colonial conservation and forestry regulation as mere disguises by a subordinate colonial science for resource exploitation and forest control. Through this approach, according to Grove, these authors overlook the innovative and complex nature of early colonial conservation policies of the British in India.[51] Indeed, compared to the systematic ecological changes caused by colonialism, the pre-colonial age might very much look like a golden age of sorts, despite—as Mahesh Rangarajan has pointed out—questions about whether the continuation of traditional land use would have been more effective than company forest departments and the post-1857 regimes in curbing deforestation for timber and other arable cultivation. Nevertheless, it is clear that the pre-colonial age was certainly not the golden age of ecological equilibrium. While there were some customary restraints, such as in the 'sacred groves' and the use of some trees was curtailed, there is enough evidence to support the fact that peasants were constantly clearing the forest for settled cultivation; and in some regimes, such as those of Mohammad bin Tughlaq in the Delhi Sultanate (1325-51), peasants were even rewarded for clearing the forest cover in order to make way for agriculture. On the other hand, there was also a close link between forests and military campaigns, meaning that apart from the need to extend agriculture, forests also became targets of attack in order to extend the military and political power of the rulers and other landed elite; once forests were cleared. In the southern part of India, the emperor Tipu Sultan is also known to have cut and burnt away several miles of trees and bushes during military campaigns. In the north-western part of the country, the Sikh rulers indulged in similar activities. The Talpur Mirs of Sind undertook an extensive afforestation programme in areas near the river Indus in the north-west part of India during the late 18th century, continuing it up to the mid-19th century, and the British had to seek permission to cut wood in these areas.[52]

Rangarajan appropriately designates the situation of forests in the immediate pre-British period as one of 'limited but significant state intrusion'.[53] This also raises the question of the distinctness of the pre-colonial situation from the colonial one as far as ecological issues are concerned. Guha and Gadgil maintain that in the pre-colonial period the village communities had control over forest management, and landlords made limited demands on peasants, quite unlike the situation in the colonial period. On the other hand, Grove has proposed that deforestation had reached significant levels even before the colonial period, and that changes in the colonial era were only a culmination of trends from the earlier period. Making an incisive critique of Grove's position, Rangarajan contends that this part of his argument is simplistic. It overlooks the fact that not only was there a qualitative change as far as deforestation itself is concerned, but it also ignores the important fact that the entire social and political framework within which the colonial regime functioned had subjected the natural resources of the subcontinent to the demands of the transcontinental compulsions under which the colonial regime operated. Moreover, there is as yet no evidence of total collapse or sharp conflicts among communities over ecological issues in the pre-colonial period like those one can find during the colonial period. Thus the comment by Rangarajan that the story of forestry can be more than a subtext in the story of the consolidation of imperial control over India can itself enable a reassessment of the nature of imperial power. The study of forestry can hence provide insights into issues of wider historical significance. His observation that colonial rule was not a seamless web, but was marked by significant changes in the attitudes and interests of rulers, and that the ecological context of imperial forestry was complex enough for it to be more than a mirror of political and economic conflicts, makes particular sense in the face of the hard-line positions. The agenda for ecological history should therefore be to rescue it from the influence of 'revisionist' ('nothing changed') versus 'golden ageist' ('everything changed') assumptions about issues of nature and environment in the subcontinent. A more historically grounded picture of ecological change should be sketched.[54]

The following works and articles have also contributed to the growth of environmental history as an important discipline in Indian universities. Ranjan Chakrabarti's[55] edited volume, *Situating Environmental History* (2007); John McNeill, José Augusto Pádua and Mahesh Rangarajan's[56], edited volume, *Environmental History: As if Nature Existed* (2010); Deepak Kumar, Vinita Damodaran and Rohan D'Souza's[57] edited volume, *The British Empire and the Natural World: Environmental Encounters in South Asia* (2011); Mahesh Rangarajan and K. Shivaramakrishnan's two-volumes, *India's Environmental History* (2012); Nandini S. Kapur's[58], *The Environmental History of Early India: A Reader* (2011), Sumi Krishna's[59] *Agriculture and a Changing Environment in Northeastern India* (2012); Dhirendra

Datt Dangwa's[60], *Himalayan Degradation, Colonial Forestry and Environmental Change in India* (2009); Iftekhar Iqbal's[61], *The Bengal Delta: Ecology, State and Social Change, 1840-1943;* Neena A. Rao's[63] *Forest Ecology in India: Colonial Maharashtra 1850-1950* (2008); Arup Jyoti Saikia's[64], *Forests and Ecological History of Assam, 1826-2000* (2011); Eric A. Strahorn's[65], *An Environmental History of Postcolonial North India: The Himalayan Tarai in Uttar Pradesh and Uttaranchal* (2009); Richard P. Tucker's[66] *A Forest History of India* (2012); S. Abdul Thaha's[67], *Forest Policy and Ecological Change: Hyderabad State in Colonial India* (2009), R. Umamaheshwari's[68], *When Godavari Comes: People's History of a River (Journeys in the Zone of the Dispossessed)* (2014) and a number of articles have shaped and inspired young scholars to write history form the environmental perspective on the Indian subcontinent.

IV

Recently some environmental historians have started to focus on regional environmental history as a way to systematise their study of the interaction between humans and nature. These regions have always existed in Indian culture for a long time. This approach inspires the historians to create a new outlook in writing of environmental history from the regional perspective. Regional history has an importance of its own particularly in a vast country like India with its numerous historical/ environmental regions. A proper study of the regional history with its historical background is necessary to understand the unique features of that particular regional environment. Modern environmental historians argue that historians need to understand the complex relationship between humans and nature on the regional level if you are to understand it at all. Dan Flores's work[69], 'Place: An Argument for Biological History' has been prominent in the making of the argument that the particularism of distinctive regions fashioned by human culture's peculiar fascination interpretations with all the varieties of topography, climate and evolving ecology that defines landscapes—and the continuing existence of such regions despite the homogenising forces of the modern world—ought to cause environmental historians to realise one of their most crucial tasks is to write well what might be called 'bioregional historians'. He argues that attention to the environment is necessary and important if we are to understand the past and if we are to create a usable past for an environmental future. But for the time being, they say, environmental historians should focus on getting it right about specific places without too much in the way of lofty purpose.

Apart from this argument there have been recent developments in the history of environment as the present environmental historians/scholars have employed the exploitation versus conservation approach in regional contexts in the Indian subcontinent. The studies so far highlighted the local peculiarities and specificities and interaction with the broad agenda of environmental changes with consequence of the transformation of landscapes into resource generating zones during the colonial period. Most of these micro level studies thinly documented the complex interaction between man and nature and its manifestations with regional peculiarities and specificities and interactions.

V

The book is divided into four thematic sections covering 14 chapters by historians, scholars and other experts on environmental history. Thus, the readers will find this book dealing with regional concepts and issues in the study of environmental history in the Indian subcontinent.

Section I: History and Environment

The main focus of this section is to understand the importance of environment and ecology in the history of the Indian subcontinent. Manash Mazumdar's chapter, *Understanding Ecology, Technology and Agrarian Expansion of Early Assam (From the Earliest Time to the 12th Century CE)* highlights the relationship between ecology, technology and agrarian expansion in the early period of Assam. The geographical expression of early

Assam basically denotes present Assam, part of the sub-Himalayan region, some portions of North Bengal and some part of Sylhet of present Bangladesh. The history of agriculture of the region can be studied in two broad aspects: pre metal and metal rather agrarian economy in hill and plains land. He has mentioned two views in understanding agricultural expansion. One view holds that the plough powered by cattle was brought by the Indo-Aryans supported by the knowledge of Sanskrit and much advance production technology. The other view holds that much in advance before the coming of the Indo-Aryans, the practice of wet rice was known to different ethnic communities. He has concluded his chapter by highlighting the progress of material advancement and progress towards new settlements within the environmental backdrop with various flora and fauna, development of agrarian technology and production therein. Nandini Sinha Kapur's chapter, *Bhils in Conservation: Aspects of Agrarian History and Sacred Groves in Southern Rajasthan* examines historical/inscriptional sources and ethnographic data in reading the trajectory of agrarian expansion and its environmental dimension in southern Rajasthan by highlighting the issues of deforestation, afforestation and also management and depletion of water resources. This chapter supports the view that the local forest officials of Udaipur district in Rajastan who mention that some of the trees in the local sacred groves are more than 500 years old. Processes of agricultural expansion parallel to state formation processes between early medieval and medieval period in Mewar was an integrative process in which Bhils from core areas (location of Udaipur and its copper belt and Zawar mines) appear in inscriptional records as village watchmen and witnesses to royal land grants by the 13th century. Thus, this chapter argues that philosophy and knowledge of environmental protection need not necessarily have been pre-historic or post-Forest Act of 1878 of the British colonial administration but can be situated in the long drawn out processes of Rajput state formation in Mewar (districts of Udaipur, Chittorgarh, Bhilwara and Rajsamand) and districts of Dungarpur and Banswara in the medieval period. Secondly, Bhils who were already worshipping goddess-cults of forests (Samoli Inscription of AD 646 about the temple of Aranyavasini) adopted the cult of Shiva by the 15th century in southern Rajasthan as is evident from the temple-text of Ekalingamahatmya (the royal temple-complex of Mewar in Udaipur district.)

Hashik's chapter, *Sacred Groves and Social Formation: Towards Environmental History of Kerala* argues that the natural environment and changes take different meanings depending on the social and cultural symbols associated with them. Combining both their physical origins and the cultural overlay of human presence, reflect the living synthesis of people and places vital to identity formation, be it local or cultural or national. Landscapes character and quality help to define the self-image of a region, its sense of place that differentiates it from other regions. There are many sacred groves attached to the shrines and worshipping places on the banks of Bharathappuzha in Kerala which eventually became the basis for the existence of different cultural practices. The entire stretch of the banks is an ensemble of many *thattaka* (jurisdiction) of goddesses and in due course it became the epi-centre of the life of the people around it. The interaction between *thattaka* and people manifest the complexity of social formation of each region. Within this backdrop an attempt is being made to delineate the sacred grove and the *thattaka* in the different regions on the banks of Bharathappuzha from an environmental perspective. Thus, the limited works produced related to the natural landscape and its influence over the cultural construction was either confined to romanticise the existence of rivers and more explanatory in nature. Thus, this chapter tries to look at the construction of regional history based on the various discourses on the natural landscapes by taking an individual river for a comprehensive study. It also helps to understand the socio-economic formations of communities from the perspectives of environmental history. Samuel Berthet's chapter, *Knowledge Systems (KS), History and Environment in South Asia* emphasises present discourses in environmental history. He argues that environmental history faces the challenges by three issues such as quantity and quality, subject to the variables of geomorphology, demography and climates; modernity and pre-modernity, colonial and pre-colonial, linked to the first issue, plus the question of the nation states and languages and systems of knowledge and value systems, linked to second issue, with the linguistic aspect as a pivotal one. He argues that ecology and environment should be studied by understanding social scientists such as Foucault, Levis Strauss, Barthes, etc. It is being articulated by more recent ones like Augustin Berque, François Jullien in the context of questioning altérité and otherness. He also emphasised how languages are a crucial tool in the mediation of environment in South Asia studies. And how and when this dimension is included development prove successful and when not inevitably seem to doomed to fail. This linguistic dimension has to be related with the language policy carried on since the colonial period in South Asia and still affecting the conception of environment during the post-colonial rule.

Section II: Colonialism, Forests and Environment

Colonialism and forest policies in India have recently been a subject matter of prolonged discussion among social scientists including historians, economists, sociologists and anthropologists. Historians today stress environmental history at the local level particularly the forest policies in various places, cultural and environmental diversity and conservation of forests in India. The colonial forest policies had a number of ruinous consequences for many nomadic and pastoral communities and for people surviving on hunting and gathering of forest produce and based on shifting cultivation. These policies enforced an unnatural separation between agriculture and forests. Many of the customary rights exercised by rural and tribal people were abolished while the use of forests was determined according to the commercial priorities of colonialism.

Geetashree Singh's chapter, *Contesting Colonial Hunting: Impact of the Wildlife Policies in Assam* examines the origin of the

British policies and legislation towards wildlife and their impact on local communities in Assam. Colonial hunting emerged as an imperial ideology that reflects the changing nature of the colonial state towards forest communities in Assam. Due to a perceived connection between hunting, power and privilege played an important role in understanding of social relations in colonial Assam. This chapter mainly discusses the impact of the wildlife policies as a part of forest polices in Assam. Most of the forest dwellers of Assam depended on the forests for their livelihood but after the acquisition of Assam by British they were considered as the greatest threat for the wild animals as they shared the same place and resources. Dinjangam Riamei's chapter, *Colonial Forest Resource Management and Ecology in Manipur* examines the forest resources management which is the main source of livelihood for the people of Manipur, especially the hills people. The forestation and subsequent use of forest land during the colonial period and their mode of exploitation of forest resources are detailed. Vulli Dhanaraju's chapter, *Colonialism, Tribals and Podu Cultivation: Studying from Andhra Agency Areas* proposes to examine how the colonial state, in the name of philanthropic strategies, imposed several restrictions on tribal areas and their *Podu* cultivation with support of local rulers who were mainly responsible for the implementation of colonial policies in Agency areas. This chapter mainly argues that the impact of the British rule over the tribal areas can be viewed as a conflict between two opposing forces. For the British it is a struggle for power and maintenance of the status quo and for the tribes it is a struggle for their very survival. In this context the chapter analyses the impact of the colonial forest policy on *Podu* cultivation in the Andhra Agency of Madras Presidency. The *Podu* cultivation essentially provides the bare requirement of tribals for survival rather than generating surplus and profit. Nevertheless, it plays a vital role in the economy of tribals as it ensures food supply almost round the year. Over the ages it has become an inalienable part of their life and culture with a number of ceremonies built around it.

Section III: Culture, Nature and Eco-Feminism

The interaction between nature and culture is central to any discourse on environment. However, concern for environment in recent times is believed to have originated from the perceived ecological crisis that seems to threaten human civilisation. Notwithstanding this newly emerged concern for the protection of environment, the relationship between man and nature and its celebration has been going on in human societies for ages. However, the pace with which human society has developed over the last few centuries (aided and abetted by progress in science and technology and spread of the processes of urbanisation and industrialisation) has resulted in casting a shadow on this relationship between man and nature that existed in the past.

Secondly, in recent years there has been a growing debate about gender and environment highlighting women's role in the use and management of the natural resources. There are a number of studies which have shown that environmental degradation is a gender process, generated mainly by human exploitative activities. These studies have shown that the poor and marginal groups especially staying in the rural/hill areas, depend directly on nature for their subsistence or survival process of environmental degradation. In the last few years the focus has increasingly been on specific suffering of the poor and marginal women especially in India.

Pradip Chattopadhyay's chapter, *Interface Between Nature and Culture: Exploring Santal Viewpoints in the Past* deals with the relationship between nature and culture among the Santal tribes in central India by exploring various perceptions in the past. Santals, lived amid nature, surrounded by hills, forests, rivers and other natural manifestations. These elements provided them their sources of sustenance and also constituted an integral part of their culture. He argues that all the past symbols of Santal identity like gods and goddesses, totem and tattoos, fairs and festivals, including numerous other beliefs and practices, were related to nature. So nature not only provided the context but also acted as an important variable for the formation of Santal identity. Any change taking place in the physical atmosphere of the region is, therefore, bound to impact upon their views and values of life. Reep Pandi Lepcha's chapter, *Traversing Mediums of Environmental Discourse: Pursuance for Panacea* has attempted that environmental discourses are communicated using various platforms. This chapter has considered two mediums like popular media and folktales to vocalise problems and discusses possible solutions. When it comes to such attempts, leading Japanese director Hayao Miyazaki spent a lifetime foregrounding issues of environmental importance through his productions at the same time providing epiphanic moments of solutions. Hence, the first part of the chapter covers an eco-critical analysis of Miyazaki's animations: *Princess Mononoke* and *My Neighbour Totoro* to concentrate on environmental predicaments prompted by human interface. In this context she explores regional aspects by contextualising the heart of environmental discourse with the help of folktales; a source of wisdom and environmental history. These narratives concentrate on a harmonious relationship shared by humans with nature and how beliefs surrounding these systems stand to reinforce and safeguard this harmony. Focusing particularly on Lepcha folktales, she considered the current state-of-affairs triggered by unbridled development on nature and how folktales have found endorsement in evoking a sense of nostalgia, thus fuelling environmental protests. Reflecting on both the mediums, this chapter summarised the apathy which plagues the conservational scenario, despite appropriate measures finding their stronghold.

Resenmenla Longchar's chapter, *Understanding the Relation Between Religion and Environment of the Ao-Nagas Through the Ritual Process* examines the different gods (*tsungrems*) associated with the environments of the Ao-Nagas and sees the ritual process of a major ceremony (*among*) *Lijabamong* observed by the people in order to balance nature from disequilibrium. It also shows how the Ao-Nagas in particular till date retain their traditional beliefs and practices, at least symbolically to endure their cultural continuities and thus establish the past-present-future continuum of their societal values and norms. The domain of religion is highly pervasive as it represents not only the cultural beliefs and practices including moral codes, rituals and spiritual ideologies but also mythology that speaks about the creation, nature and purpose of the universe and the role of a god, gods or other superhuman agencies therein. Ngamjahao Kipgen's chapter, *Forests, Ecology and Traditional Knowledge: A Kuki Woman's Perspective in the Northeast* examines the relationship between the natural resource management and ritual practices of the traditional Kukis in history. He has explored the social and ecological world of the Kukis through their folklore, rituals and stories about their use of forests and agricultural practices. This chapter draws insights from agricultural rituals relating to Kuki women and seeks to demonstrate the links between nature and culture and argues that women are close to nature and they can nurture and conserve the resources better. It is vital to remember the female's gifts and wisdom and also healing in the form of both food and spiritual sustenance comes traditionally not through men but through woman. By drawing on the literature of eco-feminism and by taking up a feminist perspective, this chapter tries to understand some of the best (socio-cultural) practices of sustainability to restore the ecological health of the environment.

Section IV: Science & Technology and Medicine

The process of industrialisation introduced modern methods of manufacturing in this country. The traditional methods of production which were based on traditional and inherited skills and poor technology started disappearing as industrialisation gathered momentum. The traditional form of manufacturing was confined to rural areas and the modern methods were adopted in urban industries. Industrialisation has brought about a great deal of changes in the lifestyle of people. It plays a great role in the development of advanced nations to such an extent that the word industrialisation has become synonymous with development. But the contemporary scientific and technological development has created a threat to environment. This threat has reached an extent that challenges the very existence of mankind. Secondly, recent works in ethno-medicine are the pioneer of natural attempts to combat human afflictions. Their history itself witnesses how they paved their way to classic medicine. The desire and effort to heal ailments has gone by the name of 'medicine' in any society, whether advanced or aboriginal. Through the ages, the knowledge, practices and innovations of worldwide ethnic communities, has been turned into traditions, whether written or oral. Medicine is one such manifestation of traditions.

Abhinandan Saikia's chapter, *Change, Cosmology, and Time in Innovation: The Idea of Non-Obsolescence in Shifting Cultivation* argues that for many scholars, adapting to change is nothing but a Schumpeterian innovation which leads to obsolescence of technology. Nevertheless the merit of this discourse is contested when technology is considered as a non-obsolescent entity, a phenomenon still prevalent in some agricultural communities. These communities practise shifting cultivation where knowledge system is primarily inherited from nature and has a relationship with cosmology. To understand this debate, a fieldwork is undertaken in Nagaland. Nagaland is a state in India which is mainly based on agricultural economy. Shifting cultivation, locally called jhum is operational in 90 per cent of the area. A mixed methodology framework is designed to carry out this study. V. Raj Mahammadh's chapter, *Environmental Diseases and Medical Reactions in Twentieth Century South India* attempts to analyse the environmental diseases and Western medical reactions in 20th century colonial South India. The main focus of the chapter is to highlight the environmental diseases and its impact on mortality and how the colonial government reacted towards the spread of epidemics and the methods they adopted to combat the diseases. Epidemic diseases have been occurring in all parts of the world since times immemorial. These affected a whole people or community, while the social and environment disruption promoted and often spread into epidemics to particular regions. Epidemics have caused a lot of morbidity and mortality among populations. The early 20th century provides valuable insights into the period that witnessed the growth of tropical diseases in the form of epidemics and their effect on millions of population in south India. The environmental diseases like cholera, plague, smallpox, dysentery, malaria, and diarrhoea, were most feared epidemics; these not only induced massive fatalities, but also caused disruption of ordinary life of people and the economy of the country. He argues in this chapter that the colonial and indigenous medicine failed to locate these epidemics in the larger system of public health and as a result the policy and administrative responses have turned out to be for a temporary period and not for setting up a system with a long-term plan of action. Nitish Mondal's chapter, *Malaria and Ecology in Northeast India: A Review* evaluated the existence of heterogeneity, variability, mortality and morbidities and transmission of malaria risks in the diverse ecological niches of northeast India. The scope and challenges in the improvement of several coping strategies, accessibility to health services, improved surveillance and forecasting technology capacities in the vulnerable populations have been evaluated and argued in relation to malaria prevalence.

The proposed edited book intends to be introspective of the historical environment by drawing attention to environmental policies, implementation and its impact at the regional level. It also proposes to draw attention to how the colonial and post-colonial Indian state, in the name of conservation, imposed several restrictions on indigenous people with support of statecraft that were mainly responsible for the implementation of environmental policies. The main attempt of the book is to find the gaps and problems in the existing research by exploration of regional environmental history and issues in the Indian subcontinent. It also explores the new areas, debates, concepts and perspectives related to mode of resources used by study of regional differences/variations which plays an important role in the broadening of the environmental history as interdisciplinary subject. This would further enable historians/scholars to study the history of the different regions from an environmental perspective.

NOTES AND REFERENCES

1. Madhav Gadgil and Ramachandra Guha, *This Fissured Land: An Ecological History of India*, Oxford University Press, New Delhi, 1994; Amita Baviskar, *In the Belly of the River: Tribal Conflicts Over Development in the Narmada Valley*, Oxford University Press, New Delhi, 2005; Richard Grove, *Green Imperialism: Colonial Expansion, Tropical Island Edens and the Origins of Environmentalism, 1600-1860*, Cambridge University Press, Cambridge, 1996.
2. The following works have greatly influenced the environmental history; William Cronon, *Changes in the Land*, Hill and Wang, New York, 1984; William Cronon, *Nature's Metropolis*, Norton, New York, 1992; Robert MacCameron, 'Environmental Change in Colonial New Mexico', *Environmental History Review*, 18:2, Summer 1994, pp. 17-39; Roderick Nash, *Wilderness and the American Mind*, Yale University Press, New Haven, 2002; John Opie, *Nature's Nation*, Holt Rinehart and Winston, New York, 1998; Theodore Steinberg, *Nature Incorporated*, University of Massachusetts Press, Amherst, 1994; Joel Tarr, *The Search for the Ultimate Sink: Urban Pollution in Historical Perspective*, University of Akron Press, Akron, 1996; Elliott West, *The Way to the West*, University of New Mexico Press, Albuquerque, 1995; Donald Worster, *Dust Bowl*, Oxford University Press, New York, 1982; Carolyn Merchant, *The Death of Nature: Women, Ecology, and the Scientific Revolution*, Harper & Row, New York, 1980; Merchant, *Radical Ecology: The Search for a Livable World*, Routledge, New York, 1992; Robert M. Rakoff, 'Doing Original Research in an Undergraduate Environmental History Course', *The History Teacher*, Vol. 37, No. 1, November, 2003, pp. 29-37.
3. The *Annales* School is one of the most important developments in 20th century history-writing, formally emerged with the foundation of the journal *Annales d'histoire economique et sociale* (*Annales* of Economic and Social History) in 1929 by Marc Bloch and Lucien Febvre. In terms of thematic range and methodological innovations, this School remained foremost in France and influenced history-writing in many other countries for decades and had followers all over the world.
4. Cited in K.J.W. Oosthoek, *Environmental, History Resources Website* (Accessed on March 12, 2015).

5. Roderick Nash, 'American Environmental History: A New Teaching Frontier', *Pacific Historical Review*, 41, August 1972, pp. 362-72.
6. Kay Milton, *Environmentalism and Cultural Theory: Exploring the Role of Anthropology in Environmental Discourse,* London and New York, Routledge, 1996.
7. J.R. McNeill, *Something New Under the Sun: An Environmental History of the Twentieth Century World*, Norton, 2001; J.R. McNeill, 'Observations on the Nature and Culture of Environmental History', *History and Theory*, Vol. 42, No. 4, December, 2003; Donald Worster, *Nature 's Economy: A History of Ecological Ideas,* Cambridge University Press, London: 1977; Emmanuel Le Roy Ladurie, *Times of Feast, Times of Famine: A History of Climate Since the Year 1000*, Doubleday, Garden City, 1971; Keith Thomas, *Man and the Natural World: Changing Attitudes in England, 1500-1800,* Oxford University Press, Oxford, 1996.
8. Donald Worster, *Dust Bowl and Rivers of Empire: Water, Aridity, and the Growth of the American West*, Oxford University Press, New York, 1978; Donald Worster, *Nature's Economy: The Roots of Ecology*, Sierra Club Books, San Francisco, 1977; Worster, Donald Worster, *Dust Bowl and Rivers of Empire: Water, Aridity, and the Growth of the American West*, Oxford University Press, New York, 1978; Worster, *Dust Bowl and Rivers of Empire: Water, Aridity, and the Growth of the American West*, Pantheon, New York, 1985; Donald Worster, *The Wealth of Nature*, Oxford University Press, 1993; Donald Worster, *Nature's Economy: A History of Ecological Ideas,* Cambridge University Press, New York,1985; Donald Worster, 'Ecological History', in Carolyn Merchant (ed.), *Major Problems in American Environmental History*, D.C. Heath and Company, Lexington, 1993; Donald Worster, 'History as Natural History: An Essay on Theory and Method', *Pacific Historical Review* 53, February 1984: pp. 1-19; Norman L. Christensen, 'Landscape History and Ecological Change', *Journal of Forest History* 33, July 1989, pp. 116-125; Richard White, 'Environmental History, Ecology, and Meaning', *Journal of American History*, 76, March 1990, pp. 1111-1116; Clarence J. Glacken, *Traces on the Rhodian Shore: Nature and Culture in Western Thought from Ancient Times to the End of the Eighteenth Century*, University of California Press, Berkeley, 1967; Keith Thomas, *Man and the Natural World: A History of the Modern Sensibility, 1500-1800,* Pantheon Books, New York, 1983; Alexander Wilson, *The Culture of Nature: North American Landscapes from Disney to the Exxon Valdez*, Blackwell,

Cambridge,1992; José Augusto Pádua, 'The Theoretical Foundations of Environmental History', *estudos avançados*, 24 (68), 2010.

9. The beginning of agriculture, considered to be a momentous event in nature-human interface, is generally associated with the Neolithic Revolution. The ground stone artifacts of this period which were well rounded and had smooth long edges made the cultivation of soil an easier process. Once man took to agriculture several very significant changes followed that may be legitimately called as heralding the beginning of a new phase in man's relationship with the environment. Human dependence on the resources of nature for survival ended. Production of wheat, barley, rice, millets, etc allowed them to get their own food. They also began do domesticate some species of animals both for supplies of milk and meat as well as for harnessing their labour for various purposes. This was a completely new relationship with the environment and its resources.
10. Eugene P. Odum, 'The Emergence of Ecology as a New Integrative Discipline', *Science* 195, March 1977; Richard White, 'American Environmental History: The Development of a New Historical Field', *Pacific Historical Review* 54, August 1985, pp. 297-335.
11. Cited in K.J.W. Oosthoek, *Environmental History Resources Website*, Accessed on Deceber 4, 2014.
12. John Opie, 'Environmental History: Pitfalls and Opportunities', *Environmental Review*, 7, 1983, pp. 8-16; John Opie, *Nature's Nation: An Environmental History of the United States*, Harcourt Brace College Publishers, 1998.
13. R. Mcneill, 'Observations on the Nature and Culture of Environmental History', *History and Theory*, Theme Issue 42, December 2003.
14. Leopold von Ranke (1795-1886), the 19th century German historian, is generally considered as the founding father of the scientific approach in the study of history.
15. Lucien Febvre, *A Geographical Introduction to History*, New York, 1925.
16. Cited in J. Donald Hughes, 'Global Dimensions of Environmental History', *Pacific Historical Review*, Vol. 70, No. 1 , February 2001, pp. 91-101.
17. Frederick Jackson Turner, 'The Significance of the Frontier in American History' in American Historical Association, *Annual Report for the Year 1893*, Washington, 1893, pp. 199-227; Walter

Prescott Webb, *The Great Plains*, Ginn, Boston, 1931; Walter Prescott Webb, *The Great Frontier*, Houghton Mifflin, Boston, 1952; James Malin, *The Grassland of North America: Prolegomena to Its History*, Lawrence, Kansas, 1947; 'Environmental History', *History and Theory*, Theme Issue 42, December 2003.

18. Cited in R. Mcneill, 'Observations on the Nature and Culture of Environmental History', *History and Theory*, Theme Issue 42, December 2003; David Lowenthal, *Man and Nature*, Harvard University Press, 1965.
19. George Perkins Nash, "American Environmental History: A New Teaching Frontier," *Pacific Historical Review*, 363, 1974, pp. 362-372.
20. J. Donald Hughes, 'Global Dimensions of Environmental History', *Pacific Historical Review*, Vol. 70, No. 1 (February 2001), pp. 91-101.
21. Jose Augusto Padua, 'The Theoretical Foundations of Environmental History', *Estudos Avançados*, 24 (68), 2010.
22. Roderick Nash, *Wilderness and the American Mind* in 1967 (Cited in José Augusto Pádua, 'The Theoretical Foundations of Environmental History', *Estudos Avançados*, 24 (68), 2010.
23. Roderick Nash coined the term "environmental history" in an article in the *Pacific Historical Review* in 1972.
24. Richard White, *Land Use, Environment, and Social Change: The Shaping of Island County, Washington*, (University of Washington Press, Seattle, 1980; (Cited in Mark Fiege, 'Towards a History of Environmental History in the National Parks', *George Wright Forum*, Vol. 28, No. 2, 2011, pp. 128–147).
25. Francis Zimmermann, *The Jungle and the Aroma of Meats: An Ecological Theme in Hindu Medicine*, Motilal Banarsidass, Delhi, 1999.
26. Irfan Habib, *Man and Environment: The Ecological History of India*, Tulika Books, New Delhi, 2010.
27. Aloka Parasher Sen, 'Of Tribes, Hunters and Barbarians: Forest Dwellers in the Mauryan Period', *Studies in History*, 14, 2,1998.
28. Ranabir Chakravarti, 'The Creation and Expansion of Settlement and Management of Hydraulic Resources in Ancient India', in Richard Grove, Vinita Damodaran, and Satpal Sangwan (eds.), *Nature and the Orient: The Environmental History of South and South East Asia*, Oxford University Press, Delhi, 1998.
29. Elizabeth Whitecombe, *Agrarian Conditions in Northern India*, Volume 2, University of California, Berkeley, 1972.

30. Mark Poffenberger and Besty McGean (eds.), *Village Voices and Forest Choices: Joint Forest Management in India*, Oxford University Press, New Delhi, 1998.
31. Ibid.
32. Chetan Singh, *Natural Premises: Ecology and Peasant Life in the Western Himalaya, 1800*-1950, Oxford University Press, Delhi, 1998.
33. Ibid., pp. 252-53.
34. Christopher V. Hill, *South Asia: An Environmental History, Nature and Human Societies,* ABC-CLIO, 2008.
35. Mayank Kumar, 'Claims on Natural Resources: Exploring the Role of Political Power in Pre-Colonial Rajasthan, India', *Conservation and Society: An Interdisciplinary Journal Exploring Linkages Between Society, Environment and Development*, Vol. 3, Issue 1, 2005, pp. 134-149.
36. Madav Gadgil and Ramachandra Guha, *This Fissured Land: An Ecological History of India*, Oxford University Press, New Delhi, 1994 .
37. Ramachandra Guha, 'Writing on Environmental History in India', *Studies in History*, Vol. 9, 1993, pp. 119-129; Ramachandra Guha, 'The Making of 1878 Forest Act; An Early Environmental Debate', *Indian Economic and Social History Review,* Vol. 27, 1990, pp. 68-75; (Ramchandra Guha,'Forestry in 'British and Post-British India: A Historical Analysis', *Economic and Political Weekly,* 20 (1985), p. 1893).
38. Ramachandra Guha, 'Writing on Environmental History in India', *Studies in History*, Vol. 9, 1993, pp. 119-129.
39. Ramachandra Guha, 'The Making of 1878 Forest Act; An Early Environmental Debate', *Indian Economic and Social History Review,* Vol. 27, 1990, pp. 68-75.
40. One of the important system in the Agency administration was the *Muttadari* system in south India. The '*mutta*' means small district or sub-divisions of a country. Groups of villages in the accessible and backward hill tracts came to be held as revenue units called '*muttas*' and the intermediary who collected the revenue and paid a certain amount of it to the government was a *Muttadar*. A *Muttadar* was only a revenue collector and not a cultivator of land. To ensure against losses in revenue collections he got a percentage as commission.
41. David Arnold and Ramachandra Guha (eds.), *Nature, Culture, Imperialism: Essays on the Environmental History of South Asia,* Oxford University Press, Delhi, 1996.
42. Vandana Swami, 'Environmental History and British Colonialism

in India: A Prime Political Agenda', *The New Centennial Review*, 2003.

43. David Hardiman, *Peasant Resistance in India 1858-1914*, Oxford University Press, Delhi, 1992.
44. David Hardiman, 'Small-dam Systems of the Sahyadris', in David Arnold and Ramachandra Guha (eds.), *Nature, Culture, Imperialism: Essays on the Environmental History of South Asia*, Oxford University Press, 1996, Delhi, pp. 185- 209.
45. Ibid.
46. David Mosse, *The Rule of Water: Statecraft, Ecology and Collective Action in South India*, New Delhi, Oxford University Press, 2003, pp. 1-27.
47. K. Sivaramakrishnan, *Modern Forests: State Making and Environmental Change in Colonial Eastern India*, Oxford University Press, Delhi, 1999. K. Sivaramakrishnan, 'Conservation and Production in Private Forests: Bengal, 1864-1914', *Studies in History*, Vol. 14, No. 2 n.s. 1998, pp. 237-264); (Also cited in Michael Mann, 'Environmental History and Historiography on South Asia: Context and Some Recent Publications', *Südasien-Chronik-South Asia Chronicle* 3/2013, S. 324-357, Südasien-Seminar der Humboldt-Universität zu Berlin).
48. K. Sivaramakrishnan, *Modern Forests: State Making and Environmental Change in Colonial Eastern India*, Oxford University Press, Delhi, 1999.
49. Ibid.
50. Richard H. Grove, *Green Imperialism: Colonial Expansion, Tropical Edens, and the Origins of Environmentalism, 1600-1860*, Oxford University Press, Delhi, 1995.
51. Ibid.
52. Mahesh Rangarajan, *Fencing the Forest: Conservation and Ecological Change in Central Provinces 1860-1914*, Oxford University Press, Delhi, 1996.
53. Richard Grove, Vinita Damodaran, and Satpal Sangwan (eds.), *Nature and the Orient: the Environmental History of South and South East Asia*, Oxford University Press, Delhi, 1998.
54. Ibid.
55. Ranjan Chakrabarti (ed.), *Situating Environmental History*. Manohar, Delhi, 2009.
56. John McNeill, José Augusto Pádua and Mahesh Rangarajan (eds.), *Environmental History: As if Nature Existed*, Oxford University Press, New Delhi, 2010.

57. Deepak Kumar, Vinita Damodaran and Rohan D'Souza (eds.), *The British Empire and the Natural World: Environmental Encounters in South Asia,* Oxford University Press, New Delhi, 2011.
58. Nandini S. Kapur, *Environmental History of Early India: A Reader,* Oxford University Press New Delhi, 2011.
59. Sumi Krishna, *Agriculture and a Changing Environment in Northeastern India,* Routledge, New Delhi, 2012.
60. Dhirendra Datt Dangwal, *Himalayan Degradation: Colonial Forestry and Environmental Change in India,* Cambridge University Press India, New Delhi, 2009.
61. Iftekhar Iqbal, *The Bengal Delta: Ecology, State and Social Change, 1840-1943.* Palgrave-MacMillan, London and New York, 2010.
62. Mahesh Rangarajan and K. Sivaramakrishnan (eds.), *India's Environmental History.* 2 Vols. Vol. 1: *From Ancient Times to the Colonial Period: A Reader,* Vol. 2: *Colonialism, Modernity, and the Nation,* Permanent Black, New Delhi, 2012.
63. Neena A. Rao, *Forest Ecology in India: Colonial Maharashtra 1850-1950,* Foundation Books, New Delhi, 2008.
64. Arup Jyoti Saikia, *Forests and Ecological History of Assam, 1826-2000,* Oxford University Press , New Delhi, 2011.
65. Eric A. Strahorn, *An Environmental History of Postcolonial North India: The Himalayan Tarai in Uttar Pradesh and Uttaranchal,* Peter Lang, New York, 2009.
66. Richard P. Tucker, *A Forest History of India,* Sage, New Delhi, 2012.
67. S. Abdul Thaha, *Forest Policy and Ecological Change: Hyderabad State in Colonial India,* Cambridge University Press India, New Delhi, 2009.
68. R. Umamaheshwari, *When Godavari Comes: People's History of a River (Journeys in the Zone of the Dispossessed),* Aakar Books, Delhi, 2014.
69. Dan Flores, 'Place: An Argument for Biological History', *Environmental History Review,* 18, No. 4 (Winter), 1994, pp. 1-8.

SECTION I

HISTORY AND ENVIRONMENT

1

Understanding Ecology, Technology and Agrarian Expansion of Early Assam (From the Earliest Time to the 12th Century CE)

Manash Mazumdar

The geographical and historical expression of 'Early Assam' denotes present Assam, part of the sub-Himalayan region, some portions of North-Bengal, and some part of Sylhet of present Bangladesh, Meghalaya and Arunachal Pradesh. The history of agriculture of the region can be studied into two broad aspects—pre metal and metal rather agrarian economy in hill and plains land. There are two views: whether early Assam introduced wet rice cultivation on an extensive scale or not. One view holds that plough powered by cattle was brought by the Indo-Aryans supported by the knowledge of Sanskrit and advance production technology. The other view holds that it was much advance before the coming of the Indo-Aryans practise of wet rice was known to different ethnic communities. Our understanding of the agrarian history of early Assam can be framed into three broad aspects—early settlement, pre-metal agrarian technology, and new agrarian society based on some material remains and interpretation of epigraphical data.

Early Settlements:

'Early Assam' vis a vis north-east India is one of the most culturally diverse areas in terms of illustrating the relationship between man and environment. The favourable climate of early Assam attracted human settlement since early times. A major shift of the tool-making technology in this part of eastern India occurred when men started domestication of a number of plants and animals and cultivation of rice and other cereals. The study will analyse major areas of agrarian activity in the pre-metal age where supposedly rice (wild variation) had been cultivated because of the region's proximity to Southeast Asia and East Asia and early human migration.

The region can be considered as an environmentally potential area for the domestication of a number of plants and animals and for making a physical and cultural bridge between India and Southeast Asia. We are quite sure that the systematic study of early settlements will reveal the earlier phase of agrarian history in this part of the region. Strategically the region is located at the junction of South Asia and Southeast Asia and its natural and cultural interconnectivity, logically explains the rich cultural diversity of the people living in the region[1].Thus, geographically, north-east India, through which India touches High Asia, is destined to play a crucial role in shaping the Indian nation in the eastern part of India.[2] There were regular movements of human races into this region from mainland India, South China and Southeast Asia. The region may be regarded as the 'Great Indian Corridor'.[3] Geologically the whole of north-east India can be divided into three distinct regions each of which has distinctive physiographic and geomorphology. The region is composed of folded and tectonically disturbed metamorphic and sedimentary rocks which were formed around five million years ago. Geologists are agreed that the Shillong plateau which formed the central part of the highland of Meghalaya is an extension of the Indian peninsular. One million years ago, the region had assumed the present geomorphologic features. The Brahmaputra valley is built up of very late alluvial flood deposits of the rivers carried down from the surrounding high lands and deposits at the foot. In course of time, most of the terrain became firm and dry suitable for human habitation with abundant supply of water and natural floods around seven thousand years before. Apart from its geological formation and strategic location, the region can claim its unique climate in the rest of India having maximum rainfall and one of the wettest places in the world with associated flora and fauna, which strongly influences the life and culture of the people of north-east India and thus provided necessary support to early human migration and settlement of agrarian people. Due to the scarcity of material (both written and excavated), it is difficult for us to reconstruct the early climatic conditions and relationship of man and environment of early north-east India. Amongst the literary references about early Assam's climate, we have the testimony of Hiuen-Tsang who says that the country (*Pragjyotisha-Kamarupa*) was 'low and damp'.[4] In 1662 AD when Mirjumla came to invade Assam, he was accompanied by Shihabuddin Talish[5] who informs us that in Assam the rain rests for eight months and even during winter there are a few rainy months. The unique monsoon climate, excessive humid and tropical forest clad mountains are unique characteristics of the climate of early north-eastern India. The rivers of Assam contain gold dust and in the valley the soils are fertile for all kinds of agricultural products that might be converted into one continued garden of silk, cotton, coffee, sugar, and tea over the extent of many hundred miles.[6] Not surprisingly, all these features attracted the early settlers to settle in the region, with regular development of the stone tool industry and domestication of plants and cereals. It appears that its physio-geographical character has brought about the fusion of elements, typically Indian and characteristically Southeast Asian in nature.[7]

It seems that the climatic condition provided the foragers to make important advances in their control of the environment and further in the area of the domestication of many plants and animals and further progress towards agriculture. Historically there occurred a transition in the region, which was already under the occupation of the nomadic hunters and food gatherers. Overall changes in tool-making technology and settlement pattern can also be noticed.

The region lies between 22° and 29°8′ north latitude and 89°40′ and 97°22′ east longitude. The geophysical division includes the hilly areas with high mountains to the north with the east-west ranges formed basically by the rocks of the tertiary period, the Meghalaya or Shillong plateau in the south composed of Achaean and Pre-Cambrian sediments and above which the younger sediments of tertiary and quaternaries are deposited. The Cachar plains constitute neo-cene fold ridges comprising sub-flysch and molasses sediment of the Mio-Pliocene age. The Brahmaputra valley in the middle, which is formed of recent alluvium was intercepted occasionally by Achaean sediments exposed in the form of denuded hillocks. Mizoram, which continued up to Arakan of Burma, was composed mainly of the tertiary formations. Thus the region developed as suitable land for early settlements supported by its varied flora and fauna around the late Pleistocene period or even earlier when migratory human beings started to develop the tool-making process. M.K. Dhavalikar in this respect observes that 'Archaeologically Assam is terra-icognita'.[8] It means very little excavation and survey was done in this region to relate the missing link of history except some stray and sporadic findings and an occasional surface collection so far as pre-history of the region is concerned.

Several colonial administrators and ethnographers took initiatives in the discovery and study of stone tools, which were found in the *jhum* field. Two shoulder specimens were found from Visvanath in Darrang district. From the district Coggin Brown[9] reported axe-grooved hammers and 'perhaps the rarest of the numerous Neolithic stone implements recorded from eastern Asia'. Some axe type Celts were noticed by Baron in the Naga Hills which the local people believed had fallen from sky. Besides these, there are a large number of stray finds from different parts of the area. J.H Hutton[10] brought to light the Neolithic cultural pattern of the region. Lubbock reported a jade Celt, which was collected from Namsang Naga, handed over to E.H. Steel.[11] Steel became so enthusiastic that he started an enquiry and collected three more jadeite axes. In 1871, Anderson collected a huge tool-kit of Neolithic implements from Arunachal Pradesh. In 1896, Peal discovered a Celt from a tea garden in upper Assam. In 1875, Godwin Austin collected a pair of polished axes. In 1939, K.L. Baruah collected two Celts one from Darrang district and another from Cachar district[12] which he compared with the Celts of Burma and Chotonagpur area. P.C. Choudhury[13] also studied the Neolithic problem of Assam in general outline. The tools, which were collected by the British officers, are now preserved in the Pitt's River Museum, Oxford University and a few of them are now housed in the Prehistory section of the Assam State Museum. However, A.H. Dani[14] made a detailed classification of all these stone tools, prepared a typological study, and argued that all the tools have an East and Southeast Asiatic affinity.

The mid-part the 20th century was very important in order to understand the nature and pattern of early settlements and agrarian activity in this part of Eastern India since many systematic excavations were conducted in order to understand the Neolithic settlement pattern in this part of eastern India. In 1963, M.C. Goswami[15] excavated the Daojalihading site with T.C. Sharma. The site is located on a ridge of a hill in North-Cachar Hill district of Assam (presently known as Dima-Hasao) between Langting and Mahur river Valleys. The excavation revealed edge tools, grinding stones, quern, mullers, flakes, chips and hammer stones, pieces of fossil wood and different varieties of potteries. It is said that edge tools were made on shale and others on grained sandstones. Excavation also reveals that fossil wood was used in a limited quantity for making edge tools. Typologically tools at Daojalihading may be classified into-(a) flake tools, (b) edge tools, (c) fully grounded tools. The edge tools were shaped initially by chipping and then finished by grinding either fully or partially. These types of stone tools could be classified into— (a) triangular Celt with flat and thin body (b) quadrangular Celt flat sides and faces (c) shoulder Celt showing two varieties– (i) curvilinear variety and (ii) rectilinear variety.

The excavation at Daojalihading of North Cachar Hill district of Assam also yielded a large quantity of potteries in broken and semi-broken condition. In most of the potteries cord, marked designs appear which T.C. Sharma,[16] H.C. Sharma, and

Dilip Kumar Medhi[17] have studied in detail. This study shows that most of the potteries contain cord-marked designs. These types of pottery are of grey colour. They are made of unevenly mixed impure clay, which is heavily tempered. All this is handmade. The final shape of the pot is given by beating the walls of the vessels with the help of a beater, which is wrapped with either a cord or string. Instead of cord-marked pottery the excavator also discovered dull red stamped ware, plain red wares, etc.

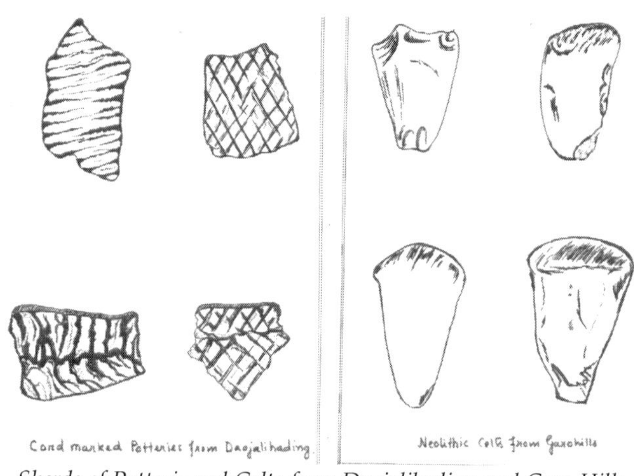

Sherds of Potteris and Celts from Daojalihading and Garo Hills

These types of potteries with the cord impression along with adzes and shoulder Celts are a very dominant tradition during the late Neolithic period in China and Southeast Asia. Therefore archaeologists have almost agreed with the fact that the cultural group who migrated to this zone in pre-historic times might have brought with them this technology and tradition of pottery making. Allchin[18] thinks that this tradition comes from Southeast Asia. Another important aspect of the Neolithic culture (though not properly dated) of Daojalihading is that the people who dwelt there were mainly food producers as the presence of stone rubbers, mullers and mealing stones strongly indicate the agrarian pattern of the settlement.

Besides Daojalihading, we have two other sites of agrarian activity in early Assam. One of them is Sarutaru. Sarutaru is located on the border of Khasi hills of the present State of Meghalaya and Kamrup District in South Guwahati. S.N. Rao[19] first exposed the site for excavation. Most of the stone tools represent shoulder Celt and other round butted axes. Handmade core-impressed pottery is also found along with the tool for the first time, the full pot was discovered in the excavation. These potteries were gritty and brown, pale brown and grey in colour.[20] The presence of cord mark wares signifies its relation with the pottery tradition of Daojalihading and a strong Southeast Asian influence.

Another important Neolithic site, which had been excavated during 1970-78, is at Dibru Valley in upper Assam.[21] There are three Neolithic sites, viz. Kanaigaon, North Kanai Garuchora and Ahutali situated a few kilometres from the east of present Dibrugarh town. The first two sites yielded stone tools of various shapes and sizes and Neolithic potsherds and ashes, the third site Ahutali contributed Neolithic stone tools, Neolithic cord-marked potsherd, ash and a Palaeolithic chopping tool. In first two sites, the excavators found the Neolithic tools, chipped and ground axes, polished axe, and polished and thin butt axe, round butt axe, straight butt axe, tenon type Celt and shoulder Celts. The study reveals that the stone tools of Kanaigaon north site is important as they are discovered along with cord-impressed potsherd, which is one of the important characteristics of Southeast Asia's tradition. Besides these sites, we have also evidence of a number of Neolithic tools in Nilachal hill area, Basita, Kalihipara, Pamohi and adjacent areas of present Guwahati city. Due to the lack of proper study and analysis, we cannot proceed further in the explanation of the findings. Very recently, we have also been informed about the Neolithic Celt at Koliabor in Amsoi which had been studied by Sukanya Sharma of the Indian Institute of Technology, Guwahati and others in the western part of Karbi-Anglong along with megalithic burials[22] The proper excavation can only reveal the hidden fact and cultural sequence of these artefacts. We can only say that throughout Early Assam Neolithic cultural evidences extended length and breadth and only the systematic excavation and study can unfold the missing chapter of this period in this part of Eastern India.

Garo hill, which is adjacent to the present state of Assam, also exposed a number of Neolithic sites. In 1968, the excavation at Garo hills by the team of Gauhati University resulted in the exposure of several Neolithic sites at Sebalgiri, Rongram Alagiri and Chitra Abri[23] in stratified context occurred at the terraces of Rongram River. The site yielded chipped and ground stone axes and crude handmade potteries, large quantities of microliths along with fluted cores in association with gritty pottery wares. Sharma[24] and others are of the opinion that the tools and other artefacts, which have been exposed in the site, can be compared with that of Southern India. Another site at Rongram which is situated on an ancient terrace of Rongram River composed of reddish silt on the top and a gravel bed yellow yielded polished and ground Celts on the top layer, below which are found large and heavy axes made on pebble stone. The site at Chitra Abri yielded a large quantity of shoulder Celts, a typical East Asiatic Neolithic tradition.

Barapani which is located between 25° 42° 26° north latitude and 91° 55° 40° longitude, about 1350 metres above the sea level is a site of ancient settlement during the Neolithic period. The site was first discovered and exposed in 1995 by a study team from North-Eastern Hill University[25] from the excavation and surface collection it reveals axes, adze Celts, points, scrapers, knives, hand axes, cores, pointed axes, shoulder Celts, etc. were found. The collection of crude shoulder Celts, is the evidence of the presence of the Southeast Asia tradition. The collection of big size crude points on quartz shows the use of this type of rock as raw material which is probably the first time in this part of Eastern India. Presence of an oval shaped hand axe in Neolithic context is an indication of Palaeolithic continuation in the Neolithic site. Another associated site at Barapani in the central part of Meghalaya is Sohpet Bneng hill of Ri-Bhoi District of Meghalaya[26] the stone tools which are exposed by excavation are shoulder tools, splayed axe, bar-Celt, axe with broad cutting edge, chisel tool, round butt axe, some flakes, points, etc. The site also exposed some handmade ceramic potsherd with cord impression, which is the typical characteristic of Southeast Asia. The tools, which are exposed from the site at Barapani, are of highly specialised functions. Apart from household and agricultural functions, these were also used for carpentry and other work which indicates the nature and pattern of the ancient settlement at Barapani in the central part of Meghalaya.

An important Neolithic settlement is found in Arunachal Pradesh which is the extreme northeast corner of the Indian subcontinent and adjoining China and Burma. Therefore, it is quite logical to think that through Arunachal the Southeast Asian cultural contact infiltrated into the region. During the colonial period, enthusiastic British officers collected a few stone Celts which are presently preserved in the Pitt's River Museum of Oxford University. T.C. Sharma[27] made a scientific analysis of the material preserved there. In 1972, M.C. Goswami[28] conducted fieldwork in the Kameng district of Arunachal Pradesh and collected eighteen Neolithic Celts .In addition to Celts there are trapezoidal, triangular and splayed axes. However, no pottery was found in the site. Parsi parlo,[29] another Neolithic settlement, yielded a number of stone tools and ceramic potteries at a different cultural level. Potteries at Parsi Parlo includes plain coarse ware, cord-impressed coarse ware, stamped coarse brown and red ware, stamped buff ware, fine buff ware and plain brown wares. Thus from the above discussion about the Neolithic settlement it appears that during the Neolithic period people chose these lands because of the availability of water flows from the hill stream and suitable ecological condition. It appears that people of Parsi Parlo practised agriculture in rudimentary form as evident by the presence of shoulder Celts and ceramic wares.

In neighbouring Bangladesh, in the district of Habiganj, archaeologists also noticed the existence of an early settlement.[30] These settlements fall within our field of research. The prehistoric site at Chaklapunji tea garden near Chandir Mazar of Chunurughat revealed a significant number of prehistoric tools from the bed of a small ephemeral stream known as *Balu*

Nadi. Altogether eighty-four stone tools were recovered from the site. Amongst them, archaeologists could identify only eight implements. These are—flake point, round bat axes, knife, unfinished points, end scraper, shoulder Celts, burin, etc. It appears that these stone tools were prepared from flint fossil wood.[31] Typologically these stone tools can be compared with stone tools of Lalmai hills of Bangladesh and some tools of Daojalihading and Garo hills of present Meghalaya. On the basis of the typological analysis, we may infer that the people of the settlement maintained contact with the people of Lalmai hills at Comilla and North-Cachar hills (Dima-Hasao) of Assam. From the study and analysis of different pre-historic sites of undivided Assam (major part of present north-east India) the process of human evolution and settlement in the region can be divided into—Palaeolithic, Mesolithic and subsequent Neolithic cultural phases. The dating of these varied tools, no serious attempt has so far been made except the state of Tripura whose Palaeolithic culture has been dated around 3050 BP.[32] As we know, that north-east India is one of the most important areas in terms of the relationship between men and environment. The region can be termed as a gift of favourable weather and climate, which naturally attracted the human races for settlement and habitation since prehistoric times. Tropical rain forest zone, humid climate, dense jungle and wild beasts could not stop the human advance to these hilly terrain to expose the land and settle there. Like West Asia, Europe and the rest of India and other Southeast Asian countries we find the evidence of the settlement pattern of early man in this part of eastern India in plateau, terraces of river, caves and even the slope of hills by adaptation of climate and environment. The presence of raw material of stone tools within the proximity of this settlement cannot be ruled out. In the following section we shall try to form an abstract or if possible concrete idea about the early form of social formation and nature of the settlement in this part of Eastern India based on the analysis of stone tools and other associated findings. Throughout the prehistory and history of early settlements of the world a major shift in the model of subsistence and tool-making technology perhaps was the period when mankind started domestication of a number of plants and production of cereals along with domestication of animals and production of cereals. In the language of prehistory the period is known as the age of advancement for permanent settlement based on mode of subsistence and domestication of animals. Though, we have no direct evidence about early men's nature of plant and animal domestication which laid the basic foundation of the early form of social formation in this part of eastern India. For the analysis and explanation, we have to form our own hypotheses and model of comparative analysis by the application of which we will try to reach a certain level to understand the nature of process of early settlement and early form of social formation in Assam.

The excavation so far conducted and reports of stray findings and collection are completely silent about the nature of plant and animal domestication and production of cereals. Till today no sites speak about remains of cereal and clues to other modes of subsistence. From the table drawn below we can form an idea about the Neolithic settlement along major rivers of early Assam and the people inhabiting there.

Table: Tentative Settlements in Early Assam During the Neolithic Period

Settlements	*Location of Early Rivers*	*Probable Ethnic Groups*
Daojali-hading	Langting and Mahur River	Tibbeto-Burmese
Sarutaru	Digaru	Tibbeto-Burmese
Rongram-Alagiri	Rongram River	Austric
Sebalgiri	Rongram River	Austric
Ganol	Ganol	Austric
Sophet-bneg	Umiam-Barapani	Tibbeto-Burmese, Austric
Parsi-Parlo	Parsi and Parlo River	Tibbeto-Burmese
Kanai-gaon, Garuchora, etc.	Dibru River	Tibbeto-Burmese, Indo-Mongolian

Though it is very difficult to say something about the agrarian activity of the tiny tool user people of different settlements, but it will be more convenient to say that location and distribution of different stone tools and their use mainly the Celts, clearly indicate some form of agrarian activity of the people in rudimentary scale.

Towards a New Agrarian Society

There are virtually no Chalcolithic and Bronze or Iron Age remains in early Assam's context. *Jhum* or even terrace cultivation is even practised in many parts of Assam. There are no subsequent cultural developmental stages of the Neolithic to early states to be addressed. The study of the agrarian history in early Assam from the points of view of its people, land, mode of production, social and natural environments and the progress of material culture is a significant historical development. We may suppose that new agricultural technology entered Pragjyotisha-Kamarupa with the Sanskritised Brahmins based on use of iron and cattle-powered ploughs and who introduced a new pattern of agricultural settlement and socio-cultural ethics in early Assam under the patronage of royal authorities. It seems that the aboriginal people who practised agriculture with tiny tools in different hilly areas and hilly settlements remained for some time out of the influence of the new agricultural technology.

Since the 4th century CE or even earlier, the rulers of Pragjyotisha-Kamarupa had started systematic grants of land to the Brahmanas along with *agrahara* settlement, the technology spread more extensively. The grant of Surendravarmana[33] significantly speaks about the construction of a cave temple of Lord Balabhadra. We may presume that by this time the agrarian activity became so widely spread that even the royal authority did not hesitate to construct the temple of Lord Balavadra. It will be logical to think that with the formation of states and with the pressure of population of different social categories, demands on land increased. These demands were applicable to all types of land *vastu, kshetra, or khila.* The extant grant of the period occasionally mentioned *vastu* and *kshetra.*[34]

The inscriptions of early Assam that so far have been discovered indicate that the lands were measured in terms of paddy (*dhanya*) and it is not surprising that it was much before the coming of the Tai-Ahoms. The plough-based cultivation was mostly rooted in many parts of the Brahamaputra Valley, which ultimately led to a well organised social system. From the geographical distribution of different grants of the periods shows that with the spread of plough technology and with the use of iron in many parts of early Assam there developed a new social system centring the Brahmanical settlements.

Iron technology definitely helped in the progress of agriculture in early Assam. Gordon[35] informs us about the indigenous iron technology of the Khasi hills of Meghalaya. H.N. Dutta[36] who first explored the archaeological sites of Doiyang-Dhansiri Valley thinks that the centres of the irons in early Assam were the Naga Hills and adjoining areas of Doiyang-Dhansiri Valley. It has been agreed by some archaeologists that from Doiyang-Dhansiri valley, irons were supplied to many places of the region. It may further be presumed that the tremendous architectural development in many parts of early Assam from the 6th/7th century onwards could not have been possible without extensive use of iron (may be crude in form) and support of a well organised state system based on surplus production.

It seems that the migratory nature of the Aryans to the eastern most zone of the region led to the emergence of the new economy in this part of eastern India. The newcomers who came to this part of this region brought with them new production technology based on the plough, and mature knowledge of crop and season which inevitably laid the foundation of a new social base based on emerging Brahmanical values and culture in assimilating with indigenous people. Nevertheless, what happened to the aboriginals whose mode of subsistence depends on slash and burning method and natural environment. Certain that, most of them clashed with the new method of production, later on accepted, and assimilated with the newcomers. The sources of the period under consideration to a certain extent indicated that the process of acculturation of ethnic groups who lived in the vicinity of the donated land started perhaps with the settlement of the Brahmanas within their midst resulting in extensive grants of land. The process might have started from the 4th/5th century CE with the beginning of land donation.

A survey of the grants of early Assam (Pragjyotisha-Kamarupa) shows that Brahmanical culture was deep-rooted in early Assam along with plough-based agrarian technology. Because of the influence of the agrarian life ownership of land became a symbol of prestige. Though in the earlier period, the agricultural activity was traditionally a taboo for the Brahmins. However around this period the agrarian activities were included in the sacred text as traditionally sacred duties of the Brahmanas.[37] The large-scale architectural development of early Assam speaks about human migration and settlement in different parts in the remote past. The grants speak of spread and extension of Brahmanical culture and agrarian economy in Nagaon-Tezpur, Doboka, and Doiyang-Dhansiri valley. The purpose of such large-scale donation of lands to the Brahmanas was to bring more and more lands under cultivation. In this context, Kosambi[38] says, "plough agriculture greatly increased food supply and made it more regular." This means that not only a far greater population, but also one that lived together in greater units. The grants were issues in most cases in the settled areas but sometimes in peripheral regions. From the 4th century CE or some earlier period onwards land grants became a common practice of the kings of Pragjyotisha-Kamrupa. Most of the grants speak of paddy fields(*dhanya kshetra*) and embankments (*Alis*).

Thus, the foregoing analysis of the agrarian activity of early Assam shows that primitive agriculture, animal husbandry, petty commodity production and plough agriculture have been identified as the principal form of production, whose relations dominated and structured the society in early Assam. Even a careful study of the extant grant of the period shows that rice was the staple food of the people of early Assam since the major part of the cultivable land of the donated village was devoted to the growth and cultivation of rice along with other products. It was this crop pattern which really decides the locale of the early settlements. Since in most cases, the granted lands were located in close proximity to rivers, streams and other natural ponds. Along with rice there were many other natural products which may have had some bearing on the material life of Pragjyotisha-Kamarupa based on an environmental backdrop.

NOTES AND REFERENCES

1. Bridget and Raymond Allchin, *The Rise of Civilization in India and Pakisthan*, Cambridge University Press, New Delhi, 1966, p. 101.
2. Ibid., p. 102.
3. Dilip Kumar Medhi, 'Potters and Potteries of Assam' in John Mikshik (ed.), *Earthen Wares of South-East Asia*, Singapore University Press, 2003, pp. 332-336.
4. Thomas Watter, *On Yuwang-Chwang Travels in India*, London, 1904, Vol. II, p. 185.
5. Edward Gait, *History of Assam* (Second Edition), Lawyers Book Stall, Guwahati, 1966, pp. 145-146.
6. John M. Cosh, *Topography of Assam* (Second Reprint), 2000, p. 133.
7. R. Gopalakrishna, 'Land and People of North-East India: An Introduction' in Jaiprakash Singh and Gautam Sengupta (eds.), *Archaeology of North-East India*, Vikas Publishing House, New Delhi, 1991, p. 4.
8. M.K. Dhavalikar, 'Archaeology of Guwahati', *Bulletin of Deccan College Post-Graduate Research Institute*, Poona, 1972, pp. 32, 137-149.
9. J. Coggin Brown, 'Groove Stone Hammers from Assam' in *Journal of Asiatic Society of Bengal*, X (4), 1914, pp.107-109.
10. J.H. Hutton, 'Prehistory of Assam', in *Man in India*, VIII, (4), pp. 228-2232.
11. Sir John Lubbock, 'The Stone Age–The Stone Tools of Upper Assam' in *Athnaeum*, 1967, London, p. 822.
12. K.L. Baruah, 'Prehistoric Cultures of Assam' in *Journal of Assam Research Society*, 7(2), 1973, pp. 35-41.
13. P.C. Choudhury, 'Neolithic Culture in Kamarupa' in *Journal of Assam Research Society*, XI, pp. 41-47.
14. A.H. Dani, *Prehistory and Proto-History of Eastern India*, Firma KLM, Calcutta, 1960, pp. 41-77.
15. M.C. Goswami and T.C. Sharma, 'A Brief Report of the Investigations of Prehistoric Archaeology in North-Cachar Hills', in *Journal of the University of Gauhati*, XIII(2), pp. 63-66.

16. T.C. Sharma, 'A Note on the Neolithic Pottery of Assam', in *Man* (2), I, 1967, London pp. 126-128.
17. Dilip Kumar Medhi, 'Potters and Potteries of Assam' in *Earthen Wares of South-East Asia*, John Mikshik (ed.), Singapore University Press, 2003, pp.126-128.
18. Bridget and Raymond Allchin, *The Rise of Civilization in India and Pakisthan,* Cambridge University Press, New Delhi, 1966, p. 121.
19. S.N. Rao, 'Neolithic Culture of Sarutaru,' in *Bulletin of the Department of Anthropology,* Dibrugarh University, pp. 1-9.
20. Dilip Kumar Medhi, *'Potters and Potteries of Assam'* in Earthen Wares of South-East Asia, John Mikshik (ed.), Singapore University Press, 2003, pp. 126-128.
21. Paban Chandra Saikia, *Stone Tools of Dibru Valley,* Dibrugarh, 1980, pp. 45-68.
22. *These Celts have been reported by Nitai Kalita of the Department of History, Koliabor College which is found in Amsoi forest area. He collected the Celt and makes a preliminary report along with Sukanya Sharma. At Karbi Anglong some Neolithic cultural sequence was found and Mr. Robin Senar, a research scholar of the Department of Anthropology of Gauhati University is presently doing research on the area.*
23. H.C. Sharma 'Stone Age Sites in Garo hills', Ph.D. Thesis, Gauhati University, 1972, pp. 82-93.
24. T.C. Sharma, 'Prehistoric Situation in North East India', in *Archaeology of North-East India,* Jaiprakash Singh and Gautam Sengupta (eds.), New Delhi, 1999, p. 49.
25. Zahid Hussian 'Who were the Prehistoric Dwellers of Meghalaya Plateau?' in *Archaeology of North-East India*, Jaiprakash Singh and Gautam Sengupta (eds.), New Delhi, Vikas Publishing House, 1991, p. 77.
26. Marco Mitri, 'A Report on the Neolithic Tools from Sohpetbeng Hill of Ri-Bhoi District in Meghalaya' in *Proceedings of Northeast India History Association*, Shillong 2005, pp. 87-95.
27. Op. cit., T.C. Sharma, *Pre-Historic Archaeology*, pp. 114-115.
28. M.C. Goswami et al., 'A Typological Study of Some Prehistoric Tools from Kameng District of NEFA (Arunachal Pradesh)', in *Journal of Assam Science Society*, Vol. XII, No. 1, 1972, pp. 29-35.
29. A.A. Asraf, *Prehistoric Arunachal: A Study on Pre-History and Ethno-Archaeology of Kamala Valley,* Directorate of Research, Government of Arunachal, 1990, pp. 1-154.
30. Md. Mujjamel Haque et al., 'Chunarughat O'Sylhet Pragitihas: Ekti Prathamik Prativedan' (in Bengali) in Sarif Uddin (ed.),

Sylheter Itihas O'Oitijja, Dacca, Bangladesh, 1999, pp. 1-42. See also, Mustakin Ahmed Choudhury, *Habiganjer Itihas,* (in Bengali), pp. 12-16.

31. N.R. Ramesh, 'A Study on Geomorphology, Quaternary Geology, and Associated Cultural Remains of West Tripura District,' Ph.D. Thesis, Gauhati University, 1989.
32. Ibid.
33. M.M. Sharma, *Inscriptions of Ancient Assam,* Gauhati University, 1978, pp. 1-3.
34. Ibid., p. 146.
35. P.R.T. Gordon, *The Khasis,* Cosmo Publications, New Delhi, 1967, pp. 57-59.
36. H.N. Dutta, 'The Art and Archaeology of Doiang-Dhansiri Valley', Ph.D. Thesis, Gauhati University, 1997.
37. Nayanjot Lahiri, 'Settlements and Economy' in Nadini Sinha Kapur (ed.), *Environmental History of Early India: A Reader,* Oxford University Press, New Delhi, 2011, p. 219.
38. D.D. Kosambi, *An Introduction to the Study of Indian History,* Popular Prakashan, Bombay, Reprint, 1994, p. 115.

2

Bhils in Conservation: Aspects of Agrarian History and Sacred Groves in Southern Rajasthan

Nandini Sinha Kapur

This chapter focuses on the aspects of deforestation and water-resources in the agrarian history of Southern Rajasthan highlighting the note of the Bhil tribe in the conservation of natural resources.

A brief introduction to the geography of the region of Mewar highlights a differentiation in space, accounting for distinct sub-regions with their own nuclear or core areas and peripheries. The sub-regions of the Mewar hills and upper Banas plain comprise the territory popularly known as 'Mewar'. It consists of the districts of Udaipur, Chittorgarh and Bhilwara. The Mewar hills cover the whole of Udaipur district except its two eastern tahsils, Mavali and Vallabhnagar, the recently formed district of Rani Samand (carved out of Udaipur district), and the south-eastern margin of Pali district. It touches the northern portion of the middle Mahi basin, which is largely occupied by the Bhil and Gerasia tribes.[1]

Agricultural activities are confined to the valley of Breach and its small tributaries and the area north of the Mahi River. This sub-region is situated between the Banas Plain and the Abu block. The highest part of the Mewar hills is the Bhorat plateau (1,202 m).[2]

The rainfall here is moderate (50-100 cm).[3] The south-eastern part of Mewar hills is densely forested and the south-west is covered with jungle scrub and grass, closely-packed ridges and valleys ridden with boulder-strewn river beds.[4] Hence, the western and southern hills of Mewar hills are unable to sustain agricultural activity. This sub-region had red and yellow soil in the north-west and ferruginous red soil in the southern part.[5] It produces crops like maize, wheat, barley, gram and oilseeds. The sub-region is rich in mineral resources, especially copper, zinc, lead and silver (Zawar mine)[6], and the major route of communication in the early medieval period ran from Delhi-Agra to Malwa and Champaner-Dohad in Gujarat via Ahada in Mewar.[7] The other significant feature of these sub-regions is the concentration of the tribal population in the Bhorat Plateau and the adjoining hills. Here the land is predominantly occupied by the Bhils. Even today, many of them practise shifting agriculture.[8] The Bhil-occupied territory of the Mewar hills is popularly known as Bhomat. Bhomat is again divided by a massive mountain range into a south-western division known as Kotra Bhomat[9] and the Merwara region that is inhabited by the tribe of Mers (Meda). Merwara is the portion of the Aravalli chain that runs between Kumbhalmer (Khumbhalgarh) and Ajmer.[10]

The upper Banas Plain is another sub-region of Mewar. This sub-region comprises the three districts of Bhilwara, Chittorgarh and Rajsamand, and the two eastern tahsils of Udaipur district, Mavali and Vallabhnagar. The Banas plain is elevated and drained by the Banas and its tributaries, the Khari Kothari, Berach, Gambhiri and Wagan.[11] The soil varies from thin to black in the western and southern parts. Extensive cultivation of maize, wheat, cotton, sugar cane and other crops is the dominant feature of agricultural activities. Cotton is predominantly grown on the black soil belt of Bhilwara and Chittorgarh districts. While the northern part, covering almost the whole of Udaipur district had a cropping incidence of 52 per cent and below.[12]

Southern Rajasthan witnessed a process of local state formation and agrarian expansion in the early medieval period. It is significant that irrigational works, both individual and royal enterprises, figure in the records in the context of land grants and rural settlements. In the kingdom of the Kiskindha Guhilas, a number of irrigational projects were owned by notable members of the rural society. The Dungarpur plates of Bhbhata refer to a reservoir and tank owned by Rongarka and Pahaka, respectively.[13] This record also refers to a well named Kaccho.[14] *(Kupakaccho)* as one of the boundaries of the donated field. For instance, the field named Pahakapabhaka yielded five units of grains *(pahakapabhakabhidhanapanchikaprimanam kshetram)*.[15]

Similar instances come from the district of Bhilwara the village of Dhavagarta (modern Dhor, in Jahazpur tahsil) was a flourishing agricultural settlement in the 7th century. The Dabok inscription of the region of the Mori king Dhavalappadeva (AD 641) refers to Saradyagraismaka fields (fields that can be tilled in autumm and summer), indicating double-cropping. The fact that the Dabok inscription refers to a large number of fields owned by different individuals indicates sufficient agricultural production. The above irrigational projects and agricultural production undoubtedly contributed to the revenue base of the local Guhila state, and indicates a stratified rural society.

Udaipur district witnessed the emergence of new settlements in the forests during this period. The Samoli inscription of AD 646 records the opening up of an akara (a mine) at Aranyakupagiri and the building of a temple of goddess Aranyavasini by a migrating community from Vatanagar (Sirohi district). The term 'Aranyakupagiri' indicates forest and a hilly terrain. The name Aranyavasini (she who dwells in the forest) indicates that the temple was dedicated to the goddess of a local tribal population.

Hence, we can deduce that the mine was be tentatively located either in the zinc-lead-silver mines of Zawar (40 km south of Udaipur), or in the copper belt around Udaipur. It is important to note that the Zawar mines came into operation in the 7th century, precisely the period of the beginning of the process of local state formation in Mewar.[16] The record points to two successive stages in the development of the settlement called Aranyakupagir. This small settlement in a hilly, forested area of the tribals already had a well (kupa), or wells, as a means of irrigation. This technology is likely to have been introduced by a migrating community in a semi-arid, hilly, tribal locality with a pre-agricultural settlement.

Some degree of limited 'peasantisation' of Bhils seems to have begun at this point. Finally, Aranyakupagir as a centre of mining and the presence of the temple of Aranyakupagir meant the emergence of a workshop-cum-exchange centre at this settlement (the temple of Aranyavasini is stated to have been visited by bards from far and near, indicating occasional festivities necessitating weekly or occasional fairs).[17] Therefore, routes connecting Aranyakupagiri with Nagda and Ahada would have resulted in some amount of deforestation. The phenomenon of deforestation assumes significance in view of the emergence of new settlements in the post-9th century. Inscriptional records list several commercial, religious and politically important centres between the 10th and 13th centuries in Mewar. The emergence of temple centres such as Ekalingaji at Nagda (north of Udaipur) and Kankroli near the copper mines at Dariba, is likely to have caused some degree of deforestation, as clearances were needed for agricultural activities of sustain temples and mathas.

It is significant that the term vana marggah (forest route), which figured in a land grant of the 7th century from the Guhila kingdom of Kiskindha[18], *is absent in the post-7th century land grant charters from Mewar, such as the Pratapgarh grant of the Guhila kind Bhartrbhatta in the Chhappan area, dated AD 942.* The Pratapgarh inscription recording the grant of a field named Vavulika by Bhartrbhatta to God Indrajaditya in the village of Palasakupika near Dasapura (modern Mandasaur), does not mention forests or forest routes as boundaries of the village. Some degree of deforestation must have been going on around the areas of Pratapgarh and Mandasaur in the 10th century. On the other hand, rural settlements dotted this landscape, as they figure in the grants made by others to the same temple complex. It is significant that royal grants were usually situated near sources of water. They were thus assured of sustained agricultural production. A separate plate of the Pratapgarh inscription, dated AD 946, records the grant of a field named

Chittullaka, in which ten manis of seeds could be sown and which was irrigated by one leather bucket.[19]

The grant was in favour of God Indradityadeva at Ghonta Varsika, made by Cahamana Devaraja. Madhava, a governor of the Pratiharas from Ujjain, donated a field irrigated by an araghatta located on the bank of a river (possibly on the northern side of Dharapadraka, identified with modern Dharavad in Mewar, near the boundary of the Pratapgarh state. Araghattas and devices like leather buckets seem to have become popular means of artificial irrigation by the 10th century. It is also evident from these records that water wheels and similar devices were suitable for fields located near river banks. These fields are likely to have been connected to rivers through water channels. The Pratapgarh inscriptions give us an idea of clusters of agriculture settlements with well-irrigated fields, drawing water from streams, rivers and wells. Society of water resource is evident which had an impact on deforestation. As the ecology to remind ourselves that irrigation works and reservoirs were owned more by individual entrepreneurs than by the Government in Mewar (southern Rajasthan) between the 17th and 10th centuries. But the Kadmal plates of AD 1083, recording the grant of revenue by the Guhila king Vijayasimha in the village of Palli (modern Pali), give us an entirely different picture. This inscription records the donation of a fifth of the produce of the village of Pali, embracing all its receipts, to Unalacarya, son of Acarya Sahiya, a resident of Nagahrada (Nagda) but whose son had probably migrated to Pali. The done was given full rights over the fifth part of every item of produce of the donated villages to the extent of its boundaries, with the exception of the income from taxes on drainage, of which he received only half (that is, a one-tenth part), the other half going to the donor himself (the Guhila kind Vijaysimha). It not identical, a similar instance comes from Bolera (Marwar division), where a royal land grant was made in AD 991 to a Brahmana, Sri Dirghacarya. It consisted of a piece of land with a share of only one-third of the water from a well (Ghaghalikupatri-bhagodakenasaha). That water was an important administrative concern in this area, is evident from royal initiative in the necessary work of construction and the nature of gift specifications.

The above evidence is important enough to prove the nature of ownership of water resources. Chattopadhyaya asks, 'How was artificial irrigation socially organised? This question is particularly pertinent to western Rajasthan where water was scarce.' An examination of the patterns of artificial irrigation works and the major beneficiaries of grants of facilities irrigation would focus on the social control of water resources. An inscriptional survey of early medieval Rajasthan reveals that grants of irrigational facilities emanated largely from the rulers who also owned an araghatta. This becomes rare in later times, although epigraphic reference to araghattas are far more numerous in the later period.

On the basis of inscriptional survey, Chattopadhyaya observes, 'in early medieval Rajasthan (there is) a certain positive correlation between... "Induced" irrigation organisation and a general growth in agricultural production .... Irrigational efforts could and did to a certain extent generate economic and social power, albeit at microscopic political-spatial levels.'

Thus, the state retained rights over water resources in the arid region of Pali. Without getting into a debate on the Asiatic mode of production, we can observe that the nature of royal grants in Pali indicates a certain amount of political control over water resources in the arid parts of Rajasthan. The point is that the Guhila state was obviously interested in diverting the resources from the newly acquired region of Pali towards Mewar through control of water resources.

Thirteenth-century records from Mewar refer to lakes/ reservoirs in the context of donated land and temple centres. The Tamtarada family, in its record of AD 1274, refers to the Kalelaya Lake in the village of Chirakupa, near which the donated land from the temples of Yogeshvara and Yogeshvari were situated.[20] Lake Kalelaya seems to have been maintained by the local elite of Chirakupa, and its water shared by them. The economic significance of this lake is clearly evident from its mention in the context of the donated land. The donated land/fields were likely to have been irrigated by the lake. One of the older tanks at the Chittorgarh fortress, Chitranga, continues to appear in 13th century records, indicating its maintenance and utility in this period. A Chittorgarh pillar inscription of AD 1287, from the reign of the Guhila king Samarsimha, records the grant of a few dramas (coins) to the temple of Vaidyanatha, situated on the bank of the Chitranga tank, by Vijada, son of Pachasiga. The Chitranga tank seems to have been an important source of water inside the fortresses of Chittorgarh for a very long time. The local elite and patrons of the temple are likely to have maintained this tank for local agriculture needs.

Araghattas continued to be an important source of artificial irrigation in the district of Udaipur in the 12th century. Royal grants continued to be made in the vicinity of araghattas. A land grant charter of King Padmasimha of AD 1194 records the grant of land in the vicinity of an araghatta named Gajan in the domain (estate) of Cahaman Rao Mokaja in the village of Kadmal, to a Brahmana named Sivaguna. The fact that the royal donations consisted of land situated near arahattas indicates the premium attached to irrigated fields in southern Rajasthan. The land donated to Sivaguna yielded a sufficient amount of crops, as it was meant for the donee's livelihood.

The process of deforestation in the tribal belt of Merwara could have begun on a limited scale in the 15th century, with the construction of the royal fortress of Kumbhalgarh by Maharana Kumbha. Maharana Kumbha granted the village of Kachhar to the Brahmana Godha Gohad, in AD 1453.[21] Land grants in the tribal tract of Merwara (occupied by the Medas/Mers) were essential for obvious political and economic reasons. However, the presence of villages in Merwara pre-dates Kumbha's arrival in this tribal tract, and indicates the emergence of rural centres under private entrepreneurship. Hence, the Guhila state alone might not have been responsible for deforestation but it is likely to have accelerated such a process around the fortress of Kumbhalgarh by building roads and bringing land under cultivation. However, the rocky nature of Merwara might have increased royal dependence of the existing village, thereby initiating deforestation around the existing village to mobilise additional resources for the administrative centre at Kumbhalgarh. Our sources indicate only one royal land grant in Merwara in the 15th century. This definitely reveals the difficulties and limitations of agricultural expansion in a hilly, forested terrain with scarce water resources.

Lakes continued to be important means of irrigation in the Nagda-Ahada belt in the 15th century. The village of Thura (near Ahada), granted to Guru Gopalabhatta by Rana Raimalla, is described as consisting of lakes full of lotuses, fruit trees, rows of rice fields irrigated by water, a fine rosary of mudgas (black bean/kidney bean) and fields of sweet sugar cane.[22] An official record choosing to highlight lakes and irrigated rice fields indicates the continuing importance of the sources of water and irrigated fields in southern Rajasthan. We are able to locate some of the villages donated to the temple of Ekalingaji in the late 14th and 15th centuries in the tribal belt of Bhomat under the Bhil dominion in the district of Udaipur. Villages west of Nagda and Chirava are plotted on a map of Bhomat.[23] These points indicate a gradual process of agricultural expansion in those areas of the forests of Bhomat which seem to have some sources of water. We are able to locate some of the villages donated to the temple of Ekalingaji in the late 14th and 15th centuries in the tribal belt of Bhomat—the Bhils dominion in the district of Udaipur. Villages west of Nagda and Chirava, such as Panavadapur, Rama, Paner, Sim-vallipur and Kathadavan, can essentially be plotted on a map of Bhomat can be best seen in the construction of a huge lake, the Rajassamudra, in the northern part of Udaipur district in the 17th century. Maharana Rajasimha has initiated the excavation of a few more lakes in the same district before the commencement of the construction of Rajasamudra. These lakes were exacavated in the villages which had the requisite water table. The Rajaprasasti Mahakavyam refers to the excavation of a new lake, 'Janasagar', at the village of Bari. The excavation of this lake cost Rs. 6,80,000. The Maharana donated the villages of Devapura and

Gunahanda to the priest Garibadas. On the same day, the crown prince Maharajakumar Jayasimha laid the foundations of 'Ranasagar' lake in the city of Udaipur.

The Rajaprasasti records the construction of the Rajasamudra Lake as follows. Crown prince Rajasimha, on his way to Jaisalmer (for his wedding) decided to construct a lake on the boundaries of the villages of Dhayonda, Sanwar, Sivali, Bhigavada, Morchana, Pasund, Kheri, Chhaparkheri, Tasol, Mandavar, Bhana, Luhana, Bansol, Gudali, Kankroli and Madha. Rajasimha acceded to the throne in AD 1618 and decided to launch the project of Rajasamudra in consultation with his chief priest. This project was supervised by different departments headed by various samantas. Details of the civil engineering are vividly described. The flow of the Gomti river was obstructed by building a mahasetu (bridge/sluice gates) between two big hills.[24] A huge labour force was deployed to dig out water. A large number of araghattas were used for this purpose. Architects and villagers were also advised regarding the water table. Water gushed out and was carried to the villages listed above by canals. The significance of these canals for irrigating fields is more then obvious. Once the water was tapped, the foundation laying was fixed for the day of Vaishakh Shukla (Monday, 13 April 1621). When the architects saw multi-coloured fish and turtles coming out from the other side of the bridge, they were able to predict the depth of the water. The next to be undertaken was the project of building a bridge at the village of Kankroli (a mining centre). Rains arrived in summer, filling up a part of the lake at Kankroli, demanding strong masonry work (the bridge) spreading over eight years, five months and six days.

A palace, Rajamandira, was built on the banks of the reservoir at Kankroli in AD 1726. A boat-launching ceremony was planned. But Rajasamudra did not have sufficient water for boats to sail. Since there was no hope of another auspicious occasion in the near future for this ceremony, Ranavat Ramasimha, the chief manager of the Rajasamudra project suggested that the lake be artificially filled with water for launching the boats. Rains arrived soon, on the performance of Varunasukta Jap (chants to please the rain God Varuna), and Maharana Rajasimha sailed in the boat. The architects closed the mouth of a canal on royal order. Simultaneous embellishments at older lakes were part of an overall project. A pavilion was built at the lake of Indrasar (Indrasarover) at Ekalingaji, along with four new gates. Details of measurements of the main bridge over Rajasamudra are mentioned, as well as details of other measurements. Four structures/altars were built at the four corners of the bridge. The altar facing Rajamandira had an araghatta (Persian wheel) which carried water to the gardens of this temple. Other bridges that were built are listed as follows: Nimba bridge, 432 gaz in length; Bhadra bridge, 144 gaz in length; bridges at the villages of Kankroli, 550 gaz in length; Asotia, 2,068 gaz in length; Vansol, 1,224 gaz in length.

The three rivers of Mewar, the Gomti, Tal and Kelva, merged into Rajasamudra.[25] The bordering area and a total of 30 reservoirs, tanks and wells, of the villages of Sivali, Bhingavada, Bhanah, Luhana, Vansol, Gudhali, Pasund, Kheri, Chaparkheri, Tasol, Mandavar, Kankroli and Sivali, were submerged by Rajasamudra.[26] The total length of the main bridge covering the lake measured 6,413 gaz. Rajaprasasti also mentions that according to the divine engineer Viswakarma, the maximum length of any reservoir should be 6,000 gaz. Hence, Ranachoda Bhata (composer of the Rajaprasasti Mahakavyam eulogised Rajasimha for having built such a long reservoir. Ranachoda mentions that Maharana Udaisimha (16th century) had made a similar attempt in the past but could not succeed; hence, he built the smaller Udaisagar. Floods on the rivers Tal and Gomti added to the waters of Rajasamudra. Architects from Lahore, Gujarat and Surat came to see the launching of boats on Rajasamudra. Markets and camps dealing in grains and foodstuff were set up on its banks. Rajasimha's queen Rani Shri Ramrasde built a well at the embankment at Debari, costing Rs. 24,000. Another queen, a Rathor princess, built a well at Rajanagar, costing Rs. 30,000.

The building of these wells and araghattas attached to

Rajasamudra indicates their irrigational capacity for the fields and gardens in all the villages listed above. The setting up of markets was an outcome of the increased agricultural productions in the villages around Rajasamudra and increased mobilisation of grading. We have already noted that canals from this lake carried water to the villages. Rajasimha made a donation of pancalangal (mahadan), consisting of five golden plough-share and the village Bhavli to Brahmanas.

However, the environmental cost of such a huge project is evident from the mention of the submergence of fields and villages during the excavation of Rajasamudra.[27] A sense of loss and compensation is evident. Ranachoda Bhatta justifies the flooding of villages in terms of the transformation of these submerged villages into pilgrimage centres and says that these villages would henceforth serve not only mankind but also aquatic animals[28] and submerged trees. Even forests were submerged. The description that forests where lions used to roar now abounded in the sound of water indicates the scale of devastation.

Ecological Ethnicities

The concept of ecological ethnicity is to refer to such small peasants and fisher folk, irrespective of caste, class, or religion. Ecological ethnicity is a social category that designates those people who have developed a certain respectful use to the bounty of nature and, consequently, a commitment to create and preserve a technology that interacts with the place and its non-human collectivity in a sustainable manner. The ecological ethnicities also includes peasants and other ecosystem people, such as fisher folk, tribals, forest dwellers, nomadic shepherds, and a host of people marginalised by development projects and the programmes of environmental modernisation. The concept of ecological ethnicity captures the fact that the practices of the rural people of the subcontinent who are heavily dependent for their livelihood and survival on their immediate environment (and on its biomass) share a great deal in common, despite differences at the level of articulated "beliefs" or worldviews."[29]

The literate classes seem to have more of a vested interest in articulating their differences and less in a direct involvement with the soil or the sea. This is particularly so with the modernising literati who either belong to or aspire to belong to what Gadgil and Guha have called the "omnivore" class. When ecological ethnicities' access to crucial biomass is threatened by developmental activities such as mining, damming of rivers, industrial agriculture, and others, they have tended to band together. This has happened especially in the Jharkhand area and the rest of middle India that has been so heavily industrialised at the expense of local inhabitants who are Adivasi, Hindu, Muslim, and Christian peasants and artisans.

The groves in Southern Rajasthan are located near the village and close to a water source; such groves are also at the top of small hillocks in the Aravalli mountain range, where people worship Bheruji Bavasi, and Mataji. Khanpa Bherji Kukawas Bheruji and Badi Roopam Mata are examples of such sites in Udaipur.[30] These sites have different forms of Hindu deities, such as Hanuman, Durga, and Siva. The presence of the temples in these groves has protected their trees. People do not harm sacred groves mainly because of their traditions, believing that those who cut or use an axe in a sacred grove may be harmed by the presiding deity.[31] These beliefs might have strongly influenced conservation of sacred groves. Continuous community protection of sacred groves has resulted in several large trees, for example, there is a large tree of Churail (Holoptelia integrifolia) growing in Amarkji sacred grove.[32] This is the largest tree of this species in India. Only fallen and ripe fruits are collected from the grove and the wood from mature trees is used only in religious rituals. The water sources found in this and other similar groves provide for drinking and irrigation.[33]

Another sacred grove near Udaipur is called Ubesvara Mahadeva with a temple dedicated to Siva. Since it is situated near a water stream, it also serves as a watering and resting place. The cowdung collected from the nearby cattle is allowed to dry and the dried dung cakes are used to cook bati(spherical traditional bread) by villagers and pilgrims. The arrangement ensures the sanctity of the grove and provides ample stock of fuel. Sacred groves also provide a meeting place for the community to discuss socio-economic issues and to resolve their personal grievances. Temple forests are managed and maintained to serve the temple. This may include religious, economic, and social functions.[34]

Temple forests are managed to meet the requirement of temples that in turn support the social functions, similarly, the Srinathji temple near Udaipur has a sacred grove located in Gautamesvara forest block. The temple management does not derive authority from the state forest regulations and protects its grove against grazing, fire and illicit felling.[35] Paoti Koda is a site at the Ved Forest Block near Mewara. The most common trees here are Bibhitaki(terminalia bellirica), Arjuna (Terminalia arjuna), and Gum Karaya(Sterculia). Among these arboreal species, several herbs, shrubs, and vines form a dense mat. In this grove, there is a natural water source.[36] Boresvara is a site at the Phalior forest block in Aspur tehsil *(Banswara district)*. On the banks of the river Mahi, skirted at the river and with rows of Negundo (Vitex negundo) shrubs is the Boresvara Mahadeva sacred grove dedicated to Mahadeva, a form of Siva characterised by the abundance of arboreal fauna and flora. The most common species of the grove are Arjuna. Tendu (Diospyros melanoxylon), Gum Bel (Aegle marmelos), Cluster Fig (Ficus racemosa), True Date Palm (Phoenix dactylifera), Kadamba (Anthocephalus cadamba), and Fig (Ficus carica). The trees in the grove are older and taller than those in the outside forest with several black langurs, squirrels, and birds in the dense canopies.[37]

Sacred Groves and Governmental Support Today

There are two trees, known as the Indian Kalpavrksa (adansonia digitata-baobab), that are present at about three miles from Banswara city in the Anand Sagar near Mahi River. Bhils call the trees Kalpadeva (lit. "tree-deity") and they are declared as national monuments by the Indian government. Of the pair, the larger one, 20-feet high, is designated as Rani (queen) and the smaller, 14-feet-high, tree is designated as Raja (king). Apparently, another tree nearby was submerged in the Mahi River a few years ago. The Bhils have immense faith in these trees and travellers always have a darsana of the trees. People desirous of having any wishes fulfilled circumambulate both the trees, keeping their wishes in mind, contemplating a return in order to perform yajna, the fire sacrificial ritual, as a token of their gratitude. By the number of such rituals being performed, it appears that the wishes of several Bhils have been fulfilled. Even during birth and death, the Bhils worship the Kalpadeva with specific rituals. The age of these trees may be over 500 years according to a local forest officer. Similarly, Mahua (Madhuca lonfolia) is also considered sacred by the Bhils.[38]

A programme called Aravalli Devvan Sanrakshan Abhiyan (Aravalli Sacred Grove Conservation Campaign) was launched in 1992. This included protection of groves, planting of indigenous species, soil and water conservation, and a participatory approach to restoration. Some of the restored groves include Moria Ka Khuna, Jhamesvaraji, Amarkji, Ubesvaraji, Dhinkli, Haldu Ghati, Banki, Khokhariya Ki Nal and Ambua sacred groves.[39]

Another major government managed environmental project, which is based on the religiosity of Bhils, is Sitamata Wildlife Sanctuary, located 30 miles from Chittorgarh and 60 miles from Udaipur in the hilly area of the Aravallis. Its area is about 400 square kilometres. It was declared as a sanctuary in 1979. In this sanctuary, around half of the trees are teak, besides these, salar, tendu, amla (phyllanthus emblica), and bamboo are also present. The leopard, hyena, jackal, fox, jungle cat, porcupine, spotted deer, wild bear, four-horned antelope, and nilgai are the animals found here.[40] The most conspicuous animal of the sitamata sanctuary is the flying squirrel, usually gliding from one tree to another after sunset.

Bhils of about 50 villages around the Sitamata sanctuary make use of these plants as the means of primary health care to cure various ailments. The study revealed the new ethobotanical uses of 24 plants. There is also a temple dedicated to Hanuman where supposedly Lava and Kusa had tied him during their encounter with Rama's army. I encountered similar mythic associations at several places in Southern Rajasthan. The most popular such temple is Ghotiya Amba. In the surrounding area of about 40 square kilometres is a dense forest of mainly sagwan trees. According to the local folklore, Rama visited the Rama Kunda during his exile, the Pandavas visited the Bhima Kunda during their exile, and they had used a tunnel as their passage during the rainy season that connects the Bhima Kunda to Ghotiya Amba.[41]

The new ritual of sprinkling saffron, Kesar Chhanta, which has helped protect several areas of forests in Southern Rajasthan is a popular method of conserving sacred groves. People collect saffron from a nearby temple and sprinkle it collectively around a natural forest patch. This puts voluntary restriction on green felling. This also protects water sources, medicinal herbs, and fruit-bearing species. For example, in Udaipur South Forest Division about 12,000 hectares of forests are being protected by Kesar Chhanta. These areas include Vijaya Talai in Salumber, Alsigarh; Bada Bhilwara, and Shyampura in Udaipur (West), Madri in Jhadol, and Nayanbara in Khairwara. This faith has also been used by the Forest Department to initiate the protection by local communities at several places. Sagwara, Kojawada, Vijaya Talai, Pargiya Pada, Ranjitpura, Jagnathpura, and Barli Padi forests are protected and managed by the people.[42]

NOTES AND REFERENCES

1. R.L. Singh, *India: A Regional Geography*, Varanasi and New Delhi, p. 557; Maj. K.D. Erskine, *Rajputana Gazetteers*, Vol. II-A and Vol. II-B, Mewar Residency (Reprinted in 1992), Gurgaon, p. 1.
2. Ibid., p. 557.
3. Ibid.
4. Morris Carstairs, 'The Bhils of Kotra Bhomat', *Eastern Anthropologist*, Vol. VIII, Nos. 3 and 4, 1953 4, pp. 169 181.
5. V.C. Misra, *Geography of Rajasthan*, Delhi, 1961, p. 173.
6. Ibid., pp. 110-111.

7. V.K. Jain, *Trade and Traders in Western India, AD 1000-1300*, Delhi, 1990, p. 111.
8. O.H. Spate, *India, Pakistan and Ceylon*, London, 1972, p. 627.
9. Morris Carstairs, 'The Bhils of Kotra Bhomat' in *Eastern Anthropologist*, Vol. VIII, Nos. 3-4, 1953-4, pp. 169-181.
10. Ibid., p. 181.
11. *Gazetteer of Chittaurgarh*, Government of Rajasthan, Jaipur, 1977, p. 15.
12. R.K. Dhabai, 'Regional Structure of Mewar' M.Phil. Dissertation, Centre for Studies in Regional Development, JNU, New Delhi, 1975 (unpublished).
13. D.C. Sircar, *The Guhilas of Kiskindha*, Calcutta, 1965.
14. Ibid.
15. Ibid.
16. Paul T. Craddock et al., 'The Production of Lead, Silver and Zinc in Early India' in A. Hauptmann, E. Perinicka and G.A. Wagner, (eds.), *Old World Archaeometry*, Bochum, 1989, p. 56.
17. *Samoli Inscription*, EI, Vol. XX, pp. 99-100, II. 7-8.
18. Grant of King Babhata of AD 688, see Sircar, *The Guhilas of Kishkindha*, p. 175.
19. Ibid., p. 187, 1.31, *(Kosavahe Chittullakakshetram manivap tensasanena pradattam.)*.
20. *Chirava Inscription*, EI, Vol. XXII, Delhi, 1986, pp. 28-92, II. 1-3, '*Sri Citrakute Citrangatadagamadhya Sri Vaidyanatha*'.
21. *Shodh Patrika*, Vol. VII, Udaipur, pp. 65-6.
22. Eklingaji Temple Dakshina Dwara Prasasti of AD 1488, *Vir Vinod*, Vol. I, Delhi, 1986, p. 87.
23. Nandini Sinha Kapur, *State Formation in Rajasthan: Mewar during the Seventh-Fifteenth Centuries*, New Delhi, 2002, p. 224.
24. Motilal Menar, *Rajprashasti Mahakavya*, Udaipur, 1973 p. 92, v. 13
25. Ibid., p. 124, v. 9.
26. Ibid., p. 125, vv. 7-9.
27. Ibid., Ch. 19, p. 2012, vv. 7-8.
28. Ibid., v. 8.
29. Studies in Social Protest, 2010, Shyam Lal, 305.8009544 L15S.
30. Pankaj Jain, *Dharma and Ecology of Hindu Communities: Sustenance and Sustainability*, 2011, Survey, UK, Chapter 5.
31. Ibid., p. 85.
32. Ibid., p. 86.
33. Prabhakar Joshi, *Ethonobotany of the Primitive Tribes in Rajasthan*, Jaipur, 1995.
34. Ibid.

35. Prabhakar Joshi, op. cit., 1995.
36. Fieldwork undertaken by Jain and documented in *Jain, Dharma and Ecology*, p. 86.
37. Ibid., p. 88.
38. Ibid., p. 89.
39. Deep N. Pandey, *Beyond Vanishing Woods: Participatory Survival Options for Wildlife, Forests and People*, Udaipur, 1996.
40. Ibid., p. 90.
41. Ibid., pp. 87, 90-9.
42. Ibid., pp. 91-92.

3

Sacred Groves and Social Formation: Towards Environmental History of Kerala

Hashik N.K.

Landscape constitutes the visible features of an area of land including the physical elements of landforms.[1] The landscapes are mainly of two types, the natural and the cultural landscapes.[2] A cultural landscape is the reflection of how humans have related to, and transformed their environment. They are illustrative of the evolution of human society and settlement over time, under the influence of physical constraints and/or opportunities presented by the natural environment and of successive social, economic and cultural forces, both external and internal.[3] The study of geographical features of an area is essential to understand the engagement of humans to their natural settings[4]. In the earlier period to the present age human life was dependent on the surrounding environment which they have inhabited. This can be attributed to have an influence on the origin and development of different types of cultures in diverse environmental zones.[5] Through various attitudes of a group, the landscape reflects the cultural character of their everyday life. This landscape is known as Historic-Vernacular Landscapes.

Kerala state is situated on the south-western part of the Indian peninsula. The land is rich in the availability of water and there are forty-four rivers flowing throughout the state, out of which forty-one flow towards the west and the rest towards the east. Several places of politico-historical and cultural importance are located on the banks of these rivers. Such rich heritage reveals how the rivers of Kerala influenced the different realms of the lives of the people.

The Bharathappuzha is the biggest of all rivers in Kerala. The river originates from the *'trimurthi sangam'* of Anamalai hills in the Western Ghats and flows through the three districts of Kerala (Palakkad, Thrishur and Malappuram).[6] Finally, the river joins with the Arabian Sea at Ponnani. The three districts have many villages on the river banks which are inhabited by different cultural communities. All the communities have their own worldview and perceptions of the river. Thus the river has influenced much on the construction of the community's identity living in and around it.

The limited works produced related to the natural landscape and its influence over the cultural construction was either confined to romanticise the existence of the river and more explanatory in nature.[7] The present chapter tries to look at the construction of regional history based on the various discourses on the natural landscapes by taking an individual river for a comprehensive study. It also helps to understand the socio-economic formations of communities from the perspectives of environmental history.

Natural and Cultural Landscape of Bharathappuzha

It is interesting to note that the water streams in Kerala are known as *'puzha'*. The Malayalam word *puzha* means a small river/stream of water or water flows. Generally in India, the large natural stream of water is known as *nadi*. The word *nadi* is derived from the Sanskrit root word *'nad'* meaning channel, stream or flow. In the case of Kerala, almost all water streams are small compared to other parts of India and the people name it as *puzha* (small water stream). In India, most of the rivers are considered as goddesses.[8] But it is interesting to note that Bharathappuzha is not recognised as a god or goddesses for the world view since the folk of Kerala perceived it as a stream rather than as a river. This is because of the very geographical locale of the state of Kerala. It is situated in a strip of territory between the Western Ghats and the Arabian Sea, infested with thick vegetation obstructing the eyes from the clear and long view of the water flows at any given point of space. In the neighbouring states the river flows are visible clearly for very long distances unlike in the state of Kerala. Perhaps due to this very physical feature, the folk of Kerala considered the river as *puzha* or *aar* denoting stream. The banks of Bharathappuzha are considered as the fertile land of paddy cultivation and is known as the 'rice bowl of Kerala'.

Bharathappuzha and Tributaries: The Appellatives

Bharathppuzha has two other names which exist in the middle and ending part, i.e. Nila and Ponnani respectively. This is the only river in India known with its name as 'Bharatha'. From Parali, Amaravathippuzha and Kalpathippuzha joins and from that place onwards the river is known as Bharathappuzha. There are many legends/opinions with regard to the existence of the origin of the name Bharathppuzha.

Table 1: River Name – Appellative Derivation

S. No.	*River*	*Attribution*		
		Male	*Female*	*Place/Visual*
1	Barathappuzha	Bharatha		
2	Barathappuzha			Parathi means wide
3	Nila			Neelam means long
4	Nila			Nilappadu Thara means the place where the Zamorin kings made decisions.
5	Nila			Nile in Egypt
6	Nila		Daughter of Neelagiri Hills	
7	Neela			Neela means blue
8	Ponani			Pon (gold)
9	Ponani	Ponan King		

Table 2: Tributaries of Bharathappuzha – Appellative Derivation

S. No.	River	Appellative		
		Male	Female	Place/Visual
1	Chitoorppuzha			Small place river
2	Shokanashinippuzha			Destroyer of sorrow
3	Kalpathippuzha			Stone path
4	Gayathrippuzha		Gayathri	
5	Thoothappuzha			Bubbles of milk
6	Kunthippuzha		Kunthi	
7	Palar			River of milk
8	Valayaarppuzha			From Valayaar hills
9	Varattar			Seems to be dried
10	Kanneerppuzha			Removal of tears
11	Paralippuzha			Through the place Parali
12	Ayloorppuza			River from Ayloor hills
13	Karimppuzha			Black river
14	Thiroorppuzha			River of good place
14	Kannadippuzha			Mirror glaze

The appellative derivation of the main river and its tributaries also comes from the very worldview of the folk. The naming of the river is almost akin to the physical appearance. Both in the case of Bharathappuzha and its tributaries the naming system of the folk is directly derived from the physical appearance of the water/river in a given geographical locale. Therefore different names are found for the same river/tributary (what the folk see and perceive is the driving force for naming). This suggests that the worldview of the Kerala folk is related directly to their physical realm. The naming system therefore is associated with the physical realm and later may crystallise drawing from mythology, etc., connected with the metaphysical realm.

The cultural phenomenon of nature reveals the human attitude towards environment. In a way, human intervention and adaptation to natural environments inevitably led to cultural landscape. In order to exploit the natural resources like rivers and streams for their sustenance the folk communities settled on the banks and made huge settlements. The constant interaction and activities of the communities with the water resources caused disruption to the course of the river flows. Nevertheless, the communities engaged in various forms using the water attributing sacrality especially with the construction activities around sacred groves and thereby conducting rituals and ceremonies at timely intervals.

To understand the emergence of different communities on the banks of Bharathappuzha one has to look for the historicity on the life on the banks of the river. During historical times, several political powers facilitated the settlements of different caste groups and communities for their sustenance. As a result, several social groups with different occupations were encouraged by the rulers to settle on the banks for the expansion of agriculture, trade, commerce and industry for augmenting their resources.

Historicity and Communities on the River Banks

The banks of the river Barathappuzha are one of the early settlements of inhabitants in Kerala. The area is very rich in megalithic monuments found in various parts of the banks of Bharathappuzha, especially on hills and forests. It is the *pazhamtamilpattu* (Sangam literature) that helps to understand the history of South India during the first centuries of AD and Kerala was part of the old *tamizhakam*. The first kingdom of Cheras was an important power in Kerala in the early centuries of the Christian era. During the 3rd century BC Jainism and Buddhism reached Kerala from North India. Brahmins also migrated to Kerala as the continuation of these people's migration. There is no unanimous opinion among the historians about the date of the migration of Brahmins to Kerala.[9] Brahmins gave ideological support and justification of the administration of the Chera kings. As remuneration, they got land and other valuable assets from the king. The other classes such as Panar (Bards of the Nayar community), Vedar (local tribe) and Kuravar (local tribe) who were getting help from the king were sidelined and downgraded their position to the lower strata of society.

After the 8th century AD, Kerala became a special political and cultural centre under the second Chera kingdom. Kerala was the totality of many territorial divisions which consisted of *nadus* (a district). The 'Nadu' was the highest administrative set up and Naduvazhi (ruler of *nadu*), a local chieftain was the head and under him were many *desham* for military purposes. *Desavazhi* (administrator of desam) is the head. After the decline of the Cheras (12-13 AD) of Mahodayapuram, the local governors raised powers and claimed the independence of their local area.[10] This was a crucial period in the social formation of Kerala. The rest of the history of Kerala after the fall of the second Chera kingdom is the history of *swaroopams.*[11] The expansion of agricultural activities and settlement patterns, the increasing domination of Brahmins, division of caste based on occupations and the rise of social order based on the administration of the temple complex were the main features during the reign of local kings.

The history of the banks of Bharathappuzha during the pre-Portuguese period is centred primarily on the kingdom of Zamorins (Calicut). Calicut was the major power in northern and central Kerala in the medieval period[12]. The banks of Bharathappuzha were the fertile lands for growing pepper and forest wealth. The Zamorins began to conquer neighbouring areas. The main aim was to capture the natural resources. Thus, when the Portuguese landed in the Kerala coast in 1498, the Zamorins were powerful sovereigns who had by then (under their control) almost all the chieftains of north Kerala including the king of Cochin as their vassals.

Vasco da Gama reached Calicut (Kappad) in 1498 and this led to the starting point for modern European colonialism in Kerala. As a continuation of European power, the Dutch had appeared in Kerala and conquered the Portuguese stronghold of Quilom, Cranganore, Purakkad, Cochin and Cannonore.[13]

The English also came to Kerala for the purpose of trade like the Portuguese and the Dutch. Meanwhile, the ruler of Mysore, Hyder Ali and Tipu Sultan conquered parts of Kerala around the Malabar region from the Zamorins. England fought against Tipu in many wars and Tipu Sultan was ultimately defeated. Finally based on the treaties of Srirangapatanam signed on February 22 and March 18, 1792, Tipu formally ceded Malabar to the British.[14] On the whole, the migrations into the land of Kerala contributed to the development of the history of the region.

An overview of the time frame of the migrations of different religious and racial groups shows that all races and groups inhabited this region. The settlement of communities on the banks of Bharathappuzha shows the distribution of communities based on occupation and engagement. They are (1) Temple servants include Brahmins and other groups (2) Occupational classes such as Kammalans, Kumbarans, etc. (3) Settlement of agricultural labourers.

It is evident that the banks of Bharathappuzha being fertile attracted many communities from historical times to the present. However, the settlement pattern reveals that the tribals and indigenous communities who are the inhabitants of the banks and hilly terrains of Bharathappuzha replaced or subdued by the process of 'Aryanisation' wherein the '*jatis*' (occupational ranking, i.e. castes) of upper '*varna*' (ritual ranking) encouraged to immigrate into the Kerala soils and expand the settled agrarian economy. As a result the social hierarchy emerged on one hand negating the 'Aryan *varna* system' and on the other incorporating it with the native hierarchical system. This paradox is quite visible in the ethno-centric overtones of the lower strata of the society and often reflected as the anti-Brahminical attitude especially, against the Namboothiri-Nayar alliance.

The major groups such as Namboothiri-Nayar from the 'Hindu fold' and Muslims and Christians have influenced the life and lore of the folk on the banks of Bharathappuzha and interestingly they themselves are affected by migrations. In other words, the religious ideology of these major communities is not native to Kerala soils but immigrated into Kerala with their immigration and settlement. As the major land owning and ritual management communities which exercise control over the land and people are from immigrant castes, their mythologies and ritual practices connected with sacred complexes also show the migratory nature wherein ritual and belief are constructed with the ideologies of non-native communities.

Sacred Groves and Construction of Territory

The worshipping form of primitive societies is varied in different parts of the world. Among all worship forms, the form of nature worship is a common tradition. Different ways of this nature worship are deeply rooted in the cultural activities of different communities. Worshipping of trees as part of nature worship is embedded in the customs of ancient pre-agrarian societies and they believed that trees were the abode of sacred spirits. Most of the communities attribute sacred character to the trees and establish beliefs and customs to ensure the protection of the sacred space of the trees.

Sacred groves (*kavukal*) consist of natural vegetation of the locality and are attributed with supernatural power (henceforth kavu/kavukal). The size of these groves starts from a few trees to kilometres of forest. Sacred groves are found in different religious beliefs in the continents such as Asia, America, Africa and Australia. Nature worship is an Indian tradition existing since time immemorial. The sacred grove is a form of nature worship and is a component of the village landscape in India. Many groves have shrines within them. It is believed that the power of gods/goddesses exist in the trees.[15] In the case of Kerala, there are no authentic survey accounts available about the number of sacred groves. In the local survey, the banks of Bharathappuzha were said to have nine hundred and seventy sacred groves. These sacred groves are the key to understand the cultural treasures of a region. The settlement pattern of the communities on the river banks and the intercommunity relations are based on the sacred grove. The village deity came into existence when people settled as an agricultural community. This would help to understand the human habitation and its relationship to nature.

The Malayalam word kavu means a garden/the multitude of trees/consortium of trees[16] and kavu is the sacred place where the goddess resides. Most of the kavus face the north. There are three stages in the evolution of kavu in Kerala, they are: (1) A stone under a tree, (2) small building constructed around the tree and there was no roof in that kind of building. It has a *srikovil* (sanctum sanctorum) (3) construction of separate building near the tree and shifted the stone of the goddess inside the building with *srikovil* and the pyramid roof of the building has small holes.[17] The edge of the roof is in pyramid shape and the bottom is in square shape. In the past, thick forests persisted in the kavus but now the entire vegetation of the kavus has been destroyed and only the shrines exist. In the above explanation about kavu, nowadays it is considered as a shrine and hereafter would use shrines to denote kavu. The banks of Bharathappuzha are known as the land of many kavus. Shrines are constructed in association with the sacred groves of deities. In some areas, they have a small place in the form of a stone, idol, platform or a single tree for worship. In the serpent kavu, generally there is no shrine but instead they worship small idols of stones representing the serpent god. The kavus of Northern Kerala exceed in hectares, whereas the kavus on the banks of Bharathappuzha are relatively small in size.[18] It is considered that the sacred grove shows the harmony between humans and nature. The symbolic representation of sacred groves is quite problematic in the present days. In order to look at sacred groves as the ecological wisdom of ancient Kerala, it also constructed the social structure of each territory through varied ritual hierarchy. Often, the sacred groves environment works as a tool to understand the environmental history of the place around it through the ritual practices and involvement of the community in a region.

The kavus has a pivotal position in the socio-economic life of the villagers. These provide a place for village gatherings during festive occasions. The *thattakam* (jurisdiction) is a territory under a goddess and each community of the *thattakam* is supposed to contribute money and paddy to the kavu during the festival period. Sacred groves are a nodal point of a divine area and the surrounding area of the shrine is a unit call *thattakam*. This place is a holy land of shrines. The concept emerged based on the settlement pattern of different communities in Kerala. Each *thattakam* has a nucleus in the form of kavu where the Bhagavathi reside, a centre which reflects the worship of Bhagavathi. This is a geographical area of the shrine where the Bhagavathi visit the people of *thattakam* during the annual festival. During the annual festival of the kavu, the *thattakam* will be in a festive mood. Most of the houses will be decorated. Bhagavathi and the oracle would travel along the streets on the elephant. The concept is that the presiding deity of the *thattakam* is personally verifying the well-being of the devotees. The members of the *thattakam* would not visit other *thattakam* and prohibit conducting marriages and other ceremonies at the time of the annual festival in the *thattakam*.[19] This attests to the fact that the identity of the territory is not defined by its interior alone and it does not deny the existence of the exterior.[20]

The kavus are numerous in Kerala and there are many myths, legends and beliefs associated with them. The beliefs and rituals performed in the kavus vary with the region, caste and patron deity of the kavu. The kavus are found in almost all regions of Kerala and more or less reduced in size, even though many of them keep the trees around it. Broadly, the kavus of Kerala are classified into three types (1) *Mrigadaivakavu* where Zoomorphic gods are worshipped (2) *Daiva* kavu where a male god is worshipped (3) *Bhagavathikavu* where a female deity is worshipped.

Further, these kavus are known under different names based on the deity to whom the grove is dedicated to. They are considered as holy places for worship and many of them have small shrines attached to them. This is crucial to understand that the *thattakam* manifest the local aspirations, idioms and ideologies thereby forming a worldview of the region.

Community Life and Environmental History: A New Paradigm

The kavu or the shrine got its name due to the local legends or the local origin myths of goddesses. If one looks at the kavus in the origin part of Bharathappuzha, it is interesting to note that most of them are under the control of the Nayar community. They are the patron *ooraalar* (hereditary trustees) and the kavus are the basic element of Nayar domination. There are some kavus where the priests are Nayars. They conduct forty-one days Namboothiri puja in a year. The Nayars were the landlords of the village and the base of all their activities was Bhagavathi. They conduct weekly rituals on Tuesday and Friday and offer *payasam* (sweet broth made of milk, sugar and rice) and *guruthi* (sacrifice) to Bhagavathi. At present, the kavus under the Nayars follow these rituals.[21] The kavu acts as an administrative centre of Nayars. Even after the transformation of the joint family system to nuclear family, many nuclear families are attached to their ancestral family by ancestral ritual practices. Nowadays, they form a committee and the patron of the kavu would be the secretary of the shrine. The members of the village are also the part of the committee for the administration of the shrine. All festivals of the kavu are celebrated under the control of this committee.

The chief festival in which the people take part in the original part of Bharathpuzha is *vela*.[22] It is mostly held in the family shrine (kavu) of the Nayar community in the Malayalam month from *kumbham* to *medam* (February to April).[23] Many kavus can be seen in each taluk and large numbers of families are attached to the shrine. Several communities were denied entering the shrine. The major *vela* in this area include Puthussery *vela*, Chandhana kavu *vela*, Thirupuraikal *vela*, Vallikode *vela*, Manappuli kavu *vela*. The original part of the Bhagavathi shrine was more or less the shrine of individual families and in due course they accommodated the other communities of the village. In a way, the sphere of influence of the *vela* festival is surrounded by the *thattakam* of Bhagavathi which is confined to a single *desham* (the term is known as the modern classification of the village).[24] Each *desham* celebrates the annual festival of

Bhagavathi in their respective shrine. The shrine of Bhagavathi in the village is the centre of the people's life around it. At present, the shrines in the origin part are under the administration of a committee which is the totality of the patron of the shrine and the members of the village. This committee will conduct all the activities related to the shrine. The designation of the patron of the shrine is known as *rakshadhikari* (protector). It is evident that the community which is getting traditionally the chief patronship due to the claim that they installed the idol and constructed the shrine for the Bhagavathi. Even today they are the prime decision-makers in the temple committees with regard to the festivals and celebration of the shrines.

The kavu is the place where the village deity resides who is trusted to protect the village and its property from natural calamities and diseases. The villagers will regularly conduct annual ritual performances in the kavu. No one can change the rituals in the kavu because most of the kavus are under the control of the kavu committee which include the members of different communities who reside around the kavu.

Graph 1: Puthoorkavu

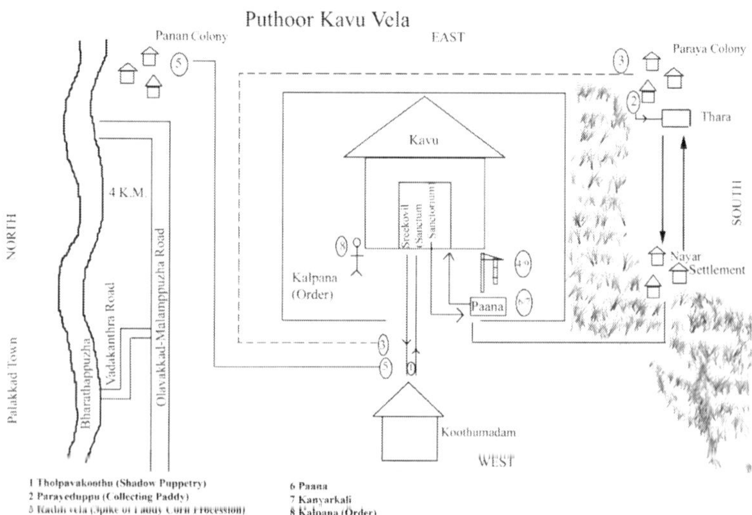

The above is the graphic depiction of the thattakam of Puthoor Bhagavathi and also the ritual space assigned to each community during the annual festival. This kavu is situated in the Puthoor area, Palakkad district (origin part of Bharathappuzha) which lies on the banks of Bharathappuzha.

Table 3: Community and Performance in Puthoorkavu

S.No.	*Ritual Event*	*Community*
1	*Tholpavakooothu* (shadow puppetry)	Nayar
2	*Parayeduppu* (collecting paddy)	Paraya
3	*Kathirvela* (spike of paddy corn procession)	Paraya
4	*Kodiyettam* (flag hoisting)	Priest and patron of the shrine
5	*Pankali*	Panan
6	*Paana*	Nayar
7	*Kanyarkali*	Nayar
8	*Kalpana* (order)	Oracle (*velichapadu*)
9	*Kodiyirakkam* (flag down)	Priest and patron of the shrine

Most of the shrines in the origin part are under the patronship of the Nayar community and they accommodate other communities such as Paraya, Panan to their festival.[25] The rest of the ritual is performed by the Nayar community and by giving the order of Bhagavathi to the villagers, the Nayar community emphasise their socio-political supremacy through the ritual performances of the shrine. The performance begins with the entering of the Nayar community's ritual performance and flag hoist the ritual command of the representative of Bhagavathi, i.e oracle. At the end of every celebration the oracle informs the villagers through his trance the nature of goddess after the festival (whether she is satisfied with the ritual or not). This shows that the reinforcement of hierarchy can be seen in the entry and exit point of the different communities in the annual ritual performances. This territory holds together heterogeneities by the expression of a commonality among the elements. Territory is a discourse of a limited space, a dynamic site for carrying out enactment and producing a sense of belonging. It also reinforces the logic of boundaries that encompasses all sorts of activities, practices and relations.

The migration outside India including the gulf countries was very low in the origin part. People of this area find new opportunities in the growing commercial area surrounding them than in migration out of the locality and country. It is very clear that the investment direction has been changed from agriculture. The transportation network and population density leads to different marketing outlets and schools in these localities. Various socio-economic and political elements create social mobility among the communities. They are able to construct their houses instead of living in a house owned by landlords. This upward mobility creates the structural changes of the relationship of the communities and leads to the rise of new land owners and the marketing of land. Breaking the feudal and patriarchal past through education helped the emancipation of lower caste/communities. The newly educated unemployed generation are not prepared to work in the agricultural sector. This caused the higher labour demand. Farmers are using land for other purposes than paddy cultivation. The large farmers who are able to get two crops a year have interest in paddy cultivation. Even though they are not ready to buy additional land for paddy cultivation.

The above reason would provide the rise of a new middle class lifestyle among the new generation. The new shift of earning income and change of lifestyle creates consequences in the social environment. The decline of common interest in the farming sector, the bond among the various local communities has weakened. People start to move in new social settings with the generality of roles and relation. The emergence of the new class in villages creates social change in the communities of the origin part. Even though structural changes have occurred in the life of the communities, they are participating in the annual ritual festivals under the surveillance of the deity of their jurisdiction. In this context, the sacred grove and the territory describes socio material contexts for a discursive space. The identity of each territory is based on its own terms and conditions. This strengthens the continuity of the nexus between the sacred grove and community relationship in the micro level of the history on the origin part of Bharathappuzha. It highlights the nature of the construction of environment on the banks of Bharathappuzha and cultural history of the communities.

The territory of the goddess is the space of societal relations which reflects through a complex set of articulations. It continues in the relations between belonging and alienation of communities, identity and identification in connection with the goddess as well as within the community. The structure of performance constitutes the territory as a lived totality in the worldview of community. The sacred grove is a location of spatio-temporal investment through an intensive relationship in the territory. The macro historical narratives of Kerala neglect these regional specific articulations of each locality of Kerala. The reciprocal relationship between the river and the scared grove (kavu) on the social formation of peoples attest the fact that, the changes in the environmental settings and its attachment to the people's life construct and re-construct the history of a region. The *janmi-kudiyan* (landlord-tenant)[26] relationship and its decline in the land of Kerala have not stopped the role of environment in the construction of history. The Nayar community did not engage in any agricultural activities during the time of the Naduvazhis. Later due to the decline of Namboothiri Brahmins power and social capital acquired through modern education helped them to be the part of government servants. This new social position helped to continue one of the strongest organised communities in Kerala in the present times.

It shows that the customs, political systems and economic pattern are all strongly linked to sacred grove worship. This interrelation reiterates the administrative systems and it has been surrounded by various hierarchies to each community. Sacred grove as the epicentre of the village life influenced the politics, trade and pilgrims. The market during the annual festival had been a key role in the economic system of the people of the jurisdiction. It visibly marks the peculiar nature of the demography and construction of space in the land of Kerala. The pattern of evolution of village discussed above must have been spread with the combination of different communities over in the geographical area on the banks of Bharathappuzha. Each place had its own segmentation of community and there is no uniformity in the combination of community in one *desham*. Thus the settlement patterns of different communities in the land of Kerala are of a different nature and it paves the way to look at the environmental history from the framework of the evolution of human habitation in Kerala. The changing relationship and engagement with the environment constitutes the need of studies to look at the change and continuity of *thattakam*. Thus, the environmental history of Kerala could focus on the regional variations and role of each *thattakam* in the construction of environmental history.

NOTES AND REFERENCES

1. The word landscape denotes that the land combines with the German verb *scapjan, schaffen'* which means literally shaped lands. Otto Schlutter (1908) first used the word 'cultural landscape' and defined geography as landscape science (*landschaftiskunde*).
2. The natural landscapes are those that originally emerged like valleys, caves, rivers, etc. The latter are those that are emerged due to the intervention of the culture, i.e. human beings with the nature.
3. UNESCO, *Operational Guidelines for the Implementation of the World Heritage Convention*, Paris, Inter-governmental Committee of the Protection of the World Cultural and Natural Heritage, February, 1994, p. 13.
4. J. Smith, *Definition and Assessment of Cultural Landscapes of Heritage Value on NCC Lands*, Canada, National Capital Commission, 2004.
5. Concept of Cultural Landscapes originated in Europe in the 15th century. The artists began to paint landscapes for people, diminishing people in their paintings to figures subsumes within the broader regionally specific landscapes.
6. The Bharathappuzha is situated almost in the central part of the state. The total length of the river is 255 km wherein 46 km flows in Coimbatore district of Tamil Nadu and the remaining 209 km course flows through Kerala state from the east to the west. The river originates from a small water stream of the '*Thrimurthy hills*' of Anamalai in the Western Ghats at about 610.26 metres above mean sea level.
7. Rajan Chungath describes the kingdoms on the banks and the

life of Kerala Brahmins on the banks. V.V.K. Vaalath analyses place names of Palakkad district and the reason behind the origin of local place names both naturally and culturally.

8. In certain cultures, the river attains either male or female qualities. In Greece, rivers are strongly masculine. According to Egyptian mythology the river Hep or Hapi, the god of the Nile River, is always depicted in the form of a man, but his breasts are those of a woman.
9. According to K.P. Padmanabha Menon, the Brahmins reached in the 3rd century AD whereas William Logan opined that it was in the 8th century AD. The modern historians opined that one cannot assume that they have come to Kerala as a big settlement group rather they came as small groups in different times and settled in various places. There are references to Brahmins in Kerala in Sangam literature.
10. K.A. Nilakantha Sastri, *The Cholas*, Madras, University of Madras, 1975.
11. There is no clear cut idea about the meaning of the word '*swaroopams*'. It could be the geographical locality under a local king. All these *swaroopams* had a centre for their administration.
12. N.M. Namboothiri, *Malabar Padanangal Zamoothirinadu*, Trivandrum, Kerala State Institute of Languages, 2008.
13. A. Galletti and Rev P. Groot, *The Dutch in Malabar*, New Delhi, Usha Publications, 1984.
14. W. Logan (ed.), *A Collection of Treaties, Engagements and Other Papers of Importance Relating to British Affairs in Malabar*, Calicut, Manuel, 1879.
15. In India, sacred groves are known under different names in different regions such as, *Dev* in Madhya Pradesh, *Saranas* in Bihar, *derais/devrahati* in Maharashtra, *Sarna/dev* in Jharkhand and Chhattisgarh, *Orans* in Rajasthan, *Devrakadu* or *Sidharvana* in Karnataka, *Kovilkadu/Thirunandavana* in Tamil Nadu and Kavu in Kerala.
16. E. Unnikrishnan, *Sacred Groves of North Kerala: Eco-Folklore Study* (Malayalam), Kannur, Sanskriti, 1995.
17. Sanjivan Azhikode, *Theyyathile Jaathivazhakkam*, Current Books, Thrishur, 2007.
18. As the abode of the spirit, the community prohibited the felling of trees, the collection of material from the sacred grove and killing of animals to ensure the protection of the place. They believe the deity would punish the people with diseases, crop failure and even death to individuals who violate the rule.

19. This segmentation of caste-based spatial distribution shows the nature of the formation of sacred groves on the banks of Bharathappuzha. It was a taboo for a caste to marry a person from the same caste in other *deshams* till the end of the 19th century.
20. Grossberg Lawrence, *Cultural Studies in the Future Tense*, Durham, Duke University Press, 2010.
21. These situations also reveal that the actual kaavu thattakam belonged to the lower community people. Ownership of the thattakam system was gradually taken over by higher classes by changing the living space of the goddess from the roof of the house of the village to the sacred grove. Even at the time of the annual festival the oracle conducts special pujas in the actual place of the deity. The interference of other communities changes the very basic nature of the relationship of community and deity.
22. The literal meaning of the word vela is work or time, whereas the people on the banks consider it the annual congregation of different communities.
23. It is considered that the Nayars may be Dravidian immigrants who were amongst the first invaders on the banks of Bharathappuzha.
24. *Census of Travancore 1891 and 1901*, Trivandrum, Government Press, 1893.
25. There were fewer Namboothiri Brahmin settlements during the 1885s in the Chittor region of Palakkad (origin part) district, whereas Namboothiri house on the other banks of Bharathappuzha was Valluvanadu 277, Ponnani 289, Eranad 120.
26. The changes in the resources especially when economic transaction has been shifted to currency exchange, the Namboothiri community became sidelined. They neglect the new education system, English language and government jobs. One side leads to poverty in the economy and the other is the absence of political power.

4

Knowledge Systems (KS), History and Environment in South Asia

Samuel Berthet

Introduction

History written within a local/regional context using local/regional sources (written, oral, anthropological, etc.) is a key to ecology. Ecology is an approach based on a contextualised science opposing de-contextualised one, as part of the modern project and KS eulogised by Descartes in the 17th century. Environmental history at the regional level uncover key issues such as scales (regions vis-à-vis the state/states, vis-à-vis other regions and smaller units, possible overlapping and shifting borders), languages and KS.

Verbal languages are part of communication systems carrying both knowledge and value systems (KVS).[1] Their development tends to favour and develop certain articulatory, sound and syntax patterns and atrophy others. They evolved specific systems that can be grouped in families sharing common features. The proposed classification are not exclusive of influences, overlapping and exchanges. Languages translate concerns common to human communities and individual beings across the globe as well as of extremely particular and specific ones. They can express those concerns both in similar and in different manners according to the different linguistic groups but also within themselves. They are the reflection of a cultural and natural diversity evolved through the recent millenniums and therefore their study both as a general phenomenon and as particular systems proves to be crucial to the understanding of environment and ecology. Furthermore the study of languages as a medium of communication and KS is not exclusive of non-verbal forms of communication. In modern societies they are part of state apparatuses, the modes of production and the market economy.

Ecology, Education and Language

Modernity changed the paradigm in education and science the world over. It did so violently and radically in the peripheries of the nation-states. The colonies suffered a double degree of *subalternity*, colonised being affected differently according to their proximity with the centres of power of the modern state. Education and modern science were framed in the colonies under the form of subaltern educational and research institutions. Their set up was based on an imperial agenda and material framework imposed and defined by the metropolis and the colonial power *in situ*[2]. It aimed at meeting the colonial financial and ideological interests. Defined in the coloniser's own terms and in its own language, by denying the cultural, educational and scientific value of the colonised culture the educational system under the British rule both supported and justified its very rule. Gradually, under the colonial rule Indian KS were marginalised in the educational and professional market undermining its economic relevance and hence its scientific one since the production of science is determined by the institutional and economic framework.

The early Orientalists' works were not attempts to prevent colonised Indians to access modern education or colonial romanticism, since modernity was not yet the mainstream discourse and the colonial agenda in India was yet to be written. In many cases, such as the French travellers' accounts of the 18th and early 19th century compiled by Jean Deleury[3] or works such as Van Rheede's *Hortus Malabaricus*[4], they were animated by a quest for knowledge finding in Indian culture and science a source to be tapped. Between the 16th to the 18th century an intense transfer of science technology occurred from South Asia to Europe thanks to the collaboration of South Asian experts with European travellers, merchants and scientists. By the end of the 18th century, this quest had further implications when developed within the discipline of philology by early promoters of the studies of Indian languages in Europe particularly in the case of Abraham Hyacinthe and Anquetil-Duperron. Philology as a comparative discipline—through the comparison between ancient Greek and Sanskrit—played an important role in humanities and social studies.

The promoters of colonisation quickly made the language one of their battlefields and a central issue in the conversion of the colonised to the colonisers' "enlightened" views. Education and the job market were the apparatuses for this conversion. By the end of the 18th century the East India Company promotion of English against Indian languages was sustained by the increasingly influent Evangelical movement pitting the scientific value of the English language—its *light* and *knowledge*—against the *darkness* of Indian languages and culture as a whole to quote the *Observations on the State of Society Among the Asiatic Subjects of Great Britain* published in 1792 by Company official Charles Grant.[5] The ensuing Orientalist controversy saw the triumph of the Evangelical views. Macaulay's famous minutes came as the official validation of a major shift.

Pioneers of ecology in India such as Tagore were particularly concerned with the issue of education and language. As analysed by Pierre Bourdieu in the general context of modern nation-states[6] and by Deepak Kumar in the case of the Raj, education was key to support a state infrastructure and a job market determined by English language sustaining a VS reflecting the colonisers' interest. Education became in itself a market with English language as both a capital and a source of income.

The linguistic policy developed later on during the 20th century by the British colonial ruler to favour the *vernacular* against English or *other European languages* was not meant at reversing the trend. It was another strategy to prevent the emancipation of the colonial subjects who to the taste of the coloniser invested with too much vigour and success the newly established formal education. English as the medium of excellence in education continued undisputed as compared to Indian languages, now considered *vernacular* or at best *classical but* irrelevant for present science and economy. The shift towards a pro-English language policy denying any scientific value and content to Indian languages and culture has far-reaching consequences for South Asia's social and economic fabric as well as for the relation to human and its environment in the region.

Why would English not cohabit with other languages in a multi-layered language structure and knowledge production system and act as a plateform? Why has English not become another *lingua franca* of the elite, like Persian before colonisation? Independent India introduced many changes such as the recognition of some Indian languages as state language apart from Hindi being made the national language along with English. The colonial legacy remains embedded in the infrastructure of nation-state: the higher educational system, research organisations, the Constitution and the judicial at the national level are based on the English medium system.

If languages are the medium of religious rites to address the invisible world, they can be described as rites in themselves. They embed social structure and power through a spectrum ranging from the implicit linguistic codes to the explicit laws. Though explicitly enunciated, the wording of laws often locate them out of reach of the non-initiated whose life they rule, even more so, in the colonial context when they were not evolved in a language system and reference system familiar to them and were meant at enforcing an imperialist agenda. The fact that almost all the South Asian leaders before and in the first decade of independence were English medium educated lawyers illustrate the intimate association between language, law and power in the colonial and post-colonial context. Education, and language provide the frame of power structure in the context of the modern nation-state.

The language/linguistic issue in India has therefore two facets: the general epistemological questioning of modernity in relation to Western languages as its vehicle (English, but also French, German, etc.) and the effect of the imposition in the colonial context of English against other languages in South Asia. Languages are battlefields, sites of power at the centre of the social reproduction.[7] They are tools in the hands of the elite to draw visible and invisible barriers with the rest of the community. English in colonial and post-colonial India has to be read in this equation between language, power, product and market. Vernacular LKS remain considered subaltern.

Critic of Modernity: Epistemology and Ecology

Language as the site of epistemology was at the centre of social scientists'concern in the second half of the 20th century.[8] The distinction between the object and the subject and its reflection between nature and culture was considered the modern man's original sin, the one responsible for nowadays' troubles between humans and the environment and the source of the very epistemological error of modernity.

Language is also at the centre of concern of today's French thinkers such as Augustin Berque and François Jullien dealing with the way human communities mediate their environment.[9] Languages are the result of the different ways of mediating the environment and in turn condition the way this environment is perceived and acted upon. Micro ecosystems and vernacular knowledge systems are keys to this approach in opposition to the transcendental and decontextualised modern one.

The modernity project is based on the definition of the subject and the object as different entities, the subjects being the only thinking entity is entitled to project transcendental truth on the object. The latter would not wield any influence on the former. According to Augustin Berque:

> The absolute-ity (*absoluité*) of the modern Western subject which correlates (nm) is the object: This transcendent position is none other than the one that the modern cogito has arrogated and that Descartes perfectly made explicit when he wrote *From this I knew I was a substance whose whole essence or nature is simply to think, and which does not require any place, or depend on any material thing, in order to exist.* (6:32–3)

The anti-ecological premises of the modernity project are laid down in this claim of a decontextualised thought. Augustin Berque shows that French language—as English—is pivotal in the building of Western modernity its very structure conveying a transcendental and unmediated relation to the object:

> In French *Marie is sad*. In Japanese, the same statement is impossible *Mari wakanashii* is impossible; one has to say *Mari wakanashisô da*, i.e. *Marie seems sad*; being *S is P for I*. In other words, in this language, the interpreter I is immanent to the appraisal *S is P*, while French can abstract it by giving it a transcending position (Berque).[10]

Other languages may propose a different relation object-subject and define a different human-non human paradigm. The overpowering paradigm at the basis of the rationale and modern thought is therefore particular to few LKS.

According to Michel Foucault in the *Order of Things*, the differences in modern thought would lie in an order of the living where human doesn't locate himself among other species. It is sustained by a vision of the world with *man* at its centre. *Man* is the *ordonnateur* or the director, the one who orders, creates order and puts in orders. Foucault saw in modern science a transcendental one in its ambitions, but an empirical in its methodology, relying on self-fulfilling prophecies and self-validating set of ideas. To overcome those limits, he proposes a paradigm shift by rethinking the location of human in the order of things:

> The true contestation of positivism and eschatology does not lie, therefore, in a return to actual experience (which rather, in fact provides them with confirmation by giving them roots); but if such a contestation could be made, it would be from the starting point of a question which may well seem aberrant, so opposed is it to what has rendered the whole of our thought historically possible. This question would be: Does man really exist? To imagine, for an instant, what the world and thought and truth might be if man did not exist, is considered to be merely indulging in paradox. This is because we are so blinded by the recent manifestation of man that we can no longer remember a time—and it is not so long ago—when the world, its order, and human beings existed, but man did not.[11]

The idea of a world without man as the director, could be considered as a premise for the radical shift of paradigm called for by ecology. Foucault mentions man as the *empirico-transcendental doublet* the *locus of misunderstanding— of misunderstanding that constantly exposes of being swamped by his own being, and also enables him to recover his integrity on the basis of what eludes him.*[12]

The other philosopher's idea of *man* under the threat of his own self is also at the very basis of the ecological thought. And he adds:

> The question is no longer: How can experience of nature give rise to necessary judgments? But rather: How can man think what he does not think, inhabit as though by a mute occupation something that eludes him, animate with a kind of frozen movement that figure of himself that takes the form of a stubborn exteriority?[13]

This interrogation calling for a new epistemology is very similar to the position of other pioneers of ecology such as Bateson and Schumacher[14]. For Foucault the reason for that stubborn exteriority lies in the fact that the roots, the inner structure and the intimate significance of language would have gradually escaped the speaker's own grasp over millenniums. In this disconnection lies the fundamental problem for humans' understanding of the world:

> How can man be that life whose web, pulsations, and buried energy constantly exceed the experience that he is immediately given of them? How can he be that labour whose laws and demands are imposed upon him like some alien system? How can he be the subject of a language that for a thousands of years has been formed without him, a language whose organisation escapes him, whose meaning sleeps an almost invincible sleep in the words he momentarily activates by means of discourse, and within which he is obliged, from the very outset, to lodge his speech and thought, as though they were doing no more than animate, for a brief period, one segment of that web of innumerable possibilities?[15]

Foucault showcases human beings under the threat of their anthropocentrism and their entanglement in a web of non-mastered codes and symbols, or signifiers and signified. The epistemological challenges caused by modernity are of ontological dimension according to Foucault. They meet the fundaments of the ecological project: where is the human in the order of things, a non-anthropocentric and a contextualised approach with the meaning of words and the structure of languages knowingly accepted, as a precondition for human's awareness of its own action upon nature, including him/herself.

Is modernity influenced and/or the result of the human genesis according to Semitic religions where humans appear at the beginning of the creation process and where the world proceeds from the word and becomes almost a processed form of the word?[16] Things exist only when and if named. Name gives life to things. The world process from the word and the verbal. Words can create things. The modernity project is based on the cultures of verbal communication. These cultures—sometimes qualified as the cultures of the book—granted an overpowering status to the verbal communication, the spoken one in a first phase and then gradually the written one marginalised all others including the verbal oral one. In a certain way, it may be proposed that the anthropocentric modern vision of the world, with man at its centre is co-existential to the central importance given to the verbal communication, and particularly its written forms, the attribute of the nation-state and its representatives. It is indeed often seen as the exclusive attribute of human, and only the most "evolved" among them, who hence would therein be the only specie able to access *articulated* thought and knowledge.

Language, KVS in a Contextualised Approach

The idea of modern languages as being the only ones able to convey scientific notions was refuted by Claude Lévi-Strauss in 1962 in *The Savage Mind.*[17] He calls the *Science of the Concrete* the sciences studied by anthropologists among what are considered non-modern communities and their KS (henceforth KSOM knowledge systems other than the modern). Lévi-Strauss first establishes the importance of order across cultures: *Any classification is superior to chaos and even a classification at the level of sensible properties is a step towards rational ordering.*[18] Then he reminds us that the belief in the superiority in one's own culture is a feature common to all societies and that so-called primitive societies when closely observed show not only a great deal of familiarity of their environment but also of concern and knowledge:

> Every civilisation tends to overestimate the objective orientation of its thought and this tendency is never absent. When we make the mistake of thinking that the savage is governed solely by organic or economic needs, we forget that he levels the same reproach at us and that to him his own desires for knowledge seems more balanced than ours. Their extreme familiarity with their biological environment, the passionate attention which they pay to it and their precise knowledge of it has often struck inquirers as an indication of attitudes and preoccupations which distinguish the natives from their white visitors.[19]

Claude-Strauss also questions the commonly accepted ideas that only modern languages offer the ability to express abstract concepts and therefore prove better for expressing scientific notions:

> It has long been the fashion to invoke languages which lack the terms for expressing such a concept as *tree* or *anima* even though they contain all the words necessary for a detailed inventory of species and varieties. But, to begin with, while these cases are cited as evidence of the supposed ineptitude of *ineptitude of primitive people* for abstract thought, other cases are at the same time ignored which make it plain that richness of abstract words is not a monopoly of civilised languages[20] and quoting Robbins, Harrington and Freire-Marreco: "The ordinary individuals among the whites does not distinguish (the different botanical species). Indeed it would be possible to translate a treatise on botany into Tewa."[21]

Similarly in India, the scientific value of pre-modern botany had attracted the attention of Europeans as illustrated by the work *Hortus Malabaricusa unique and pre-eminent position among all the early publications on botany in general and Indian plants in particular* (K.S. Manilal, C.R. Suresh and V.V. Sivarajan: 1997).[22] This work by Van Rheede, the Dutch Governor of Cochin, composed at the end of the 17th century was based on the

Ayurvedic system for the classification of plants in Malayali. This study in turn influenced the modern taxonomy laid by Van Linnen still relevant today. It is a case of Indian pre-modern constructed science scientifically relevant in its geographical and temporal context as well as beyond.

Claude Lévi-Strauss goes a step further by calling *micro-adjustment* practices some rituals:

> "(Rituals) are explicable by a concern of what one might call micro-adjustment—the concern to assign every single creature, object or feature to a place within a class"[23] and further "magical rites and beliefs appear as so many expressions of an act of faith in a science yet to be born (...)"[24] and earlier: "One may readily conclude that animals and plants are not known as a result of their usefulness; they are deemed to be useful or interesting because they are first of all known."[25]

Micro-adjustment brings KSOM close to ecology. Claude Levi-Strauss assesses as scientific the approach of the studied KSOM and sees their knowledge of environment as predating the choices made of the particular uses of its component, restoring the idea of choices and ethics. The anthropologist challenged also the perception of KSOM being unable to experiment and innovate:

> Each of these techniques assumes centuries of active and methodical observation, of bold hypotheses tested by means of endlessly repeated experiments. A biologist remarks on the rapidity with which plants from the New World have been acclimatised in the Philippines and adopted and named by the natives.[26]

Before Jasper Diamond's radical reading of human civilisation in his article *Agriculture: The Worst Mistake in the History of the Human Race* in 1987,[27] Claude Lévi-Strauss had already opened the door to a different understanding of the shifting to agriculture and the Neolithic period:

> It would be impossible to understand how he (human) could have come to a halt and how several thousand years of stagnation have intervened between the Neolithic revolution and modern science like a level plain between ascents. There is only one solution to the paradox, namely that there are two distinct modes of scientific

> thought. These are certainly not a function of different stages of development of the human mind but rather two strategic levels (...) two different routes, one very close to, and the other more remote from, sensible intuition.[28]

History of agriculture brought since more nuanced views on the so-called Neolithic revolution and brought also to light the many changes and evolutions which occurred between the beginning of agriculture and the modern times.[29] The point here is Levi-Strauss proposed that there are different strategies and *routes* not to be related one to another by a hierarchical order but by different choices and ethics. The study of KSOM by the anthropologist raised crucial issues for ecology in bringing new lights on allowing different perceptions and translations of the relation between humans and environment.

Languages and the Narrative

Not only were KSOM—and sometimes are—considered as unable to convey a scientific thought and abstract notions, they were also deemed incomprehensible by the tenets of modern thought. South Asian pre-colonial literatures, religions and sciences were often seen by the colonisers—who very rarely had any direct access to their original forms and were truly unfamiliar with their reference systems—as a jumble of incomprehensible myths and speculations. Furthermore, to understand KSOM or any knowledge system, the language is a prerequisite but is not a sufficient condition. Languages are part of complex webs of socio-cultural, non-verbal and emotional build up and references.

In 1975, Roland Barthes proposed an analysis of the inner coherence in narratives. In *distortion and expansion*, he first put into perspective what is mistaken for unrealistic or incompatible to the factual truth in non-modern narratives:

> Generalised distortion gives the language of narrative its unmistakable character: because it is based on a relation, often a distant one and because it mobilises a sort of implicit trust in one's intellective memory, distortion is a purely logical phenomenon, and as such, it constantly substitutes meaning for the pure and simple facsimile of narrated events.[30]

Barthes calls the second structural aspects of narratives *Mimesis and Meaning*. The intricacies of the structure of narratives accordingly perform integrative functions:

> In the "language" or narrative, the second important process is integration: what has been disjoined at a certain level (a sequence for instance) is joined together again at a higher level (whether it be a sequence elevated in the hierarchy, a signified subsuming widely scattered indices, or an action affecting a whole class of characters). The complexity of a narrative can be compared to that of an organigram capable of integrating backtracking and forward leaps; or more correctly, integration makes it possible to compensate for the seemingly uncontrollable complexity of units situated on one level. Integration helps direct the comprehension of fragmented elements, at once contiguous and heterogeneous (as they occur in the syntagm which responds only to one dimension: succession).[31]

This is a well-known process to traditional storytellers who convey their messages in contorted patterns with twists and bounces, a process mobilising the affective collective memory. As Amadou Hampate Bâ (1988) explained in his introduction of the Peul epic *Kaidara*, there are various layers of readings overlapping in a single narrative, the purely entertaining, a more social-educational one and finally a metaphysical one.[32]

The integration mentioned by Barthes might result in intricate plots. The Sanskrit epic *Kathâsaritsâgara* by Somadeva could be considered as a classical instance of such a structure as well as the *One Thousand and One Nights* or *Sindbad*. Most epics and narratives at the regional level in the Indian subcontinent reveal structures fitting the one described by the semiotic specialist. Narratives play a very important role in KSOM as both vehicle and expression of knowledge activating intellect processes different from the modern ones. Recollecting with KSOM require therefore a different approach of narrative, an approach that cannot be based only on their written collection or record. They are themselves contextualised expression of KVS requiring an intimate familiarity with the socio-cultural pattern of the society they belong to.

It might be objected that in the case of small communities'

language whose livelihood relies on a particular ecosystem their KVS is limited to this particular environment. Since ecology looks at contextualised interactions within an environment these KS are relevant vis-à-vis a generic knowledge often unable to include the complex set of socio-biological parameters particular to an ecosystem.

The Home(s) and the World

Let us take an example of the concrete application of a proper reading of a contextual human-environment pattern through a local KSOM. ODR collaborative project in Mithalanchal-Bihar aimed at the reconstruction of houses after the Kosi river's flood damaged 1,50,000 houses.[33] This owner-driven project engaged in the use of local material, local *mistris* and local narratives. As the Owner Driven Reconstruction (ODR) team was surveying the area the *mistris* narrated them the local myth and narratives around the Kosi river:

> As the enraged Kosi floods overtopped its banks, destroyed and carried everything in its path down to the Ganges and into the sea, the sea is pleased. He asks, "You bring me rich gifts from your land, but why don't you ever bring me the bamboo?" Ganga replies, "All those who rigidly try to obstruct my angry waters must be destroyed. Only the bamboo bends low and touches my feet, quelling my anger. So I spare him."[34]

ODR then used local *mistris'* architectural knowledge as well as ability to introduce to the future house owners the advantages of bamboo as a sustainable material for the reconstruction drive.

> And central to their life is the bamboo—they say' from birth to death' every step in their lives, is supported by the bamboo. However, they build such that the degrading material is changed without bringing down the structure. Sustainability was not something that people in north Bihar needed to learn. In fact that was something they could teach, to anyone who listened."[35] In this dialogue the role of local *mistris* familiar with the context proved pivotal. In collaboration with the latter, the project team worked out "incremental improvements"[36] to the known structures and technics. Furthermore, the owners had the capacity to maintain, repair and modulate the use of their house if necessary

> with the help of local *mistris*. They were not depending on imported technology, engineers and materials. The state government then decided to replicate the process.

This example very briefly described here confirms most of the analysis brought forward previously regarding to the relevance of KSOM in dealing with local environment/livelihood issues through languages and narrative. The concepts brought forward by Levi-Strauss' *Science of the Concrete* and Barthes' analysis of the narrative both find here concrete application. KSOM proved scientifically relevant to local environmental issues. The collection of regional/local history plays an important role in the environmental studies, not as a mainstream scientific narrative to be taken literally of course, but relevant in its social and economic context.

The micro-adjustments relevant to the necessary adaptations to the micro-conditions specific to ecosystems are often part of these KSOM considered as informal. The narrative carried in the vernacular language carried solutions designed at answering the eco-system constraints. The compatibility of KSOM with innovation was also confirmed, as in the case of the incremental improvements of existing technics. Those solutions proved also relevant to the sustainability of a local market in terms of natural resources, technical skills, manpower and free and informed choices of the concerned users. The KSOM has given a central role to the local market in terms of resources, manpower, technology, products and choices. It has allowed a development paradigm different from the usual governance criticised by the pioneer of ecology (the bigness of capital intensive and imported technology and material escaping capacity of the local manpower and users). This case is particularly relevant since habitat sets the organising pattern for social, economic and cultural life.

The idea is not to develop a romantic perspective on the vernacular languages and knowhow but to restore the social, economic and environmental relevance of locally evolved knowledge systems based on local languages in an inclusive and adaptive dynamic. KSOM can contribute a wide range of approaches and concrete solutions to be devised regarding the management of local resources. This can help building another development paradigm where intervening agencies would first have to reconsider the subject-object relation along the lines drawn by the critics of modern epistemology and become familiar with the epistemology evolved by the population they work with in their own knowledge system in order to work out adaptive and adapted approaches. It would trigger a shift from Descartes' decontextualised and disembodied mode of thought and restore the dynamic of *environmentalisation of the subject*. In this context, regional history has a multiple and necessary contribution to bring to the environmental debate. It is indeed a prerequisite to a truly relevant ecological discourse, contextualised, multidimensional, which can contribute to the better understanding of today's environmental issues with humans at the centre.

REFERENCES

1. From here onwards verbal language(s) will be considered under the term "language(s)".
2. Deepak Kumar, *Science and the Raj*, Delhi, Oxford University Press, 1992.
3. Jean Deleury, *Les Indes florissantes, Anthologie des voyageurs francais, 1750-1820*, Paris, Bouquins, 1991.
4. Dan H. Nicolson, C.R. Suresh, K.S. Manilal, *An Interpretation of Van Rheede's Hortus Malabaricus*, Konigstein, Koeltz Scientific Books, 1988. Grove, Richard "Indigenous Knowledge and the Significance of South-West India for Portuguese and Dutch Constructions of Tropical Nature", *Modern Asian Studies 30* (1): 121–143, February 1996.
5. Evans, S., "Macaulay's Minute Revisited: Colonial Language Policy in Nineteenth-Century India", *Journal of Multilingual and Multicultural Development*, Vol. 23, No. 4, Hong Kong, 2002, pp. 260-281.
6. Pierre Bourdieu, Jean-Claude Passeron, *Reproduction in Education, Society and Culture*, London, Sage, 1990.
7. Pierre Bourdieu, *Language and Symbolic Power*, Harvard University Press, 1991.
8. We will not address the issue of thoughts outside the realm of verbal communication.

9. François Jullien, *Vivre de paysage ou l'impensé de la raison*, Paris, Gallimard, 2014.
10. Augustin Berque, "Renaturer la culture, reculturer la nature, par l'histoire", p. 168, in *Entropia* n 15, Le Bourg, Parangon, 2013, pp. 161-172 . Translated by the author of the article.
11. Michel Foucault, *The Order of Things*, p. 321, New York, Pantheon Books, 1971.
12. Ibid.
13. Ibid., p. 322.
14. Gregory Bateson, *Steps to an Ecology of Mind: Collected Essays in Anthropology, Psychiatry, Evolution, and Epistemology*, University Of Chicago Press, 1972; E.F. Schumacher, *Small Is Beautiful, Economics as if People Mattered*, London, Harper Perennial, 1989.
15. Michel Foucault, *The Order of Things*, op. cit., p. 322.
16. Retaining therefore only one of the at least two interpretations of the Genesis myths where the world is created by the medium of the word. The word can be considered a purely physical phenomenon as a wave-vibration or the word can be considered in its semantic aspect seen as embedded in his linguistic structure.
17. Claude Lévi Strauss: "The Science of the Concrete" in *The Savage Mind*, London, Weidenfeld and Nicolson, 1966.
18. Claude Lévi Strauss: *The Savage Mind*, op. cit., p. 15.
19. Ibid., p. 3.
20. Ibid., p. 1.
21. Ibid., pp. 5-6.
22. Dan H. Nicolson, C.R. Suresh, K.S. Manilal, *An Interpretation of Van Rheede's Hortus Malabaricus*, op. cit.
23. Claude Lévi Strauss: *The Savage Mind*, op. cit., p. 10.
24. Ibid., p. 11.
25. Ibid., p. 9.
26. Ibid., p. 14.
27. Jared Diamond: "The Worst Mistake in the History of the Human Race", in *Discover*, 1987. http://discovermagazine.com/1987/may/02-the-worst-mistake-in-the-history-of-the-human-race/.
28. Claude Lévi Strauss, *The Savage Mind*, op. cit., p. 15.
29. Jean-Paul Collaert, *Céréales, La plus grande saga que le monde ait vécue*, Paris, Rue de l'échiquier, 2013.
30. Roland Barthes : "An Introduction to the Structural Analysis of Narrative", p. 267, *New Literary History*, Vol. 6, No. 2, *On Narrative and Narratives* (Winter, 1975), pp. 237-272.
31. Ibid., 269-270.
32. "I am at once futile, useful and enlightening". Amadou Hampate

Ba, *Kaidara: recit initiatique peul*, preamble, Paris, Julliard, 1969. Translated by the author.

33. Vivek Rawal, Sandeep Virmani, "Sustainable Construction, Story of Orlaha and Puraini in Bihar", in *Architecture+Design*, March 2012, Exposure Media Marketing Pvt. Ltd., pp. 48-58.
34. Ibid., p. 49.
35. Ibid., p. 50.
36. Ibid.

Section II

COLONIALISM, FORESTS AND ENVIRONMENT

5

Contesting Colonial Hunting: Impact of the Wildlife Policies in Assam

Geetashree Singh

> Both the Asian and African rhinoceroses have been murdered for their horns to provide the Far Eastern market—and formerly the European market too—with raw materials for dubious medical and magical remedies. Once it would have been unthinkable that these two magnificent animals would ever be in danger of extinction, so great were their numbers and so extensive their ranges. But, today, both are in grave danger. Bans imposed on trading in these products are flouted by the international racketeers in the business.
>
> *–E.P. Gee.*[1]

Colonial hunting emerged as an imperial ideology that reflects the changing nature of the colonial state towards forest communities in Assam. A perceived connection between hunting, power and privilege played an important role in the understanding of social relations in colonial Assam. The British forest policies had a huge impact on wildlife. Owing to the British wildlife policies there was a huge loss of human and animal life. The extermination of carnivores preyed on herbivore species that were preferred for hunting by the elite and restricted the use of forests, grasslands and other areas.The wildlife legislation in India started with the British need of controlling the extraction and transit of forest produce to extend their power over the forest resources including wildlife. On the other hand, the British forest policy tried to have full control over the access of forest resources by eliminating the local tribes from the cultural rights over the access of forest resources. Most of the forest dwellers of Assam were dependent on the forest for their livelihood but after the acquisition of Assam by the British they were considered as the greatest threat for the wild animals as they shared the same place and resources. Gradually forest legislations debared tribes from any kind of rights over forests and were denied access to the forest products including wild animals.

This chapter mainly focuses on the nature of forest policies in British India as part of the colonial necessities that primarily earn the revenue from forest resources and timber for ship building, railways, industries and exports made it essential for the government to control the forests. The extension of agricultural lands into forest areas was crucial to the state to maximise taxes. The increase of tea plantation after the 1860s led to the clearing of huge forest areas which were thrown into the direct human-animal conflict zone in colonial Assam. The paper also discusses the policies adopted by the British government such as reward giving, distribution of guns and gun licenses and appointments of professional shikaris to kill wild animals which ultimately resulted in the destruction of a large number of wild animals in Assam.

Hunting: A Privileged Game

The British were unfamiliar with the concept of hunting before coming to India. Being highly influenced by the Mughal lifestyle they started imitating their lifestyle.[2] Hunting was one such feature which was practised by the Mughals in their leisure time.This brought the concept of the British game hunting. The practice of game hunting by British officials is evident from the large number of British records.[3] The British officials attached the hunting of wild animals with 'their masculine power' and on the other hand criticises the practice of the indigenous people. M.S.S. Pandian argued that *shikar* or game hunting was one of the aspects on which the colonial government tried to construct and affirm the difference between its 'superior'self and the inferior 'native' other.[4] While they presented themselves as risk-taking, preserving and super-masculine the native people were considered as utilitarian and effeminate.[5] The British regarded the wildlife hunting as a sort of character-building 'masculine power' and marking good hunters as "potentially good soldiers, pioneers, explorers and leaders of empire."[6] It became one of the aspects of elite class culture. The British officials on one hand call their hunting practice superior and on the other hand associate cruelty with the hunting practices of the tribes of Assam. The best example of such emphasis on cruelty on wildlife by native hunters of Assam was M'cosh's *Topography of Assam*. It mentioned, "The Singphos kill them by poisoned arrows fired from a musket, and after striking out their teeth, leave the carcasses to be devoured by beasts of prey."[7] The British officials tried to show their method of hunting as sophisticated and more civilised against the indigenous method of hunting. However, strychnine (poison) was extensively used by the British officials for the destruction of wild animals.[8]

In the middle of the 19th century, Major John Butler of the 55th Regiment of the Bengal Native Infantry found the sport in Assam as an exciting pastime for the English sportsman. He observes, "From the vast extent of waste or jungle land everywhere met with it in Assam, there are perhaps few countries that can be compared with it for affording diversion, of all kinds for the English sportsman."[9] Butler mentioned various forms of sport namely, tiger, elephant, rhino and deer sport.[10] In one day's hunting it was not an uncommon event for three or four sportsmen to 'shoot thirty buffaloes, twenty deer and a dozen hogs, besides one or two tigers.'[11] Captain Pollock, a military engineer responsible for laying down the road networks in the Brahmaputra valley in the 19thcentury, an anecdote claimed, shot dead one rhino or buffalo for every breakfast.[12] Sharing his hunting experience he further says, "I followed a rhinoceros for some way, but it had got into a tangled brake, where it was safe. I then came across some buffaloes, and shot a couple of bulls, one with very curious horns, forming nearly a circle, and all but meeting at the points."[13] This is how the British officials shared their hunting experience but there are no statistics which can show what numbers of wild animals were killed for game. Seeing these descriptions, there is no doubt that a large number of wild animals were killed by the British officials for game.

Extension of Cultivation

The British attempted to clear the jungle for the extension of the cultivation which helped them to earn revenue. Moreover the tea plants grew wild in the jungle and the British government attempted to give tea plantation a more civilised form by establishing tea gardens over the wastelands. This subsequently brought several acres of forest land for tea plantation. The British officials were keen to spread the tea plantation where ever the jungles were cleared.[14] B.H. Baden Powell of the Bengal Civil Service, noted that "The discovery of indigenous tea in Assam gave a great impetus to the establishment of tea-gardens, and naturally the special rules for grant of considerable areas of waste to capitalists (as distinct from the ordinary miles for occupation of plots of agricultural land) had in view chiefly the extension of tea-cultivation."[15] The extension of tea gardens to waste land reduced the forest land for wildlife. Mahesh Rangarajan argued that there is no doubt that there were points of conflict between mega-mammals and people before the coming of European rule but these acquired a sharper edge during British rule.[16] There was no attempt at the elimination of wildlife prior to the British rule but the British government attempted at total annihilation of wildlife. In Assam the need for clearing the jungle was felt for the extension of tea cultivation, which was not possible without the annihilation of wild animals. Jayeeta Sharma argued that, "protecting nature necessitated that indigenous forests be transformed into the tea gardens which imperial science and commerce required."[17] The extension of opium cultivation could also be assigned as one of the causes for the clearance of jungles. In 1860 the government monopolised the opium cultivation in the state and there was no serious attempt at discouraging the opium cultivation till 1921, when Mahatma Gandhi visited the province and discouraged the consumption of opium. Not only for the extension of tea cultivation but also to save the paddy fields from the attacks of the wild animals specially from elephants, tigers, rhinoceros, buffaloes and hogs attempts were made to clear the jungles.[18] The numbers of the wild animals decreased fast in consequence of the people having suffered much from the destruction of their crops by the wild animals.[19] Offering of a substantial monetary incentive for killing female wild animals and their cubs aimed at stopping of reproduction of these animals. In this way the eradication of the species helped in the extension of cultivated arable land.[20] The gradual extension of cultivation and opening out of the country led to the decrease of population of tigers and leopards in later years.

The extension of tea plantations was the main cause which led to the decrease of the waste land. This also caused the destruction of a large number of wild animals. "The new tea growers carved out great plantations in Assam, Ceylon, Indonesia, and later Africa and South America. Vast tracts of forest were levelled and countless animals destroyed to make way for the orderly rows of tea bushes."[21] E.P. Stebbing, F.Z.S., F.R.G.S., also agreed that the extension of cultivable land for tea plantation had affected the number of wild animals in Assam.[22] Similarly, a tea planter Mr. Barker commented on the clearance of jungles for tea plantation.[23] He affirmed that the clearance of jungle disturbs hundreds of monkeys. The clearance of jungle also affected the population of rhinoceros in the province. Mr. Barker viewed that, "Many rhinoceros have been shot within the last few years in the vicinity of Julpaiguri but there, partly owing to being constantly hunted, and partly owing to the clearance of large tracts for tea cultivation, they are rapidly becoming scarcer, and the sportsman must travel still farther east before he finds them at all plentiful. In the eastern portion of the Bhutan Dooars and in Assam, wherever there are heavy reed jungles on the banks of rivers or on the margin of swamps, rhinoceros may be met with, and occasionally several congregate in one covert."[24] In this way rhinoceros became extinct from those places in which once they were numerous. Thus, the clearance of jungles led to the destruction of a large number of wild animals.

Commodification of Wildlife

The British officials soon realised that wildlife and trophies could also be a commodity for trade. Human greed, trade and political expedience led to the destruction of elephants. Rhinoceros were killed for ivory and their horns were sold to the far eastern market as raw materials for making decoration materials and also dubious medical remedies. Rhinoceros horn was used in oriental medicine since long back.[25] The main user of this was China. It was used as traditional Tibetan medicine and was mainly used as an anti-pyretic and also as an aphrodisiac. It was used for making dagger handles and other decorative materials. During the *Ahom* period, skin of buffalo, rhinoceros, and deer was used to make *dhal* (shields) as an instrument of self-defence.[26] According to Captain Welsh's *Report on Assam* (1794), elephants' teeth, have always been an article of export. Rhinoceros horn were trifling articles of export.[27] The horn and skin of wild animals were extensively used for making decorative articles as described by Captain J.T. Newall, a soldier and sportsman, in his words, observed: "Samber {Ccifusaristotelis), the largest of the deer tribe, is common to all parts of India. In Kashmir, the noble Barasingha, and some other allied species in Assam, and the south eastern parts of Bengal, can compete with this fine animal in size and appearance; but they are not distributed generally as is the sambur. The horn of the stag is three-typed, and when mature very massive. Its skin, when dressed as leather, is in great esteem for the manufacture of shoes, belts, saddle covers, and numerous other things. It is far softer, yet tougher, than common cow leather; and in consequence articles made of it fetch a higher price."[28]

Ivory carving was one of the thriving professions during the British rule. The ivory carvers were known as Baktars or Baktar-Khanikars. Ivory articles constituted the major portion of royal gifts to visiting grandees as well as distant dignitaries. The Baktars used to work on deer horns along with ivory carving. Deer horn artifacts were mainly made only for decoration.[29] But later by the end of the 19th century the number of ivory carvers declined in Assam. The Census Report (1881) reported 917 number of elephant dealers in Assam. This was an important profession in Assam. However, it says that the number could have been more than recorded. The capitalist people were mostly involved in this business whose main profession was not elephant catching and those who were called elephant dealers were professional employees of the capitalists who took hunting licenses from the government.[30] But, this profession declined in the later part of the 19th century as the Census Report (1891) reported only four ivory carvers.[31] The decline of elephant population by the late 19th century could be the probable reason for the decline of the profession of elephant catchers. The decline of ivory was said to be the cause of disappearance of the art. Tribal hunters beyond the inner line sold out tusks to the traders who in turn sold them in Calcutta (Kolkata) with a good margin. The Marwari dealers used to buy tusks in Assam and sold them in Calcutta which fetched them more profit.[32] Colonel Pollock stated that, "Although the horns are contemptible as trophies, the native Assamese and Marwaris prized them greatly, and will give as much as Rs. 45 a seer (2 lbs.) for them. They were also greatly prized by the Chinese. Two officers, Cock (afterwards killed in the Naga campaign) and Bunbury, just before I arrived at Gowhatty, made a good bag of these beasts, and by the sale of the horns more than repaid all their expenses. They live in apparent harmony with wild elephants, and I have seen them lying down in the same mudhole with a buffalo."[33] Debrugarh was an important centre of the tusk trade. Ivory articles were luxury items for the common men. The price of the ivory articles shows that these were beyond the means of average households. From 1898-1900 the well-known ivory articles and their price was as follows, (a) comb for Rs. 5 to Rs. 20, (b) back-scratcher Rs. 20 to Rs. 50, (c) spoon and fork Rs. 30 to Rs. 50, (d) toys-elephant from Rs. 30- to Rs. 55, horse Rs. 8 to Rs. 10, fish Rs. 1.8 to Rs. 8, cart Rs. 50 to Rs. 60, (e) bracelet Rs. 8 to Rs. 10, (f) knife handle Rs. 3 to Rs. 8 (g) ring Rs. 4 to Rs. 6 (h) Tema (small box) Rs. 4 to 6, etc.[34]

Rhinoceros horns were also profitable and good for trade.

A confiscated rhinoceros horn weighing 40 *tolas* has been sold by auction for Rs. 600 in Darrang. Almost every portion of a rhinoceros has a ready market value, the dried blood being especially prized. It is for this reason poaching was so rife.[35] Rhinoceros horns have always been valuable in India because of some supposed aphrodisiacal virtue but apparently still more so in China, the demand for horns in the market caused the extermination of *Rhinoceros sondaicus* in Burma except for a few individual specimens closely guarded by the forest department. China was undoubtedly after one horn rhinoceros (rhinoceros Indicus) with the consequence that a rhinoceros horn became worth more than a good pair of elephant tusks.[36] British officials agreed that there was too much money in this business.

The business was so lucrative that it appeared that snags were common in connection with the trade. For at one time the local Marwaris lamented that the Cacharis had palmed off on them bamboo roots, blackened and faked to look like rhinoceros horn the Cacharis went one better and sold them faked pieces of buffalo horn, it was not known if any 'acid test' was devised by that time.[37] A rhinoceros horn was worth about half its weight in pure gold in the open market, but the value of ivory was decreasing very greatly by 1931.[38] Other than this, taxes were also imposed on elephant hunting, elephant catching, rhinoceros hunting, etc.[39] Killing of tigers for trade also existed. Tiger's skin value was more in the market then the amount paid as bounty[40] and thus it was in large number. Even as early as 1871, Captain Rogers agreed that there was lakhs of amount in selling of skin of wild animals.[41] The killing of wild animals for trade was common. F.C. Daukes, Secretary to the Chief Commissioner of Assam also agreed that wild animals were killed for trade specially the smaller animals like pigs, deer, etc. In his words, "It is, however, observed from the returns received from all districts in which government guns are given out these guns are more frequently used for purposes of sport and the killing of buffaloes, pigs and deer for sale than for the destruction of dangerous animals."[42] Thus the colonial rule in Assam led to the commodification of wildlife.

British Policies Towards Wildlife

The British government raised a fight against wildlife. The exploitation of forest resources and clearance of jungle for cultivation led the British government to adopt measures for the extermination of wildlife. Wild animals like tigers, buffaloes, stags and other animals made cultivation difficult which was the main source of revenue.[43] The British officials argued that the killing of wildlife is needed for the safety of life and property. This led the British government to initiate various measures for the destruction of wildlife. At the initial stage, there was a debate among British officials as to what measures to be adopted for the destruction of wildlife. After some of the earlier experiments it was decided by the Government of India as well as by the Provincial governments that giving of rewards was recognised as effective method. Reward giving became the most popular method of the destruction of wild animals during the British rule. Prior to British rule the reward giving was never practised by any ruler. Mahesh Rangarajan argued that the system of reward giving for the destruction of wild animals was 'utterly unknown to the original rulers of India.'[44] The British began fresh infringements on the animal world with their systematic measures of extermination.[45] The introduction of rewards involved the local inhabitants, *shikaris* called from neighbouring provinces in the process of extermination of wildlife primarily for the sake of rewards and secondly for trade purposes. Mahesh Rangarajan argued that "Bounties aimed to eliminate cattle-marauding tigers. Saving draught cattle would help extend the area that was under the plough. Fewer tigers meant more cultivation and more revenue, their elimination a blessing of imperium after the elimination of an oriental despot. Unprecedently, larger rewards were given out for killing tigress, and special prizes for finishing off cubs. This was to be a war where no quarter was given."[46] Large sums were given for the destruction of females and cubs of wildlife to stop the reproduction of wildlife.

The scale of reward varies from animal to animal. Reporting on the measures adopted in the provinces for the destruction of wild animals, the Secretary to the Chief Commissioner stated the following measures: different rates of rewards were paid for the destruction of wild animals according to the nature of animals. For example, the highest reward was paid for the destruction of rogue elephant, viz. Rs. 100 compared to other wild animals. The lowest reward paid was Rs. 2 for the destruction of hyenas. The paying of rewards also depended on the nature of destruction in any districts. For the destruction of a full-grown tiger was paid Rs. 25 in North Cachar Hills, Sibsagar, Lakhimpur, Garo and Naga Hills but in other districts only Rs. 20 was paid. For the killing of leopards Rs. 5 was paid in all districts of the province, for wolves and bears Rs. 10 was paid. For the destruction of snakes rewards was not paid in all the districts but in some districts like Gauhati and Sibsagar a reward of Rs. 2 annas was paid. Other than, reward giving the gratuitous distribution of guns and ammunition in Assam Valley, Khasi and Jaintia Hills districts for the protection of human lives, cattle and crops from wild beasts also caused the destruction of wild animals in large numbers.

The pattern of use of weapons also changed with the introduction of modern weapons. Prior to the British rule, the local inhabitants used traditional weapons like bows and arrows, spears, and *daos* through which not many wild animals could have been killed but the supply of modern weapons like guns and rifles made the killing of wild animals easier than ever before. The free licensing of guns added to the destruction of wild animals.[47] The increase in the destruction of wild animals was more particularly after the distribution of guns among the villagers. Guns were mostly used by *shikaris* and license holders for killing of game for trade and not for the protection from wildlife. In addition to the free grant of licenses under the Arms Act (1878), government guns were gratuitously distributed to persons living in dangerous localities for protection from wild beasts. It was not only used for the purpose for which it was given out but it was used for the purpose of sports and pleasure.[48]

Appointment of the professional *shikaris* for keeping down

the number of wild animals was common during British rule. There were attempts to encourage men of the *shikari* class to keep down the wild animals. However, very few natives of the *shikari* class were in the province. It was confirmed by Colonel Pollock, Madras Staff Corps, during one of his hunting expeditions in the province said that, "we had no shikaris, as none exist in Assam."[49] Thus, *shikaris* from the neighbouring province, Bengal were called up to Assam to keep down wild animals. Even the reward giving was not successful to control the wildlife in the absence of professional *shikaris*. The Secretary to the Chief Commissioner of Assam observed that "The success of the system of rewards, in fact, depends a good deal on the existence of a professional *shikari* class, who can be attracted by them to engage in the destruction of wild animals as a means of livelihood."[50] Even the increase of the amount of reward paid was not successful in keeping down the wild animals in the absence of professional *shikaris*.[51] The use of poison like 'cobra poison' and *dakara* (aconite), was also in practice during the colonial period for the destruction of wild animals.[52] Apart from these, sports by the British officials and elite class also contributed to the destruction of wild animals. According to Rangarajan, "the deliberate and organised destruction of carnivores under government patronage was a novel feature of the British period."[53]

Impact of Wildlife Policies

Human interference in wildlife habitation brought destructions of life and property by wild animals. If the natural food chain was not disturbed by the British to fulfil their greed the destruction by wild animals might also be missing in history except occasionally. The killing of herbivores by professional *shikaris* like deer, pigs, and dogs for trade caused a natural food crisis for the large carnivore. This led to massive destruction of human life and cattle by wild animals. Wild animals killed fewer people than cattle. According to the available statistics (1875-1915), wild animals were accounted to have killed an average of 14,931 cattle each year. On the other hand, human beings were killed on an average of 358 each year during 1875-1927. Snakes were very destructive for human life. According to the available statistics 18,604 people were killed during 1875-1927 by wild animals including snakes. Out of it 9,880 were killed by snakes alone which is 0.9 per cent of the total number of people killed by snakes and 8724 by wild animals which is 6.3 per cent of people killed by wild animals in India. Snakes alone caused more than half the deaths of the total deaths of people during 1875-1927.

The British policies led to the extermination of wildlife in the province as in other provinces of the Indian subcontinent. As argued by Mahesh Rangarajan that "The British came to the Indian subcontinent with a long history of a systematic campaign to exterminate carnivores in the British Isles."[54] The policies of the Government of India led to the destruction of a large number of wildlife and also brought some of the animals on the verge of extinction. Balakrishna Seshadri argued that, "nowhere in the world has destruction of the natural wilderness —the habitat of wild life—proceeded with such speed and totality as on the Indian subcontinent. It has been the most decisive factor in the catastrophic diminution of India's wildlife —within and outside the sanctuaries—in the last twenty-five years."[55] The clearance of jungle was mainly to provide timbers for the newly constructed railways. In the initial years of the British rule wild animals were seen as pests whose elimination was encouraged with monetary incentives. Each year around thousands of wild animals were killed for rewards. According to the available statistics a total number of 1,68,112 wild animals including snakes were killed in fifty years (1877-1927). Out of which 90,102 were snakes which is 1.1 per cent of the total number of snakes killed in India and 78,070 were wild animals which is 9.2 per cent of the total number of wild animals killed in India. Out of 78,070 wild animals 21,541 leopards, 17,316 tigers, 12,823 bears and 155 elephants were killed. Wolves or hyenas were less in Assam valley unlike in other provinces of India where the British government attempted to exterminate wolves along with tigers and leopards. In Assam the destruction by wolves or destruction of wolves was less compared with the other province of Assam. The reason could be the killing of these animals might not be reported. Only 48 hyenas and 53 wolves were reported to have been killed during 1877-1927.

The colonial rule witnessed huge destruction of wildlife. The need of the extension of tea cultivation led the British government to adopt measures like rewards giving, sanction of special rewards, liberal distribution of guns and gun licenses, calling up of professional *shikaris* and use of poison. The reward system contributed to the killing of a large number of wild animals during the British rule. The calling of professional *shikaris* not only led to the destruction of carnivores but a large number of herbivores like deer, pigs, buffaloes were also killed for their skins and horns. Prior to the British rule traditional weapons like *dao*, bows and arrows, etc. were used to hunt but the British government supplied guns to the cultivators and villagers for protecting life and property from the attacks of wild animals. Guns were also given to professional *shikaris* to eliminate wild animals which had a huge impact on wildlife. The destruction of the wild animals was justified by the British as it was dangerous for human life and property. However, there were conflict of opinions between the British officials, some of them argued that the destruction of large numbers of carnivores led to the increased population of herbivores which were destructive for crops, thus, and the food chain was disturbed. Rhinoceros was mostly killed for sport and trade. Very few statistical records reveal the killing of rhinoceros. However, it was killed in large numbers as during the early part of the 20th century rhinoceros was on the verge of extension. It became extinct from areas where once they were numerous. Thus, the British rule led to the destruction of huge wildlife population in the province of Assam.

REFERENCES

1. E.P. Gee, *The Wildlife of India*, Sterling Publishers, New Delhi, 1986, p. 7.
2. William Dalrymple, *The Last Mughal: The Fall of Dynasty, Delhi, 1857,* Bloomsbury Publishing, New Delhi, 2006.

3. C.E.M. Russell, *Bullet and Shot In Indian Forest, Plain and Hill*, W. Thacker & Co, London, 1900; Nuttall, W.M., Fauna, *Bengal and Assam, Behar and Orissa: Their History, People, Commerce and Industrial Resources,* The Foreign and Colonial Compiling and Publishing Co., London, 1917, pp. 631-640; Pollok, C., and W.S. Thom, *Wild Sports of Burma and Assam*, Hurst and Blackett, London, 1900; Moray Brown, *Shikar Sketches with Notes on Indian Field-Sports*, London, Hurst and Blackett, 1887, pp. 207-280; Jguy Fleetwood Wilson, *Letter To Nobody, 1908-1913*, John Murry, London, 1921, pp. 119-124; Colonel Kinloch, *Large Game Shooting In Thibet, The Himalayas, and Northern India*, London, Thacker, Spink and Co., 1885; Pollock, C., *Sport in British Burma, Assam, Cassyah and Jyntiah Hills*, Chapman and Hall, London, 1879.
4. M.S.S. Pandian, 'Hunting and Colonialism in the Nineteenth-Century Nilgiri Hills of South India', in Richer H. Grove, Vinita Damodaran and Satpal Sangwan (eds.), *Nature & The Orient: The Environmental History of South and Southeast Asia*, New Delhi, Oxford University Press, 1998.
5. Ibid.
6. K. Shivaramakrishnan, *Modern Forests; Statemaking and Environmental Change in Colonial Eastern India*, New Delhi, OUP, 1990, p. 90.
7. J. M'cosh, *Topography of Assam*, Bengal Orphan Military Press, Calcutta, 1837, p. 45.
8. C. Pollock, *Sport in British Burma, Assam, Cassyah and Jyntiah Hills*, Chapman and Hall, London, 1879, p. 120.
9. J. Butler,*Travels and Adventures in the Province of Assam, During a Residence of Fourteen Years*, Smith, Elder and Co., London, 1855, p. 215.
10. Ibid., pp. 215-220.
11. Ibid., p. 217.
12. P.D. Stracey, Quoted in Thaper, *Battling for Survivals: India's Wilderness Over Two Centuries,* OUP, New Delhi, 2003, p. 218.
13. C. Pollock and W.S. Thom, *Wild Sports of Burma and Assam*, London: Hurst and Blackett, 1900, p. 437.
14. D. Datta, *Cachar District Records*, Vol. 2, The Asiatic Society, Kolkata, 2007, No. 180 of 1853, p. 308.
15. Powell Baden, *A Manual of the Land-Tenures and of the System of Land-Revenue Administration Prevalent in the Several Provinces*, Vol. III, Low Price Publications, Delhi, 1990, p. 410.
16. Mahesh Rangarajan, *India's Wildlife History: An Introduction*, Permanent Black, New Delhi, 2005, p. 23.

17. Jayeetha Sharma, 'Making Garden, Erasing Jungle, The Tea Enterprise in Colonial Assam' in Deepak Kumar, Vinita Damodaran, and Rohan D'souza (eds.), *The British Empire and the Natural World: Environment Encounters in South Asia*, New Delhi, Oxford University Press, 2011, p. 126.
18. E.R. Grange, 'Extracts from the Journal of an Expedition into the Naga Hills', *JASB*, Vol. IX, Part II, pp. 947-53; Verrier Elwin, *The Nagas in the Nineteenth Century*, New Delhi, Oxford University Press, 1969, p. 214.
19. E.R. Grange, op.cit., pp. 947-53.
20. Mahesh Rangarajan, Computing the Numbers of Tigers Killed for Rewards in British India, 1875-1925, NMML, New Delhi, 1996, p. 6.
21. S. Krech, J.R. Mancill, and Carolyn Merchant (eds.) *Encyclopaedia of World Environmental History*, London, Routledge, 2004, p. 1187.
22. E.P. Stebbing, *The Diary of a Sportsman Naturalist in India*, London, John Lane, 1920, p. 129.
23. G.M. Barker, *Tea Planters Life in Assam*, Calcutta, Thacker, Spink & Co., 1884, p. 126.
24. Colonel Kinloch, *Large Game Shooting in Thibet, the Himalaya, and Northern India*, London, Thacker, Spink and Co., 1885, p. 61.
25. A. Choudhury, *Kaziranga: Wildlife in Assam*, New Delhi, Rupa & Co., 2004, p. 8.
26. Lila Gogoi, *The Burangjis: Historical Literature of Assam (A Critical Survey)*, New Delhi, Omsons Publications, 1986, p. 214.
27. N.N. Acharyya, *Historical Documents of Assam and Neighbouring States*, New Delhi, Omsons Publications, 1983, p. 24.
28. J.T. Newall, *The Eastern Hunters*, London, Tinsley Brothers, 1866, p. 453.
29. R. Saikia, *Social and Economic History of Assam (1853-1921)*, New Delhi, Manohar Publishers, 2001, pp. 56-57.
30. *Report of the Census of Assam for 1881*, Calcutta, Office of Superintendent of Government of India, 1883, p. 122, Section 224.
31. R. Saikia, *Social and Economic History of Assam (1853-1921)*, Manohar Publishers, New Delhi, 2001, p. 56.
32. Ibid.
33. C. Pollok, *Incident of Foreign Sport and Travel*, London, Chapman & Hall, 1894, p. 67.
34. Ibid., p. 58.
35. *Quennial Review of Forest Administration of the Province of Assam, 1924-25 to 1928-29*, Shillong, 1929.
36. *PRFA for the Year 1929-30, AGP*, Shillong, Para. 20, 1930, p. 4.

37. *PRFA for the Year 1929-30*, AGP, Shillong, 1931, para 20, p. 5.
38. Ibid., Para 20, p. 5.
39. R. Sakia, 2001, op. cit., p. 30.
40. Cited by Mahesh Rangarajan in Wildlife In India: Two Essays. NMML, New Delhi, 1996, (H.P., December 1890, Nos. 360-407, Note by J.P. Hutchins, September 30, 1890)
41. (NAI), Home, Public, 1870, August, File No. 71-73.
42. (NAI) Home, Public-A, November, 1889, File No. 236-269.
43. Gunnel Cederlof, *Founding Empire on India's North-Eastern Frontiers 1790-1840, Climate, Commerce, Polity*, New Delhi, OUP, 2014, p. 183.
44. M. Rangarajan, *Fencing the Forest: Conservation and Ecological Change in India's Central Provinces 1860-1914*, Delhi, OUP, 1996, p. 145.
45. Anon. 'The Game and Game Laws of India', *Qly Review*, Vol. CCCXXXIII, 1888, p. 91, cited from M. Rangarajan, op. cit., 1996, p. 145.
46. M. Rangarajan, *India's Wildlife History: An Introduction*, New Delhi, Permanent Black, 2005, p. 23.
47. (NAI), Home, Public-A, December. 1885, File No. 69-101.
48. (NAI), Home, Public, 1890, December, 360-407.
49. C. Pollock, *Incident of Foreign Sport and Travel*, London, Chapman & Hall, 1894, p. 42.
50. (NAI), Home, Public, December, 1884, File No. 109-140.
51. Ibid.
52. A.M. Smith, *Sports and Adventure in the Indian Jungle*, London, Hurst and Blackett, 1904, pp. 103-104.
53. M. Rangarajan, Computing the Numbers of Tigers Killed for Rewards in British India; 1875-1925, NMML, New Delhi, 1996, p. 6.
54. Mahesh Rangarajan, op. cit. 2006, p. 145.
55. Balakrishna Seshadri, *The Twilight of India's Wildlife*, John Baker Publishers, London, 1969, p. 13.

6

Colonial Forest Resources Management and Ecology in Manipur

Dinjangam Riamei

Introduction

The mountain state of Manipur has a, total area of 22, 329 sq. km. The land mass of Manipur constitutes 0.68 per cent of the geographical area and 0.19 per cent of the population of India. The state lies between latitudes 23.80°N to 25.68°N and longitudes 93.03°E to 94.78°E. Manipur is one of the border states in the north-eastern part of India, bounded by Nagaland on the north, Assam on the west and Mizoram on the south and along the east it shares a 398 km international boundary with Myanmar. Geographically, the state is divided into two main relief features, the oval-shaped central plain at an elevation of 792.4 mtr (2600 ft.). The valley is about 2,600 feet above sea level with drainage from north to south and the highest mountains in the hill rise to nearly 10,000 feet above sea level.The entire forests of Manipur are included in the Himalayan system.

This chapter looks into the history of forest resource management under Manipur state as well as by the hill people and the changes, which had taken place with the British intervention during the colonial period. Most importantly, it looks into the interface between forest and ecology in the state of Manipur during the colonial period. The study of environmental history remains largely in its adolescent stage in the state (Manipur) although much has been done especially in the context of Western countries. The study lies in promoting environmental consciousness by looking at the past, and more importantly investigates the importance of forests and the changes to the ecology during the colonial period (based on the issues of regional environmental history in the Indian subcontinent, particularly to Manipur state).

Environmental resource management is the management of the interaction and impact of human societies on the environment (involves all components of the biophysical environment, both living and non-living). The forest has a profound influence on the economy as well the environment. The socio-economic activities of man are greatly influenced by forest and forest resources. Besides, the most important roles which fewer visible to the common man is the ecological role of forests that controls the extremes of heat in summer, but that as a general rule also modify the extremes of cold in winter.[1] It is found that Indian forestry is different from that of any other country as noted by the British colonial rulers during their regime in India. Every kind of climate and every type of vegetation from the alpine forests of the Himalayas to the tropical evergreen forests of the West Coast, from the desert forests of Sind and the Punjab to the bamboo-clad hills, which form the eastern most frontier between India and Burma.[2]

Trade (Pre-Colonial Manipur)

A range of historical evidence to explore the conditions of Manipur forest before the colonial intervention and various courses of changes that took place during the colonial period, it is worth highlighting the study of (traditional) the system of trade and the forest resources management for the perhaps counter intuitive insights, which they offer into the pre-conditions for sustainable resource management. Since time immemorial, agriculture was the predominant occupation of the people of Manipur. They had also engaged themselves in an activity of trade within the state as well with other Indian states[3] and the neighbouring countries like southern China and Burma.[4] With the introduction of bell metal coins by King Maharaja Ura Konthouba the commercial activities of 558-668 AD[5] made much more advanced in the pace of commercial activity in the state. People traded mostly in buffaloes, cows, mithuns, dogs, fowls, poultry, earthen pots, wooden tobacco pipes, mortars, plates, mugs, cane baskets, mats, rain proofs, etc.[6] in exchange for their agricultural product goods[7] and the jungle products of bee-wax, tea seeds, black resin, ores, elephant tusks, etc. were traded by Nagas.[8]

As connection with the Burmese (trade) it may be stated that the Manipuri traders used to bring goods (buffaloes, ponies and bricks from across the border) through three land routes[9] (1798-1801 AD) and exported silk to Burma. Regarding the Manipuri trade link with China, merchants of far Yunan Province of China visited Manipur in 1630 bringing with them goods like silk, paper, tea, etc. and carried back home commodities like wax clothes, cotton, ponies, etc.[10] It is seen that before the colonial intervention of Manipur forests, the process of commercialisation of state forests were not found in the state or did undergo a timber business.

Prior to the colonial intervention of Manipur forests, the state forests and its resources were not touched by scientific methods. Nevertheless, when British-trained foresters entered the picture, the forests were more highly refined and exposed to the scientific changes. On the other hand, the early British forests are evident, much focused on the revenue by imposing several terms and conditions on forest conservancy.

Manipur forests are abundant with plants, and mineral resources. In this connection, Pemberton noted:[11]

> In different parts of this mountainous chain is, as might have been anticipated from its extent and elevation, most various and abundant. On the lofty summits and ridges around the Muneepur valley, Oak and Fir of very superior growth are procurable. On the heights around Kubo, Teak alternates with the Fir and Bamboo, and the valley itself is entirely filled with magnificent forests of the Sal, Gurjun, and Keo tree. Among the valleys bordering on the Cachar frontier, Jarul, Nagisur, Cham, Ana, and Toon abound. The same valuable description of timber is found along the whole western face of the chain, as low down as the sources of the Kuladyne river, where Teak again appears; but the difficulty of floating it down that river, and the Morusang, adds so

> considerably to the expense, that it is found much cheaper to import it from Rangoon, and Leemeenah in Bassein, on the Ava side of the range, where this most valuable timber grows in luxuriant profusion.

Forests were reserved and managed under a certain scheme of forest conservancy so also exploited under specific rules and regulations under State Forest Reserve.

Colonial Laws Enact to Conserve/Protect Forest Resources

The study mainly focused on the exploitation of major forest produce of timber, fuel wood, etc. other than the exploitation of minor forest products, i.e. animal, cane and bamboo, stone and earth, grass and fodder, incense and perfume, cardamom, orchids, etc., under the colonial state, which was never before.

When Lord Dalhousie took up the Charter of the Indian Forest Act, 1855 for the first time,[12] all the teak in the country was retained by the state after 10 years, the Forest Act, 1665 enacted and it gave the government full power over all sorts of forests in the country, under the jurisdiction of the British Government.[13] The Act not only turned all the communal property into state property but also alienated the ownership and management of forests. Finding that the Indian Forest Act, 1868 was inadequate to meet the requirements of the government, another Act was passed in 1878. Under the new act of 1878, the Indian forests were classified into Reserved, Protected and Village forests and prohibited the people from having any right over the Reserved Forests.[14] By the beginning of the 20th century, the colonial authorities further tightened their control over forests or water over India and Manipur in particular. That the Indian Forest Act, 1927 empowered the provincial government to declare any forest or water, which was the property of the government as Reserved Forests.

Types of Forests in Manipur

I	II	III	IV	V
Moist Tropical Forests	**Dry Tropical Forests**	**Montane Sub-tropical Forests**	**Montane Temperature Forests**	**Sub-alpine Forests**
Tropical wet evergreen forests	Tropical-dry deciduous forests	Sub-tropical broad-leaved hill forests	Montane-wet temperature forests	Sub-alpine forests
Tropical seal evergreen forests	Tropical-thorn forests	Sub-tropical pine forests	Himalayan moist temperature forests	Moist-alpine scrub
Tropical moist deciduous forests	Tropical-dry evergreen forests	Sub-tropical dry ever-green forests	Himalayan-dry tempera-ture forests	Dry-alpine scrub
Littoral and swamp forests	-	-	-	-

Manipur forests abound in varieties of plants, animals and mineral resources, characteristics of any tropical rain forest areas. Captain H.W.G. Cole, Officiating Political Agent Manipur talking to the Belgian gentleman visiting Manipur (M. Chandoir) noted:[15]

States that for the last few days his diet consisted principally of green parrots and monkeys.

However, these forests were gradually brought under the general forest policy of the government of forests in the country, under the jurisdiction of the British Government. The Act not only turned all the communal property into state property and alienated the trees from the ownership and management of forests but also tilted in the destruction of forests as the people had no responsibility over them. The following were the forest general rules and regulations set by the colonial authority.[16]

i) Indiscriminate cutting of wood in this valley village reserves is prohibited and no one can cut wood there for sale. If any village is found doing so there will forfeit the privilege of free wood for their personal use.

ii) The village may be held responsible for the theft of wood committed in the State Reserve near their valley village Reserves as there is little chance entering the Reserves by the outsiders without their knowledge.

iii) None can grass cattle in the Reserves except with a permit from the Forest Member, M.S.D. or from an officer to whom the issue of permit is delegated.

iv) None can fell or cut trees from the Reserve without a permit from the Forest Member, M.S.D. or from an officer to whom the issue of permits is delegated.

With the above Acts and Regulations, gradually the people lost their indigenous rights over their own forestland. The Manipur state forest management under the colonial government was begun from 1891-92.[17] The Cachar Reserve Forest was the earliest State Reserve Forest that, declared as a protected forest by the colonial authority in Manipur.[18] Followed by Burma/Myanmar Border Teak Forests (lies along the Indo-Burma border, i.e. extreme east along the international border with Burma/ Myanmar/on the foothills of Kabow valley along the Burma border around the Tamu Township of upper Chindwin district).

The 1878 Indian Forest Act of Colonial India affected Manipur, curtailing the right of the forest-dwellers (over forest) in Manipur by surveying and declared as protected forests under the 'State Forest Reserves' that the whole forests areas overlooking the Manipur valley. Thereby, Maxwell the Political Agent of Manipur[19] declared the following forests as "State Forest Reserve" forests in 1895;[20]

I. the Langol forest

II. the Khuga forest and

III. the Heingang forest

All the Tera trees and silk cotton trees of the valley overlooking forests were made the property of the government and placed under the charge of the Forest Department.[21] In 1897-98, the pine trees (some oak trees and mixed evergreen trees) virgin forest of Uhkhrul, confined in the present Uhkhrul district of the state were taken over by the state and declared as State Forest Reserves. The colonial authorities in 1939-40 declared the Sugnu forest of the hill district of Chandel in the southernmost part of the state even re-demarcated the boundaries of the pine reserves to regenerate. All these efforts, the pine reserves in the state including those of Heingans and Kambung were taken over by the colonial state. Therefore, the unrestricted rights of the indigenous people over forests were curtailed by the Forest Department in manifold ways from time to time.

The major sources of state revenue income were collected from the forests produce itself (both of minor and major forest). Prior to the British rule, the forest department *Urungba Loishang* and the *Urungpurel* (Forest Officer) or *Urungpurel Achouba*[22] (Chief Forest Officer) mentioned in the court of the Maharajas of the land were not mentioned under any circumstances by the British colonial rule. Although the Urungba Loishang under the maharaja's rule neither have a definite forest policy nor trained personnel to manage it in scientific management nevertheless they did not used the forest and exploit the forest as the colonial authority did.

The early British rule in Manipur did not have a separate forest officer and as a result forestry affairs were looked after by the President of the Manipur State Darbar.[23] The forest servants drew allowances with His Highness consent.[24] The early British occupation of the state, underwent a hectic negotiations with the Assam government for years for export of timber to British India, but due to heavy imposition of duty, the same could not be done except minor items (tea seeds, ivory, agar wood, etc.) were exported and timber to some extent. The state forests were managed in an ill-defined way under the control of the Assam Forest Department for their management and in a similar vague manner within the sphere of influence of DFO, Cachar Division Assam. However, the actual commercial extraction of forest produce started through the DFO Cachar Division in 1898 with the agreement of the Assam Government with a revenue sharing of 25:75 between the state of Manipur and the Cachar Forest Division.[25]

With a view to develop the state forests a separate forest department, the State Darbar began to be established in the year 1931 under the charge of a member of the former Manipur. In 1932 (under the presidentship of Capt. C.W.L. Harvey of the political department) the Manipur State Darbar assigned D.C. Kaith[26] to survey the forests of Manipur and to submit a proposal for their better management. And thus, with Kaith's report, a brief forest policy was highlighted under which the following four types of forests in Manipur State Darbar (Resolution No. 10 A) were envisaged.[27]

State Reserve	• To be put under strict state protection
Valley Village Reserve	• For the villages situated in the valley by depending on the nearby forests for meeting their requirements
Hill Village Reserve	• Known as 1/4 miles reserve maintained around each recognised hill village (Pawa Reserve)
Open Reserve Open	• For commercial and domestic requirements of the people of Manipur under permission

However, due to lack of trained staff and communication or the socio-economic condition, the method of scientific forest management was not yet touch. Only in the year 1932, the State authority took the interest to appoint a Forest Officer of State, D.C. Kaith, who was on deputation from Himachal Pradesh and he was given the first task to make a note of Manipur forests by the Darbar mainly of Jiri Barak drainage forest which at present covers the Western Division, Southern Division, Jiribam Division and Tengnoupal Division.[28] And as per, he divided these areas into 19 (nineteen) timber blocks for proper management and extraction.[29] These units are the management units. Kaith's Report was very comprehensive and was regarded as the foundation of forestry in Manipur.[30] But with the Darbar (Resolution No. 2A of November 23, 1932)[31] made bound every decision of forests and its members, to the Darbar. Also, the Darbar was not even to recommend the permanent appointment of Kaith as Forest Officer.[32]

The foremost objective of colonial policy was to collect a revenue. Thus, soon after the assumption of political power in 1891, they set in to start on managing the forest (resources) of Manipur by the Darbar's declaration on March 29, 1933:

> Considered Memo No. B/608 of 15-3-33 and B/654 of 18-3-33 from the Deputy Conservator of Forests, Cachar Division forwarding a copy of the state of the Manipur State timber and bamboo blocks. The Darbar approved the revised sale notice forwarding with the latter Memo.[33] Considered the Forest Officer's Report regarding the fall of Forest Revenue in the State's Forests on the Cachar border.[34]

The colonial authority for both commercial and other purposes as noted by Pemberton extensively used the forest products:[35]

> Bamboos of every variety, from the most delicate and small, to the most gigantic, cover the faces of all the inferior heights; and the margins of the different nullahs and torrents abound with a rich variety of ratans, some of which vary from 80 to 190 feet in length, and are particularly useful in the construction of the rustic bridges, which the mountaineers are frequently in the habit of throwing across the most formidable torrents, during the rainy season. The Gurjun, red Jarul, and Toon tree grow most profusely on the banks of the two great estuaries, Teks Naf and Myoo, in Arracan; and since our occupation of the province, have been extensively used for ship and boat building purposes.

The forests of Manipur were thus exploited (selling of timber and bamboo) which was never exploited for any commercial purposes (especially of the Cachar border forest) before. At this time, the Darbar was prepared to allow the Forest Officer, in consultation with the Divisional Forest Officer, Cachar, to give loans to certain reliable contractors, if they could be found, up to a limit of Rs. 6,000, for the immediate working of forests. The Forests Officer and the Assam Forest authorities would make them.[36]

The trees were also cut down and cleared the forest areas for economic development and road expanding, the Darbar resolved the following under the heading agenda:

> Cutting trees within 50 feet of road area. 4. Considered authority

> the S.E. to cut all thus jungle growing within 50 feet of the road between miles 7½ and 8 Burma Road.

It was also resolved to warn the owners of the trees and jungle that "all trees and jungle must cut down such trees and jungles if within 50 feet of the Burma between miles 7½ and 8, and that if this is not done within 30 days of notice being served on them, the S.R. may cut such trees and jungle, which when cut will be headed over the owners B.R. to serve notice to this effect on the owners."[37] For better or easy reach of the forest resources, the state authority, even in the last part of their rule in Manipur opened up numbers of new forest branch offices.[38]

Therefore, the colonial rule brought changes that the long-standing rights of the hill men were deprived by not only the facilities of earning but also they were made to buy the resources from their own land. They were made to buy the monopoly right of village resources from their own land. Furthermore, the prices at which hill men might sell the forest produce were also fixed.

Systems of Selling Forest Produce

The following methods were the systems used by the colonial power to sell the state forest produce as under:

a) By auction (the timber and poles are generally sold through auctions)
b) Tender allotment and
c) Permit system.

The monopoly right to extract timbers from each block was given to different contractors. The sale of forest products by public auction in this system involved the leasing of forest blocks to registered forest contractors for extraction of timbers under certain terms and conditions prescribed by the government. The contractors had to make a security deposit and the minimum and maximum amounts of timber to be extracted were fixed. They were required to bid in a public auction and the highest bidder was given monopoly rights to extract forest products from a block for a first period, generally three years. Royalty on forest products was subject to revisions according to the prevalent market rates.

Timbers were sold by categorising the quality of the wood as fuel wood trees (assumed less valuable value) and the Forest authorities dealt with valuable trees like Uningthou, Laihou, Tairel and Na-U separately.[39] The contractors paid royalty plus monopoly fees to the government. The forest members issued permits to the Manipur State Darbar. The Reserved forests were sold by auction in the month of August every year.[40] Besides, timber, the thatching grass overlooking the valley Imphal where area grasses were found growing (fit for sale) were also sold by leasing out to the contractors. Thus the traditional rights of the indigenous people to use unreservedly forest produce were in the hands of the rich and influential contractors.[41] [The right was with the President of Manipur State Darbar]. This losing of traditional rights by the indigenous people resulted in conflicts with the leases and the villagers.

During the fall of forest revenue receipts the authorities even offered an assistant in the form of loans to continue the commercialising, mostly of timber.The Darbar prepared and asked to allow the Forest Officer (in consultation with the Divisional Forest Officer, Cachar), to give loans to certain reliable contractors, if they could be found, up to a limit of Rs. 6,000, for the immediate working of forests. The Forests Officer and the Assam Forest authorities would make them.[42] Besides, some well-defined areas were also leased out to traders on payment of definite instalments on a definite date with a view to help the timber traders (Darbar sanctioned Rs. 250 for removal of boulders from the stream which caused obstruction to the extraction of the timber).[43]

Under the management of Deputy Forest Officer (DFO), timber merchants and traders made a pressing rush for exploitation of the matured and valuable trees. As said, the main objective of the authority was only to secure the 25% share of the tax paid by the state for the supervisory role in the management of the forests. The DFO of Cachar was instructed by the Assam government not to work for the improvement of the forests except for the work of collection of royalty [D.C. Kaith reported].

Commercialisation of Forestry and its Impact on Environment

The colonial forest officers view on Manipur forest resource as an agent of state revenue.The colonial intervention of the Manipur forests brought manifold changes both of positive and negative perspectives. The positive aspects are the introduction of conserving the natural (forest) resources based on the scientific methods and so also conserving the virgin forests with the foremost objective for commercial purposes with scant concern for the harmful effects to the other side. Their conquest extensively brought a plunder of natural resources of the state with indifference towards environmental protection. The British administrators earned a revenue of about Rs. 20,000 from the Cachar forest itself a year. The authority pointed out 'if the rich resources of this forest (Cachar Border) were judiciously worked, the state could get as much as Rs. 4,037, as the forest revenue even before proper management on the forest began in 1891-92'.[44]

And, the forest resources of the State had become commercialised and constituted a main state revenue receipts. Several forest policies were framed by the state, to manage the fluctuations of the state revenue from time to time, (i.e. imposition of a higher limit of cutting down trees, i.e. 4/6 at breast height, felling of even the immature trees by the unscrupulous timber traders and removal of boulders from a stream which caused obstruction to the extraction of timber, etc).Collection of taxes from the forest products were done through a number of toll stations which had been established at different places on all the routes leading to Imphal town. In this connection, J.C. Higgins, the Vice-President Manipur State Darbar reported that a few stations were to set up with Darbar resolution No. 7R of 14.11.Forest Tolls.4.

A few steps and proposals were also taken up, in order to manage the forests around Manipur state by appointing a number of forest officers (like Maxwell, Rowbowthem, A.J.W. Milroy and D.C Kaith) who had expertise in forest management. However, the degree of commercialising the forest produce were excessive exploitation sometimes even exhausted the forest with scant regard for the natural environment. In this connection, Battacharya noted:

> There was no restriction imposed on the extraction of trees (without technical advice).[45]

The British colonial failed to check the over-extraction,[46] the nature and as well the rights of the indigenous people were gradually lost their rights over their forests which they had cherished and enjoyed from the early period. Thereafter, they were at the mercy of the timber trader, whose interest was to take as much as possible.

Conclusion

Thus, the forests were left unexploited only with the means of road and transportation system found difficult. The extractable forest resources were exploited by creating a number of State Forest Reserves, which were again leased out to the different contractors. Mostly in the hills areas steps were also taken by the Political Agent for effective peaceful extraction of timbers by installing two *Lambuses* with strict instructions, posted in the bordering forests areas to avoid the strained relations between the local people and the timber traders. The fact cannot be ignored that the colonial state undertook a 'afforestation scheme' to some extent in some part of the State's reserved forest areas but the operation of forest resources by the state was judged against the degree of exploitation. The exploitation of forests became a 'source of considerable and steady income' for the colonial state with little care for the environment to the maximum advantage of the state. The foremost aim was to collect a percentage royalty with a small amount invested for the conservation of the state reserve forests in Manipur.

NOTES

1. *Department of Education, Health, and Land*, File. No. 41, Diary No. 41/F, New Delhi, National Archives of India, 1937, p. 1.
2. Ibid.
3. Assam, Cachar, Lushai Hills, Tripura, Naga Hills, etc.

4. R.B. Pemberton, *Eastern Frontier of India*, Delhi, Mittal Publications, 1979, p. 3.
5. It was the beginning of monetisation of the barter economy in the state. See also K. Gangmumei, *A Brief Note on Loiyamba Shiyen: A Royal Edict on Social Distribution of Economic and Administrative Functions*, Shillong, NEIHA Proceedings 1982, p. 31.
6. W. Shaw, *Notes on the Thadou Kukis,* Gauhati, Government of Assam, 1929, pp. 85-86.
7. Like beads, spear, clothes, etc. from the Meiteis of the valley.
8. R. Brown, *Statistical Account of the Native State of Manipur and Hills Territory under its Rule*, Delhi, Sanskara Prakasak, 1873, p. 10.
9. K. Gangmumei, *History of Manipur: Pre-Colonial Period,* Vol. 1, Delhi, National Publishing House, 1991, p. 10.
10. R.B. Pemberton, *The Eastern Frontier of India,* 1929, op. cit., p. 3.
11. Ibid., pp. 13-14.
12. A. Vaidya, *A Backgrounder on Forest Governance and Forest Management Legislations in Pre-Independence and Independent India, Leading up to the Forest Rights Act 2006,* WWW: http://infochangeindia.org/, (accessed August 15, 2014).
13. Ibid.
14. S.N. Lokendra (ed.), *Land Use System of Manipur Hills,* New Delhi, Rajesh Publications, 2004, pp. 84-85.
15. H.W.G. Cole, *Tour Diary,* Political Agent and Superintendent of Manipur, Imphal, 1897, p. 3.
16. *Manipur State Darbar,* Resolution FM's Memo No. 31M.F/11-18, Imphal, Manipur State Archive, 1936, p. 14.
17. *Administrative Report of Manipur State* (*1891- 92*), Imphal, Manipur State Archives, p. 9.
18. This forest is confined to a narrow halt of trees along the Barak River and its tributaries, viz.-Jiri, Tuivai, Irang, Leimatak and Makru.
19. *Administrative Report of Manipur State* (*1891- 92*), op. cit., p. 6.
20. *Administrative Report of Manipur State* (*1891- 92*), op. cit., p. III.
21. *Manipur State Darbar* (*1941*), *Resolution No. 22,* op. cit., p. 60.
22. N. Ibobi, *The Manipur of Administration 1709-1907*, Imphal, S. Manglem Singh Publications, 1976, p. 117.
23. The Darbar is a policy-making institution. The management of the State was over to His Highness the Raja and his Darbar functions like a court of law. During the colonial period the Raja as the President (the titular head, power were based on the Vice President, the European), the Vice President a European officer

(I.C.S. officer). The strength of the Darbar was seven, excluding the Raja, quorum was four.

24. *Manipur State Darbar,* 1937, op. cit., p. 99.
25. *The Survey Report on the Distribution of Bamboo Species in Manipur,* Imphal, Forest Department, Government of Manipur, 2004, p. II.
26. Kaith was the first Forest Officer in Manipur, graduated (B.Sc.) from the University of Edinburgh.
27. *The Survey Report on the Distribution of Bamboo Species in Manipur,* op. cit., p. 12.
28. Ibid.
29. Ibid.
30. The next officer of the state was Hari Singh, a product of Edinburgh, Scotland who stayed in Manipur for a year. He was succeeded by K.V. Reddy who worked in the state upto 1942. During this period, the Indian Forest Act, 1927 was adopted in Manipur. During 1939-41, a Ranger was trained in the Forestry course for the first time and the entire state was under a Forest Division. After Reddy a local officer took charge. R.K. Bijoy Chandra Singh worked till 1969 as Chief Forest Officer.
31. It is published for the general information: The Darbar desires that appeals from the Forest Member's orders in the Forest and other miscellaneous cases should be considered by the Darbar and from that court in the ordinary way to His Highness.
32. *Manipur State Darbar,* 1933, op. cit., p. 22.
33. *Manipur State Darbar,* 1933, Resolution No. 07, op. cit., p.116.
34. Ibid.
35. R.B. Pemberton, *The Eastern Frontier of India,* 1997, op. cit., pp. 13-14.
36. *Manipur State Darbar,* 1933, Resolution No. 08, op. cit., p. 86.
37. Ibid., p. 146.
38. *Manipur State Darbar,* 1947, op. cit., p. 406.
39. *Manipur State Darbar,* 1946-47, op. cit., p. 12.
40. *Administrative Report of Manipur State (1915-16),* op. cit., p. 11.
41. Ibid.
42. *Manipur State Darbar,* 1933, Resolution No. 08, op.cit., p. 86.
43. *Manipur State Darbar,* 1923-1924, op. cit., p. 12.
44. *Administrative Report of Manipur State (1891-92),* op. cit., p. 9.
45. M. Bhattacharya, *Gazetteer of Manipur State,* Calcutta, Anushilan Press, 1963, p. 21.
46. *Administrative Report of Manipur State, 1936-37,* op. cit., pp. 13-14.

REFERENCES

Primary Sources

Archives

Administrative Report 1891-1947, Imphal, Manipur State Archives (56 Volumes).

Foreign Department, *Political Proceedings*, New Delhi, National Archives of India, 1940-1947.

Department of Education, Health, and Land, File No. 4, New Delhi, National Archives of India, 1937.

Tour Diaries

Tour Diary of Officiating Political Agent of Manipur [Cole, W.H.G.] 1897.

Darbar

Proceedings of a Meeting of the Manipur State Darbar, 1932-1947.

Published Materials (Books)

Brown, R., *Statistical Account of Manipur*, New Delhi, Superintendent of Government Printing, 1873.

Pemberton, R.B., *The Eastern Frontier of India*, Delhi, Mittal Publications, 1835.

William Shaw, *Notes on the Thadou Kukis*, Gauhati, Government of Assam, 1929, pp. 85-86.

Secondary Sources

A. Books and eBooks

Gangmumei, K., *History of Manipur: Pre-Colonial Period*, Vol. 1, Delhi, National Publishing House, 1991.

Lokendra, N.S. (ed.), *Land Use System of Manipur Hills*, New Delhi, Rajesh Publications, 2004.

Ibobi, S., *The Manipur Administration 1709-1907*, Imphal, S. Manglem Singh Publications, 1976.

Vaidya, A., 'A Backgrounder on Forest Governance and Forest Management Legislations in Pre-Independence and Independent India, Leading up to the Forest Rights Act 2006', WWW: http://infochangeindia.org/, (accessed August 15, 2014).

Van, V.S.S., *Forest for the People, Policy and Legislation*, Bombay, 2002.

B. Report

Economic Survey of Manipur 2009-2010, Imphal, Directorate of Economics & Statistics, Government of Manipur, 2010.

C. Website

www: http://infochangeindia.org/.

7

Colonialism, Tribals and *Podu* Cultivation: Studying from Andhra Agency Areas

Vulli Dhanaraju

Introduction

Land as a unit of thought can have several meanings. It is an area to be owned and used for agricultural purposes or as an area over which one wields political power. To the extent that it serves the biological imperative within a subsistence economy, it may be viewed as merely an area to be owned and used for agricultural purposes. But to the extent it crosses the boundaries of subsistence economy and enters the area of surplus generation, it begins to be viewed as a tool for acquiring political power and control.[1] From the political and economic point of view it involves access to resources, control over people and social relationships. The powerful non-tribals by virtue of their social, economic, and political advantage exercise power and control over the tribals as seen in the acquisition of their lands thereby depriving them of their every source of livelihood. In a sense, the entire phenomenon of the alienation of tribal land by non-tribals may be viewed as a conflict between two opposing forces. For the former it is a struggle for power and maintenance of the statuesque and for the tribals it is a struggle for their very survival.

This chapter proposes to examine how the colonial state, in the name of philanthropic strategies, imposed several restrictions on tribal areas and their *Podu* cultivation with support of local rulers who were mainly responsible for the implementations of colonial policies in Agency areas. This paper mainly argues that the impact of the British rule over the tribal areas can be viewed as a conflict between two opposing forces. For the British it is a struggle for power and maintenance of the status quo and for the tribes it is a struggle for their very survival. In this context, this paper analyses with the impact of the colonial forest policy on *Podu* cultivation in Andhra Agency. The *Podu* cultivation essentially provides the bare requirement of tribals for survival rather than generating surplus and profit, nevertheless, it plays a vital role in the economy of tribals as it ensures food supply almost round the year. Over the ages it has become an inalienable part of their life and culture with a number of ceremonies built around it. K.S. Singh[2] argues that the entry of colonialism into the tribal regions of India through various philanthropic strategies of the communal tribal mode of production and attributed judicial nature of the regions by way of adopting survey and hence, the emergence of the private right on land. The very entrance of the colonial state into these areas was resisted violently by the tribals of the Agency areas.

Nature of Economic Organisation in Andhra Agency

In Andhra Agency areas, Jatapus, Konda Reddis, Savaras, Porjas, Konda Doras and Khonds subsist mainly on agricultural activity and most of them depend on *Podu* cultivation[3]. Besides *Podu*, they also raise horticultural crops. Their main activity is supplemented by food gathering and collection and sale of minor forest produce.[4] The material equipment of all these communities consist of simple tools such as bows and arrows for hunting, digging sticks, *'Konki boriga'*, hoes and sickles are used in agricultural activity.

Even though dress, decoration, political structure and behaviour patterns of tribals in this region were undergoing rapid changes due to long-standing and increased contact with the general population, their agricultural practices and other methods of exploiting nature remained relatively unchanged. Both advanced and primitive tribal groups still subsist on *Podu* cultivation. There were two types of *Podu*, namely *'Chelaka Podu'* and *'Konda Podu'* in vogue. While the *Podu* practised in plain jungle clearance and flat lands is known as *'Chelaka Podu'*, the *Podu* confined to hill slopes is called *'Konda Podu'*.[5] Both the types involve shifting of cultivation site from one patch to another after the fertility of the patch is exhausted. The cycle of shifting is determined by agro-climatic conditions locally prevailing. In *Konda Podu* primitive implements like hoes, digging sticks, hand axes and sickles are used, for *'Chelaka Podu'* the implements employed by the settled cultivators are used. *'Konda Podu'* operations start with the onset of summer to the accompaniment of certain rituals. After selecting a patch of land the trees and bushy growth are cleared and allowed to dry. Before the onset of the monsoon this is burnt. This process marginally increases the fertility.

The *Podu* cultivation essentially provides the bare requirement of tribals for survival rather than generating surplus and profit. Nevertheless, it plays a vital role in the economy of certain tribal groups as it ensures food supply almost round the year. Over the ages it has become an inalienable part of their life and culture with a number of ceremonies built around it.

Women and children play a vital role in the economic activity of the tribal household. Women participate in every economic activity particularly in agriculture (except ploughing) and non-agricultural activities. They freely accept wage labour when opportunities are available besides collecting forest produce. The tribal children from the tenth year onwards help their parents in family pursuits by tending cattle, weeding fields, chasing birds on the standing crops, etc. When the parents are engaged in their family occupation, the younger children are left to the care of the elder children usually girls.

The geographical location and the tracts of wooded hills offered little scope for stable forms of agriculture other than shifting cultivation or slash and burn cultivation on hill tops, which was practised from time immemorial called *Podu* in the Andhra area. After reaping a few harvests the land was left fallow and agricultural work started afresh on new ground. This practice of shifting cultivation patterned semi-nomadic life. At each new place, they erected field houses or thatched huts for living, out of material taken from the surrounding jungles. After selecting hill-slopes, they felled trees and then burnt a part of that jungle which was followed by sowing. The plough was not used but they used digging sticks for making holes to sow seeds of jowar and pulses. The crops grown were jowar, millet (*jonna*) redgram (*kandi*) maize, *korra* and other kinds of grains and pulses.

Ever since they learnt the use of metal implements, the tribals depended on craftsmen of plains, living on the fringes of the forest. These contacts led no doubt to the other exchanges with more advanced civilisation. The tribals exchanged neither luxuries nor armaments, but only necessary goods and even those on occasional transaction. In fact, they carried on little or no commerce[6].

Earlier in 1946, in the Report of A. Aiyappan, the following tribes were considered as fit subjects for inquiry and all these belong to the Agency areas of the four districts.[7] These are:

District	*Names of the Tribes*
Godavari	Koyas, Konda Reddis
Srikakulam	Jataps, Savaras, Paidis, Kondalus
Visakapatnam	Bhagathas, Khonda Kapus, Khondas, Gadabas, Khonda Doras, Muka Doras, Ghazis, Jutas, and Dombos, Dhulias, Valmikis, Kammars, Ojas, Mulias, Ojinbes, Ronas and Gnads

Even this list is comprehensive, and sometimes it is overlapping. There are tribals like Runas, who are identical with the Bagathas. The tribes like Ojas and Runas are not found in the agency parts. The former belongs to the northern area of Orissa province while the latter are essentially a matter of Karaput Agency. Nevertheless Ayappan's list was taken as the criteria in the matter of giving protection to the agency tribes. The government should revise the list and include all the tribes that have been omitted in the schedule of the list. No accurate figures were available with regarding to the population of each tribe. Since the estimation of the census was not readily available, the figure of the 1941 census alone should be accepted. According to the information received from taluk offices about agency population shows an increase of 10% over the figure recorded in 1941 the total then being 498,026.

The population figures of some of the tribes, according to the census report of 1941 are mentioned as follows:[8]

Tribe	*Population (in numbers)*	*Percentage (%)*
Bagatha	14,642	6.18
Domb	20,305	8.58
Gadaba	11,190	4.73
Gond	480	0.20
Jatap	12,453	5.25
Khond	39,648	16.75
Knda Dora	19,843	8.38
Parja	14,080	5.95
savara	12,842	5.43
Koya	91,279	38.55
Total	2,36,762	100

Debating Colonial Forest Policies

How does one can study formulation of colonial forest policy and its impact on tribal society in India today? One could start with the insight offered by Edward Said,[9] who argues that all knowledge is a historical construction and it cannot be adequately understood without referring to contemporary politics and power. Further, practices of knowledge or the description of the practices of knowledge not only produce discourse but "are embedded in technical processes, in institutions, in forms of transmission and diffusion".[10] There are also minute alterations in fields of power that keep past and present firmly connected. The transformation—partly juridical, partly real, partly ideological—of people from colonial subjects to sovereign citizens suggests a changed moral context, as Clifford Geertz[11] has suggested.

Therefore, the study of colonial discourse is important, especially with regard to the nature of colonial intervention and its impact on the native institutions[12]. Key continuities in the hegemonic discourses about forest management in the aftermath of decolonisation may be noticed, and these can help assemble the pieces that went into realising colonial discourses and their manifestation in state authority structures. Many Orientalist ideas about primordial Indian ways of living informed the approach to forestry in the 19th century. There was the idea of the ancient monarchic state presiding nominally over self-governing, village communities that appears in the writing of Henry Maine, Marx, Weber and Louis Dumont. This could, in turn, feed the notion of forest communities engaging in pre-capitalist forms of forest use that were ecologically sustainable.

The restrictions imposed on tribal people by colonialism through their law enforcement, had endangered the 'freedom of the natives', and forced them to question the imposition of new types of authority. Due to the imposed British policies, a segment of the new native ruling authority emerged, which exploited tribal people in various forms. Their challenges had taken the shape of insurrections witnessed in all the tribal belts of the country from time to time. In every part of India the impact of British rule led to new social formations among the tribal people. The imperial needs dictated the British interest in the Indian forest resources, which resulted in the establishment of control over forest resources.

During the initial stages of the East India Company rule, the evolution of forest policies were closely associated with both Bombay and Madras Presidencies, as the teak-stocked districts were situated in these presidencies. In order to meet the teak wood demands of the Bombay Dockyard, the Company government initiated interest for the forest policies.[13] The earliest attempt of European merchants' involvement in teak trade was made in the formation of the timber syndicate in Malabar district in 1796 under the leadership of Machonochine, who was an employee of the company's medical service. Though this syndicate had survived only for a short time, it had its influence on the subsequent attempts in connection with the supply of teak timber to the Navy requirements.[14] But these collapsed owing to stiff resistance from the native merchants.

During the period from 1800 to 1850, the East India Company followed the policy of limited intervention in the forests of the Madras Presidency. The forest exploitative activities were mainly confined to the teak forests. There were no serious exploitative and conservation operations undertaken by the government as they were very expensive and time consuming. In 1840, the Court of Directors, while reviewing the forest administration argued that there would be no advantage in purchasing more land than was actually required to make for teak wood.[15] In this way, at the initial stage, the forest policies in the Madras Presidency were confined to simple extraction of the teak wood that was required for shipbuilding and other necessities of the government.

From 1860 to 1882, the history of the forest policies in the Madras Presidency was mainly the struggle between the Forest and Revenue departments to control the village jungle lands. An introduction of railways in India in the mid-1850s created a massive demand for timber and compelled the colonial state to formulate strategies to exploit the forest resources in India in a sustained form. The commencement of the railway network in various parts of British India resulted in two simultaneous processes: one, it led to wanton destruction of forests and second, in order to have continuous supply of wood for railway network they exploited the tribals and used them as labourers in clearing the forest. Ramachandra Guha argued that the Indian forest department was established in order to provide the wood requirements to the railway network systems that were introduced in the 1850s.[16] The wood necessities of the railways had exercised significant influence on the Madras government forest policies.

The hostile relations between the Forest and Revenue departments on the issue of control over the forest and waste lands had a significant bearing on the debates on the forest legislation in the Madras Presidency. The Board of Revenue and the revenue officials consistently opposed the proposals sent by the Government of India on forest legislation with an innovative counter argument. They argued that forest tracts in South India were communal property, enjoyed by the people since time immemorial. Some of the studies on the colonial forest policies argued that the forest acts enacted by the British were formulated after intense debates within the colonial bureaucracy.

After the 1860s, the colonial state attempted to acquire control over the forest resources in India, not only to meet the wood supplies for the railways and various other government departments, but also to generate revenue from forest resources. This was the first step in this direction for the promulgation of the Forest Act of 1865.[17] This Act imitated a new legal and administrative regime in the forest management system in India. It was the first attempt in the legalisation and bureaucratisation of the forest landscape to meet the timber requirements of the colonial state in India. One of the important features of the Forest Act of 1865 was that it categorised the Indian Forest landscape into 'reserved forests' and 'unreserved forests'. Under this scheme, reserved forests were declared as state property, wherein people's access was prohibited. In unreserved forests, peoples were allowed to access forest produce with certain restrictions.[18] The object of this categorisation was to impose state monopoly on the forest resources in India.

The promulgation of the Madras Forest Act of 1882 had initiated new legal and administrative regimes for forest management in the Madras Presidency. The Act asserted that the forest landscape in the Madras Presidency belonged to the state. It empowered the Madras Government to undertake demarcation, reservation and settlement of forests as state property. This articulation of the revenue officials on the protection of the communal rights of people in the Madras Presidency was not reflected in the Act as it was promulgated. Brandis, the main architect of the Madras Forest Act, felt that the general framework of the Indian Forest Act of 1878, the Burma Forest Act of 1881 and The Madras Forest Act of 1882 were similar. But, he pointed out that the Madras Act of 1882 possessed two peculiar features: one, it did not have a chapter on village forests and two, it created the forest courts for allowing people to appeal against the decision of the Forest Settlement Officer.[19] The forest courts were incorporated into the Madras Forest Act of 1882 in order to address the public discontent during the implementation of the forest settlement process in the Madras Presidency.

The Madras Forest Act of 1882 did not propose the communal forest that was advocated by the Board of Revenue and revenue officials in the Madras Presidency. It describes the fact that the articulation on the communal rights was a rhetoric used by the revenue officials to oppose the expansion of the forest department. In other words, the nature of the colonial state policies at one level were identified with sensitive discourse on the protection of people's rights, and at another level, pushed the colonial state to a higher pedestrian.

By 1900, most of the forests in the Madras Presidency were brought under reservation. Consequently, tribals that were critically dependent on forests for survival for day-to-day needs were excluded for the customary access in forest tracts.

Impact of the Forest Policies on *Podu* Cultivation

As I mentioned in the above discussion one of the important means of livelihoods for the tribals in the Andhra Agency area was the *Podu* cultivation practised for subsistence needs. The shifting cultivation in the Northern Circars districts was called the *Podu.* There were two important areas where this system was practised: one, in Godavari region and another was in Vizagapatnam and Ganjam districts.

It was reported by the officials from Vizagapatnam that important forest tracts were cleared away by shifting cultivation. The *Podu* therefore, was depicted as the main factor responsible for destruction of forests on mountain slopes. In 1873, Colonel Beddome, the Conservator of Forests, reported that "This plateau (3000 feet plateau) is wonderfully well weaved by numerous streams, when all have their rise in the woods which more or less clothe all the small raising hills. These latter were all, at a very recent date, covered with fine forests, but this is fast disappearing owing to the ruinous system of hill cultivation. Numerous hills have already been turned into bare rocky waste, or only clothed with a few date bushes or the protest description of stunted growth, and if the present way of cultivation is allowed to go on unrestricted the entire trees disappear of all woodlands, is only a question of time."[20] However, the ideas on forest conservation for protecting surface drainage and rainfall were questioned by revenue officials in the Madras Presidency.

Prior to the reservation of forests, the tribals enjoyed considerable freedom to undertake *Podu* cultivation in hill areas. It was restricted by the government after reservation of hills of exploitation of timber. In order to acquire forests silviculture operations, the Forest department imposed ban on the *Podu* in reserve forests. For instance, in Andhra region, strict regulations were imposed on the practice of *Podu* cultivation within the 100 yards of reserved forests in 1905. It was argued by the forest officials that "not only were large areas of forest destroyed for *Podu*, escape fire from the burnt clearings swept over many square miles of forest every year. Therefore, for conservancy to be through, it was necessary to exclude all *Podu* cultivation from the limits of the reserved forests, and to curtail the privilege of the hill tribes within rich areas".[21]

Thus, regulation on *Podu* cultivation was justified with the arguments that unless it should be prohibited, forest conservancy was not possible. However, in some cases, the forest department allowed tribals to live in reserved forests and practise *Podu* cultivation on the condition that they should work for the forest department.[22] In other words, wherever, the colonial state required labour in the interior forests they followed a policy of attracting tribal labour. Thus, the Madras Government followed a cautious policy and tried to use their labour in the forest conservation operations.

The nationalist intelligentsia also responded to the *Podu* issue. As M.V. Ramamurthi, the president of the Parvathipuram

Taluk Congress Committee pointed out that: "Most of the hillmen live on what is known as *Podu* cultivation. Dry crops are raised and the yield is very much less than the plain dry lands. Herein they come into conflict with forest authorities of the zamindars. These slopes or tracts on hill sides throw back on other sources of living as coolies, etc; this is a problem which requires careful consideration."[23] Thus, the *Podu* cultivation, which was an important means of livelihood for tribals, was restricted by the forest department.

Unlike the plain peasants, the tribals could not articulate their grievances in the form of written petitions. They demonstrated the discontent on forest rules in the form of burning reserved forests and attacking subordinate forest staff. For instance, reserve forests in Dhankonda and Sanivaram in Vizagapatnam distrcts were burnt by tribals in opposition to regulations imposed by the government on *Podu* cultivation.[24] These sporadic protests sometimes brought concessions to hill men. The tribals living near the reserved forests of Dharakonda and Sanivaram in Vizagapatnam district were given concessions for grazing and *Podu.* These concessions were often cancelled under the pretext of disloyalty of tribals to the forest department. The concessions granted to tribes in Ganjam district were cancelled under the pretext of disloyalty of tribes to the forest department.[25]

In spite of government concessions, tribals continued to violate the forest rules, which had restricted their means of livelihood. For instance, in Vizagpatnam district, 3000 areas of reserved forests were damaged by tribals in Kondasantha village by setting fire. [26] The *Khond* tribals who lived in Ganjam and Vizagaptnam district frequently engaged in burning reserved forests for practising *Podu* and thus created problems to the Forest Department. Thus, the legitimacy of the forest rules was questioned by the tribals by violation of rules and damaging reserved forests. It was this necessity that compelled the colonial state to incorporate the contestations of people for accessing forests, if not as a general policy, at least on a case-by-case basis. For instance, in Godavari district, the *Koya* and *Konda Reddy* tribals were given concessions for accessing forests on the condition that they should help forest officials in fire tracing and other conservation operations in reserved forests.[27] The major problem that created hostile relations between the Forest department and tribals was the harassment by forest guards and watchers, for such interference undermined the tribals in day-to-day life. The Madras government took cognisance of this problem and cautioned the district collectors to minimise the harassment by lower forest officials.[28]

There were two factors that compelled the forest administration to adopt a cautious policy towards tribes: one, the need to use their local knowledge of forest routes ad timber trees in silviculture operations and secure labour in forest conservation operations and two, to prevent tribal revolts in opposition to the interference of the forest reservation in day-to- day life. The tribals were employed by the forest department as watchers and labourers in boundary clearing operations and fire patrolling activities in Andhra Agency.

The forest settlement procedure was not conducted in the Madras Forest Act of 1882. The reason attributed for this was that the tribals could not come up with proper claims at the time of forest settlement due to lack of understanding of the procedure. To address this problem, the Madras government directed the Forest Settlement Officer to leave sufficient forest areas at the time of the forest settlement in the tribal areas. In pursuance of this policy, the Forest Settlement Officer in the Palakonda and Golgoada taluks of Vizagapatnam informed that he had left sufficient forest land for the use of tribals at the time of forest settlement.[29] The reservation of forests as estates resulted in far-reaching demographic changes and displaced the tribals from their ancestral places. For instance, at the time of forest settlement, some of the tribal villages were included in the reserved forests in the Atikonda reserve in Vizagapatnam district. Consequently, the tribals were forced to move out from their ancestral lands.[30] The Forest Settlement Officer in the Karaka reserve in Vizagapatnam district mentioned that several villages were included in the reserved forests.[31] However, the forest department was happy to keep the tribals inside the reserved forests, because it required their labour in forest conservation operations and for the patrolling and fire-tracing operations.

The forest settlement process was slow in the agency areas of Andhra. Because the survey and settlement of the forests became a hard task for the Madras government for want of information. In 1890, the collector of Vizagapatnam district informed the government that he could not undertake the forest reservation due to lack of clear information on the land tenure pattern in the district.[32] He reported that the *Muttadars* and *Mokshadars* claimed the property rights on the forests proposed for conservation and created problems for the forest settlement process. As a result of this, the forest conservation process moved at a slow pace in Vizagapatnam.

While reserving the forest land in the tribal areas of Andhra region, the settlement procedure that was prescribed in the Madras Forest Act of 1882 was not followed. The main reason for this was, these areas consisted of valuable timber trees on the one hand, and ecologically sensitive zones, on the other. Owing to these reasons, the Madras government attempted to reserve hill forest tracts. It justified the reservation on the ground that sufficient forest areas were left for the access to the tribals for continuation of their customary rights. But, in most cases the tribals failed to understand the demographic changes initiated by the forest reservation. This had created serious problems in the later days.

Before the intervention of the colonial state, the hill areas in the Andhra region were managed by the *Muttadars*[33], who were the hereditary hill chiefs. Due to harsh environmental conditions and lack of communication, the British could not acquire control over these areas.[34] The *Muttadars,* imposed a small tax on cultivated lands, but did not disturb the traditional relationship between tribals and forests. Penetration of the colonial rule through forest policies exposed the tribal areas to wider exploitation both by the state and plain traders. After realising the potential of resources in the hill areas, the colonial state initiated its efforts to acquire control over these areas. However, the state attempts were resisted by the *Muttadars*. There was a series of revolts against the British intervention in Vizagapatnam and Gunjam districts between the years 1830 and 1840.[35] In spite of revolts, the British gradually acquired control over the tribal areas by promulgating the Act of XXIV of 1839. Under this Act, the hereditary rights of *Muttadars* were disallowed.

Thus, restrictions on *Muttadars'* hereditary rights on the one hand and tribals' discontentment due to the restrictions on *Podu* on the other, manifested in massive tribal uprisings in Rampa areas of Godavari district in 1879-1880.[36] This shows that the British intervention and imposition of restrictions on tribals' access to forests created grievances in tribal society. In this context, introduction of organised forestry and imposition of the state monopolistic control over forests in tribal areas led to deprivation of tribals.

Conclusion

The following observation has been made in the study of colonial policies impact on *Podu* cultivation in Agency areas of Andhra.

Firstly, the tribals have a certain specific relationship with forests. They always interact for their sustenance and try to recreate the forests with their traditional conservation systems. But the progressive assertion of state monopoly rights over large areas of forests turning them into 'reserves', has resulted in large-scale eviction and uprooting of traditional tribal villages. The relationship that existed between tribal social organisation and the forest was completely upset as a result of forest policies. This large-scale commercial exploitation of forests not only destroyed the source of livelihood for tribals but also adversely affected the ecology of the area. The tribals were not only denied their means of livelihood, but also became victims of exploitation and harassment in the hands of forest officials and contractors.

Secondly, the colonial forest policies implemented in the tribal areas had initiated far-reaching changes. The British policy of conservation of forests and restriction of *Podu* to certain areas was intended to prevent destruction of forest wealth. The irony is that tribals had their own conservation methods. In fact, the land used by the tribals for agriculture was not thick or wooded jungle. Moreover, such forestland in the course of 10 years or so would reproduce itself. Ramachandra Guha (1985) has rightly observed that the importance of forests in hill life had given rise to a natural system of conservancy that took different forms, either by drawing a protective ring around the forest or by dedicating hill slopes to deities and preserving trees and slopes around such places.

Thus, the colonial system of forest management was continued even after 1947 with minimal modifications. The exploitation of forest resources for market needs and imposition of restrictions on tribals' access to forests generated discontent on government machinery among tribals in the Andhra agency areas. This discontent was expressed in forms of rebellions that took place in Andhra. The primary reason for the tribals' exclusion as per this chapter lies at the deep structural level. The superimposition of the pyramidal power structure of the British organised on the principles of a centralised bureaucratic system over the inverse pyramidal power structure of the tribal society has resulted in discontent among the tibals in colonial Andhra.

REFERENCES

1. Philip Viegas, 'Land Control and Tribal for Survival', *Social Action*, Vol. 37, 1987, p. 326.
2. K.S. Singh, *Tribal Society in India: An Anthropo-Historical Perspective*, Manohar, New Delhi, 1985.
3. Report of the Special Agency Development Officer, Malayappan Report, 1952, Madras.
4. Furer Haimendorf, *Tribes in India: The Struggle for Survival*, Oxford University Press, New Delhi, 1992 and *The Reddis of Bison Hills, A Study of Acculturation*, Macmillan & Co, London, 1945.
5. Furer Haimendorf, *The Reddis of Bison Hills, A Study of Acculturation*, Macmillan & Co, London, 1945.
6. The Fifth Report of the Select Committee on East India Company Affairs, 1812, Vol. II, New York, 1969 (Republished), p. 110.

7. A. Aiyappan, *A Report on the Socio-Economic Conditions of the Aboriginal Tribes of the Province of the Madras*, Madras, 1948.
8. Ibid.
9. Edward Said, *Orientalism*, Vintage, New York, 1979; Also see K. Sivaramakrishnan, 'Colonialism and Forestry in India: Imagining the Past in Present Politics' in *Comparative Studies in Society and History*, Vol. 37, No. 1 (January, 1995), pp. 3-40.
10. M. Foucault, "History of Systems of Thought." in *Language, Counter-Memory, Practice: Selected Essays and Interviews*, D.F. Bouchard (ed.), Oxford University Press, 1977, pp. 199-200.
11. Clifford, Geertz, *Works and Lives: The Anthropologist as Author*. Stanford University Press, Stanford, 1988.
12. Nicholas B. Dirks, "The Invention of Caste: Civil Society in Colonial India", *Social Analysis*, Special Issue, 1989, pp. 42-52.
13. E.P. Stebbing, *Forests of India*, Volume series, first two volumes are published by John Lane, London in 1922 and 1927; Vol. III was published by A.J. Reprints, New Delhi, in 1982 and Vol. IV, Oxford University Press, London, 1962, pp. 61-62.
14. Berthold Ribbentrop, *Forestry in British India*, Indus Publishing Company, New Delhi, 1989, p. 67.
15. E.P. Stebbing, Vol. I, op. cit., pp. 80-87.
16. Velayuthan Saravanan, "Commercialization of Forest, Environmental Negligence and Alienation of Tribal Rights in the Madras Presidency, 1792-1882", *Indian Economic and Social History Review*, Vol. 35, No. 2, 1998, pp. 125-146.
17. Berthold Ribbentrop, op. cit., pp. 97-98.
18. Ibid., p. 12.
19. Ibid., p. 2.
20. *Andhra Pradesh District Gazetter, Vizagapatnam*, Vol. I, first published in 1907, and republished in Hyderabad, 1994, pp. 117-118.
21. R.B. Corwell, *Working Plan for the Godavari Lower Division, 1934-44*, Government Press, Madras, 1937, p. 28.
22. The Board of Revenue Proceedings, L/R, dated November 30, 1906, F. No. 1265.
23. A. Ayappan, 1948, op. cit., p. 15.
24. *Annual Administrative Report of the Forest Department in Madras Presidency*, Government Press, Madras, 1908-1909, p. 11.
25. Ibid., 1912-1913, p. 8.
26. Ibid., 1914-1915, p. 8.
27. Ibid., 1908-1909, p. 33.
28. Ibid., 1912-1913, p. 21.

29. The *Board of Revenue Proceedings*, F. No. 352, Miscellaneous, March 14, 1894.
30. The *Board of Revenue Proceedings*, F. No. 451, dated July 9, 1894.
31. Ibid., F. No. 297, dated May 9, 1895.
32. Ibid., F. No. 130, dated April 28, 1886.
33. One of the important administrations in Agency areas of Andhra was the Muttadari system. The '*mutta*' means small district or sub-divisions of a country. Groups of villages in the accessible and backward hill tracts came to be held as revenue units called '*muttas*' and the intermediary who collected the revenue and paid a certain amount of it to the government was a Muttadar
34. M.S.R. Anjaneyulu, *Vizagapatnam: A Study of the Relations Between the Zamindars and East India Company*, Visakhapatnam, 2007, p. 65.
35. P. Kamala Mohan Rao and D.L. Prasada Rao, " Tribal Movements in Andhra Pradesh", in K.S. Singh (ed.), *Tribal Movements in India*, Vol. 2, Manohar, New Delhi, 1982, pp. 353-372.
36. David Arnold, "Rebellious Hillmen, The Gudem-Rampa Uprisings 1839-1924", Ranjit Guha (ed.), *Subaltern Studies*, Vol. II, Oxford University Press, Delhi, 1982, pp. 82-142.

Section III

CULTURE, NATURE AND ECO-FEMINISM

8

Interface Between Nature and Culture: Exploring Santal Viewpoints in the Past

Pradip Chattopadhyay

The interaction between nature and culture is central to any discourse on environment. However, mankind's approach to and perception about nature has continued to evolve over the ages. In the past, natural phenomena have been regarded as divine in human society. Further if past myths and legends are to be believed, we get an idea that ancient society was regarded as the modifying agent in the natural world.[1] In Sumerian myths as well as in the writings of Greek and Roman thinkers references are copious to show how landscape shaped the characters of people. In ancient Greece great scholars like Panaetius, Posidonius, Cicero and others have graphically sketched the changes produced by men in the environment. Their main focus, as revealed by Clarence J. Glacken was to show that man's mission on earth was to improve the order designed by God. The achievements in different fields, such as, irrigation, drainage, mining, agriculture and animal husbandry were seen as complements to divine order. Man was considered as an assistant of God in His superintendence of the earth. There was not much of a change in this approach to view nature in the Christian Middle Ages. Since this approach can be best characterised as the increasing hold of religion on the minds of men, it gave way to philosophic trends and transcendental forces to play a decisive role in shaping the destiny of mankind. To the monkish chroniclers everything that appeared as good or bad served as a link in the long chain of divine planning and that mankind blessed with the ability to work had to help God and himself in the improvement of the earth. In Christian theology, however, the earth was regarded as a transit station, the higher object being always to realise God with all his manifestations. In modern times with the multiplication of scientific discoveries including a great leap forward achieved in the field of technological advancement a significant departure from this approach is discernible. Nature is no longer viewed as merely a domain of God nor does mankind remain satisfied in playing the role of a second fiddle to God. Man's increasing attempt to use nature for his own interests has become the buzzword which is reflected in his attempt to act as the steward of land, manipulate the courses of rivers, manage marshes, ponds, lakes and to cut down trees for the cause of advancement of civilisation. This is pretty evident when Georges Louis Leclerc, the count of Buffon said in the 18th century, "it is me and only me who can make it nice and livable."[2]

However concern for environment in recent times is believed to have originated from the perceived ecological crisis that seems to threaten human civilisation.[33] Debates are widespread pertaining to interaction between nature and culture. However debates on sustainable or eco-friendly development or human engagement in industrialisation and urbanisation processes at the cost of nature have attracted attention most in recent times.

Notwithstanding this newly emerged concern for the protection of environment, the relationship between man and nature and its celebration has been going on in human societies for ages. However, the pace with which human society has developed over the last few centuries (aided and abetted by progress in science and technology and also by the spread of the processes of urbanisation and industrialisation) has resulted in casting a shadow on the relationship between man and nature that existed in the past. A faint glimpse of this relationship, may be discernible in the tribal societies in modern times as tribal people are reported to have retained many of their past beliefs and practices even today.[4] Also the process of their evolution to modernity is believed to have been slow compared to the caste society. Indeed, for generations the tribals had shunned external influence and remained content with their peripheral existence. Throughout the ancient and medieval periods tribals had virtually stayed marginalised from the mainstream and their exposure to the forces of modernisation and change only began with the advent of the colonial rule. Thus, in many respects the tribal world view and perceptions of environment are not only distinct but also may be said to be the representative of the past notion of people about nature and culture.

There existed in ancient India the ethos of worshipping mountains, rivers, forests and animals. The inhabitants of the Indus region worshipped gods in the form of trees, animals and human beings. The Harappan people looked upon the earth as a fertility goddess and worshipped her in the same manner as the Egyptians worshipped the Nile goddess Isis. Animals were worshipped in Harappan times and many of them were seen as represented on the seals. A male deity on a seal is surrounded by an elephant, a deer, a rhinoceros and a buffalo.[5] At his feet appear two deer. The four animals surrounding the deity look towards the four directions of the earth. The protection of elephants became a serious business during the time of the Mauryas. The Arthasastra mentions the rules for protecting elephant forests.[6] Other types of forests are also preserved for animals and for protection of special species of trees. Forests always occupied a place of distinction in ancient India as they were considered to be the abodes of the pantheon of gods and goddesses. In fact this tradition of worshipping nature is also visible in tribal societies.

Social scientists across disciplines have developed a number of analytical frameworks for defining the relationship between the tribals and their natural environment. Tribals have been defined as an ethnic category sharing a distinct kind of relationship with nature and they have also been delineated as backward and living at different stages of evolution. Recent revisionist scholars have tended to rewrite tribal culture as somewhat inseparable from its ecological settings and have criticised the colonial discourse for overdrawing the separation between forested landscape and livelihood patterns including agricultural relations of the tribals.[7] Even today, tribal societies represent exemplary dependence on nature for their culture and survival. It is said that the identity of the Adivasis is closely linked to the natural resources and the environment amidst which they live. Land (jamin), forests (jungle) and water (jal) are the main components of their survival which are also synonymous of their identity. Environmental interests and aspects are believed to have a direct bearing on many of the socio-religious beliefs and practices in tribal societies. Their round- the-year engagements in agricultural works, in gathering fruits and other essentials from forests, hunting and healing practices including celebration of fairs and festivals bear testimony to their relationship with nature. Besides, there are other issues which bear a direct reflection to the tribal notion of environment. This study seeks to examine some of these beliefs and practices of the Santals in the past where their notion of environment appears to be more direct and distinctive.

Sentiments for Land and Forests

Santals, for example, lived amid nature, surrounded by hills, forests, rivers and other natural manifestations. These elements provided them their sources of sustenance and also constituted an integral part of their culture. In fact, all the early narratives of colonial ethnographers and administrators have harped on this issue in no uncertain terms that Santal settlements had developed with natural defences all around. 'The Santal villages border those in the Santal Parganas and are situated in the narrow strip of broken high country west of the East Indian Railway, lying between the hills of the Santal Parganas, which approach the Birbhum border on the one side and the alluvial soil of the plains proper on the other. Where these hills recede from the border as in the south west of Murarai thana there are practically no Santal villages.'[8] Thus, their fascination for hills, forests and soil, particularly, laterite soil[9] as essential components for developing settlements was noted by early colonial ethnographers. In fact, all the past symbols of Santal identity like gods and goddesses, totem[10] and tattoos, fairs and festivals, including numerous other beliefs and practices, were related to nature. So nature not only provided the context but also acted as an important variable for the formation of Santal identity. Any change taking place in the physical atmosphere of the region is, therefore, bound to impact upon their views and values of life.

The Santals used to nourish a special sentiment for land, it being regarded as synonymous of their identity. The loss of land meant the loss of identity to them. 'The traditional land base holds an important symbolic and emotional meaning for them as the repository of ancestral remains (Sasans), clan origin sites and other sacred features important to their religious system.'[11] The land system of the Santals modelled on their traditional ideas and beliefs was fundamentally different from the agrarian system and structure of their non-tribal brethren. When the land was first reclaimed, the manjhi or the village headman acted as the sole spokesman for the entire village and engaged in a settlement with the superior landlord in relation to land rent. After consultation with his co-villagers, he agreed to pay a fixed amount of rent, which he collected from all the cultivators of the village. The headman then distributed the land among his co–villagers, making them responsible for the rent to be paid as per settlement. The headman too had to pay his share of rent for the land he held. He was however given a portion of the village land, around two to four bighas, in addition to his own share of land (nij jote), which he held rent-free. Such lands were called man/khem lands. But the headman, as also the other officials of the village who held man/khem lands by virtue of their position, could not claim any special privilege.[12] Thus, it was not a farming system in the ordinary sense of the term because the Santal *mustagir* or headman/farmer did not derive any profit. He was merely a rent-collecting individual and one among equals. Further, as the settlement was made verbally, it lacked the defined contractual character of the ordinary system.[13]

Like land the Santals also cherished a sentiment for forests. In most cases they cleared forests before establishing villages. But they only cleared as many forests as they needed for setting up villages or creating agricultural land. Also trees were sometimes cut down for acquiring fuel-wood or building houses. Before the advent of the British, the Santals used to enjoy customary rights over forests. The place in the forest thick with Sal and Mahua trees was earmarked by them as a *sacred grove*. The Santals regarded this place as sacred and inviolable and the entire vegetation of the place was protected from encroachment. Forests not only played an important role in the economic life of the Santals but also provided materials for their magico-religious beliefs and practices including health care. The Santals had a profound knowledge of several medicinal plants and herbs which helped them to maintain their physical well-being. Indeed, forests also constituted an integral part of their nature-worship. Hills, forests and rivers usually acted as natural defences for their villages. Thus, the life of the Santals in the past was nature-oriented and the whole gamut of magico-religious beliefs and practices including festivals were in a sense aimed at celebrating their relationship with nature.

Myth Relating to Earth's Creation

Santal creation narratives[14] contain references to different elements of nature and their role in creating this earth as well as the stages that preceded the emergence of mankind. It is said that at the beginning there was only water and below the water was the earth. Then aquatic plants and animals came into being. The legend says, then *Thakur Jiu* at first decided to create human beings of clay. But before he could infuse life into them the horse *sin sadom* (which had been kept close) trampled on them. Then *Thakur Jiu* decided to make birds so that they would remain relatively free from getting killed or trampled on by other creatures. He therefore made birds *Has* and *Hasil* from material scalding off his chest. The birds came to life as soon as *Thakur Jiu* blew into them and they immediately flew away. But they had nowhere to sit and rest since there was water all around.

So, after a while they came down and sat on *Thakur Jiu's* hands. Meanwhile the horse felt thirsty and began drinking water. While drinking water it left some froth from his mouth in the water. It floated and produced more foam on the water. *Thakur Jiu* told the birds to go and sit on the foam which they did but soon they complained that though they could roam free by sitting on the foam water but they had nothing to eat. Hearing this *Thakur Jiu* called upon all his aquatic animals that he had created earlier, namely, the alligator, the lobster, the raghop boar fish, stone crab, earthworm one by one asking them if they could collect earth from below the bottom of the sea. All had failed except the earthworm. Then *Thakur Jiu* levelled the earth with a harrow. 'While harrowing, the earth got heaped up in some places, these became mountains. When the earth was put in order the floating foam of the water got stuck to the earth'. On this foam Thakur sowed mauricatus seed (*sirom*) and then further sowed various grasses and trees. Thus forests came into being. The birds, created earlier could now rest and build their nests on trees. Soon the birds lay two eggs on nests. 'After some days from those two eggs emerged two human beings one boy and a girl'. As the two human beings were growing the anxiety of the birds also kept growing concerning where to keep these two.' The birds then started flying at the advice of *Thakur Jiu* in search of a proper place for a human beings. They flew towards the place where the sun sets taking the human beings on their back and landed in Hihiri Pipiri. The birds then became untraceable. The human beings came to be known as Pilchu Haram and Pilchu Budhi. Soon they met Lita who claimed to be their grandfather. Lita then taught them the art of preparing liquor and asked them to drink it after offering a part of it to their god Marang Buru. Thus they became intoxicated and at night slept together involved in procreation. In the morning they felt ashamed of their bodies and covered them with the leaves of the banyan tree. In course of time they got seven sons and daughters. The tradition goes on telling how the community grew, how the first generation of the community was destroyed by *Thakur Jiu* by fire from heaven because of their sin, how one pair survived the disaster and how the next generation grew up and wandered from place to place in the past, etc.

The narrative mentioned above is popularly known as Skrefsrud's version of Santal creation narrative which is said to have been taken down by Rev. L.O. Skrefsrud in 1870-1871 from an old guru named Kolean Guru. It is contained in the Santali book *Horkoren Mare Hapramko Reak Katha*. In addition to this, another version of the same is also available published by Rev. A. Campbell entitled *Santal Tradition*. The essence of the story in both the versions is more or less the same except a minor change in character and a more detailed delineation of the growth of early human beings featuring in Campbell's version.

In this narrative the belief of Santal ancestors on *Thakur Jiu*'s role in creating this earth and human beings is clearly pronounced. Successive stages of creation beginning with water to aquatic plants and animals, to birds and finally the creation of human beings is clearly spelled out which bear a close resemblance to creation narratives of other traditions. In fact these narratives also indicate how the minds of past people used to work pertaining to nature and its various manifestations paving the way for the belief that all creations in this earth followed the divine wish and were united in a chain system sharing essential links with each other. Human beings were thus regarded as a part of the process of the same divine creation that also witnessed creation of water, earth, forests, aquatic animals and birds. The only difference, however, is that mankind perhaps emerged only at the end of this creation process to be preceded by all other living or non-living organisms. Thus, human beings in the Santal creation narratives were not assigned any special position of respect or recognition for their intellectual calibre, thinking faculty and ethical supremacy and were merely treated as one among the other creations of god. This creation tradition of the Santals, it is clear, stands in contradiction to the creation narratives of caste people as they attach much greater importance to the agency of human beings in the kingdom of God. Indeed this approach of the Santals has imparted among them not only a sense of gratitude and respect towards nature but also has bred a sense of awe and fear for supernatural forces capable of causing death and devastation if hurt or displeased. This very approach to nature may also be said to have laid the foundations for all their socio-religious beliefs and practices.

Sacred Grove

The existence of the notion of the sacred or holy grove in tribal culture may be interpreted as an indigenous way of preserving forests or at least a part of it, dotted with rare varieties of trees, scrubs, herbs and plants that have been revered by tribals through the ages. The groves have always been considered to have links with certain cults and the entire vegetation in the grove surrounding that cult is regarded as sacred and inviolable. 'No vegetable matter, not even dead wood would be removed from the grove without incurring the wrath of the gods.[15] The only possible exception was fallen fruit that may be gathered.' However the groves seldom appear to be totemic in origin since no specific sacred tree species need be present in a sacred grove but it can be said that groves served to create a proper setting for the cult rites.[16] 'Kosambi mentions the occurrence of groves among mother goddesses of the Atonga tribe of West Africa in which secret rites of the cult are performed by a sisterhood of priestesses. Any man entering the grove by accident is required to join the sisterhood and to dress and live like a woman for the rest of his life. There is a similar tale in Indian mythology of Manu's son Ila who entered the grove of the mother goddess Parvati by mistake and was transformed into a woman.'[17] Among other taboos denial of accessibility to males in the groves is significant.

In Santal culture groves appeared as a sacred place of worship for only the male members of the villages. Such groves were also storehouse of many plant species with medicinal value absent from the entire region. Forests of Bankura and Midnapore are full of sal and segun (teak) trees and the holy groves of the Santals contain these trees in abundance. Taboos and stories are in wide circulation relating to groves. It is said that attempts by individuals to cut down trees or to hunt animals in the groves have often resulted in death or severe injury of the encroachers. This lends credulance to the belief that 'the protection extended to the vegetation in the grove by the reigning deity is, or at least used to be, quite absolute.'[18]

Religious Beliefs and Practices

Religious beliefs and practices also constituted important elements of the ethnic identity of the Santals in the past. The religious world of the Santals was comprised of hordes of *bongas* and *spirits*. These *bongas* were believed to have control over various natural phenomena and calamities. So, the Santals always tried to appease them through magical and religious practices. These *bongas* were often worshipped and propitiated with the sacrifice of animals, offerings of rice beer and the blood of the sacrificed animal. The village tutelary spirits of the Santals consisted of *Marang Buru, Morenko Turiko, Jaher Era, Gosal Era, Parganas Bonga* and *Manjhi Haram Bonga.*[19] Also the sun, the moon and other manifestations of nature had an important place in the Santal pantheon. However, the nature of Santal worship was primarily congregational and the approach-collective. The religious festivals of the Santals spanning the year were closely connected with their agricultural activities. The most important of the festivals were *Soharae Sim, Baha, Erok Sim, Iri-Gundhi, Nawai* and *Janther*. Besides, other important festivals like *Karam, Jom Sim,* and *Mak More* were also important. Every festival had two aspects, one the magico–religious, which covered the sacrifice and offerings to appease the deity and the other, the recreational, which provides entertainment and enjoyment including drinking, dancing, singing, etc.[20] Charulal Mukherjee has commented that, "It seems as if the very heart of the tribe beats in unison with the advent of these tribal events, for it is here that the Santal plunges into his primitive herd-life to worship the tribal deities, to sing the advent of the agricultural season, to make merry over a bumper crop and to ward off by magic, the pests that hinder the sweet and even flow of their common life."[21] In fact Santals in the past felt that various aspects of their economic life were needed to be guarded by appropriate ceremonials and rituals to the tribal deities, so that the beneficient may protect the harvest and the malevolent bongas may be shorn of their malign influence. These sacrifices and libations to deities and ancestor-spirits are closely associated with all Santal public festivals. The life of the Santals in the past was threatened by natural calamities and disasters of various kinds. For example, there might be insufficient rain or too much of it. Locusts might consume the corn grown and as the people revere to these baffling mysteries of existence, they look for confidence and want to secure good luck for themselves and their tribe. 'Through these festivals the Santals wanted to establish a communion with the super-human powers by first of all propitiating them with the hope that they in their benevolence might influence the destinies of the tribe at such turning points in the material life of the tribe.'[22]

Healing Practices and Superstitions

Traditional healing practices and associated superstitions were also in many ways related to their perception about natural environment. Earlier the belief was that the diseases and calamities occurred due to god's wrath and influence of evil spirits. Anything that disturbs the normal course of life, be it in the form of sickness, disease or a natural calamity was conceived as unnatural by the Santals. According to P.O. Bodding,[23] Santals suffered from many peculiar ideas about these evil spirits and their mode of operation. They considered that natural objects like, trees, hillocks, etc., could be 'possessed' by evil spirits but it was not possible to know in advance which tree hillock or physical object would be possessed by an evil bonga. However, it was believed that if a boy falls down after climbing up a tree and suffers an injury, it was indicative of the tree being possessed by an evil spirit. Such a tree then became an object of worship. If for some reasons the tree dried up, the popular interpretation was that the tree could not stand the impact of the evil bonga possessing it. Sitakant Mahapatra[24] has explained that there is nothing called 'accident' in the life of the Santals.

Whenever they faced accidents like drowning in a stream, snake-bitting or devouring by a tiger resulting in death or perpetual maiming, they attributed them to 'unnatural situations.'

Santals accepted death as ordained by the Marangburu. The issue of death never seemed to bother them in the past. Like most other primitive communities, they also displayed lack of obsession with regard to death as they were more concerned about the pleasure and pains of life and the joys and sorrows of daily existence. Of course, they too suffered from pathos and bewilderment with the death of their near and dear ones but death appeared to them as something that they could not do much against. Probably due to their total surrender to the inevitability of death the spirit to enjoy the present life reigned supreme in them.[25] Santals belonging to the present generation may differ from this attitude but it is true that their counterparts in the past hardly had any fear about death or the nagging old age. Suicide was also extremely rare among them in the past.

The most striking aspect of the traditional Santal attitude towards health was their belief in the role of supernatural forces in maintaining physical well-being including existence on the earth. This notion had indeed blurred their real awareness about pain or disease and instead prepared them to accept or tolerate pain as a part of earthly existence. Apart from this, even sufferings and miseries were considered as necessary in the purificatory process to be recompensed in the next life. This culture of attributing mishaps and misfortunes to divine providence had in fact dented Santal initiatives to seek a realistic approach to disease and death.[26]

Witchcraft existed as an integral part of the religio-magical beliefs of the Santals in the past. A.B. Chowdhuri has mentioned that the extent of the problem of witch-killing including tortures of varying degrees practised by the Santals has been very widespread in West Bengal as well as in other states.[27] The Santal belief in witchcraft is believed to have originated from their respect for and fear of the bongas. Among the Santals, the principal element in the assumption of supernatural power was the concept of the bongas, the power that controlled nature.

Earlier the Santals believed that these bongas, at times, could become wrathful and make life miserable. The witches had a liaison with these spirits or bongas and therefore, they also had the power to cause harm to man.[28] This belief in the malevolent bongas, and the possible relationship between the witches and the bongas had, in fact, made the phenomenon of witchcraft in Santal society very difficult to bear. Though Santals in general did not always believe in wrathful bongas since they had been worshipping the bongas for centuries, some of them at least, shared the idea that the witches or others might have actually turned the bongas against them and that only the witch-doctors could identify such witches.[29] In the Santal society there were witch-doctors known as ojhas or jangurus who were in charge of warding off evil bongas or spirits by worshipping gods, observing rituals, making sacrifices and performing religio-magical practices.

The witches' role as shamans or traditional healers is also a much talked about issue in present times. Riane Eisler has commented that witches were traditional healers and witch accusations were aimed at discrediting the healing knowledge of women. Studies from different regions in India also hint at women's shamanistic roles. Verrier Elwin, for example, talks about Saora women's shamanism and that they were custodians of black magic and had unrivalled knowledge of herbs and plants. Skaria says dakans were often thought to be good at gathering. In Chotanagpur the relationship of women with nature and forests and their knowledge of roots, herbs and plants were quite established in the community domain and belief system.[30]

Thus Santal views relating to the causes of death and disease may be categorised into three heads—the natural, the malign and the divine. The remedy for natural illness or sickness would be sought in herbal medicines while those caused by malevolent bongas/spirits or withches would be addressed through incantations, charms and sacrifices administered by the ojhas or jangurus. A third category that caused death and devastation on a larger scale was attributed to gods and goddesses and elaborate arrangements to propitiate them were in place in the society of the Santals.[31]

Understanding tribal perception of nature is thus significant to understand the approach of the past people to the natural environment. Indeed, it was this perception that had shaped their world-view, including ideas and attitudes to life. The distinctive element in it was the recognition that nature was a domain of God, an area of God's manifestation in all its flora and fauna. Accordingly, dependence on nature for survival and economic use of natural resources became an integral part of their religo-cultural ethos. However, this ethos has undergone changes with the passage of time and with the achievement of progress in science and technology. The spread of the processes of industrialisation and urbanisation all over the world and the consequent material advancement that came alongside has made men overconfident to randomly exploit nature, the ill effect of which has resulted in frequent visits of natural calamities like cyclones, tsunamis, floods and earthquakes.

REFERENCES

1. Glacken, Clarence J., *Huellas en la playa de Rodas,* Ediciones del Serbal, Barcelona, 1996, p. 163.
2. Leclerc, George, Louis, *Historia Natural,* Vol. 12, Paris, 1764, pp. 85-86.
3. Debates are widespread pertaining to interaction between nature and culture. However debates on sustainable or eco-friendly development or human engagement in industrialisation and urbanisation processes at the cost of nature have attracted attention most in recent times.
4. Kosambi, D.D., 'The Contribution of D.D. Kosambi to Indology' in Thapar, R. (ed.), *Interpreting Early India,* New Delhi, Oxford University Press, 1992, p. 91. According to D.D. Kosambi, 'historians in India were in a particularly happy position since so much of the past survives in the present ... the survival within different social layers of many forms that allow the reconstruction of totally diverse earlier stages.'
5. Sharma, R.S., *Ancient India,* New Delhi, NCERT, 1980, p. 40.
6. Chakrabarti, Ranjan (ed.), *Situating Environmental History,* New Delhi, Manohar, 2007, p. 13.

7. Agarwal, A. and K. Sivaramkrishnan (2001), *Social Nature: Resources, Representations, and Rule in India,* Delhi, Oxford University Press, 2001, p. 2.
8. McAlpin, M.C., *Report on the Condition of the Santals of Bankura, Birbhum, Midnapore and North Balasore,* Calcutta, Firma KLM, 1981, p. 4.
9. Ibid., p. 6.
10. Mukherjee, Charulal, *The Santals,* Calcutta, A. Mukherjee & Company Pvt. Ltd., 1962, p. 108.
    The author here shows that the clans are totemistic in origin. Certain relationships exist between the clans and some physical phenomena or some tangible objects such as an animal, a bird or even some plant or grass. Thus, Murmus revere the Nilgai, Hansdak hold the duck sacred, Marandis salute if they happen to cut Marandi grass. The general rule is that a member of the same totem will never kill or hurt the object he derives his name from nor will he tolerate intermarriage within the clan.
11. Areeparampil, Mathew, *Struggle for Swaraj,* Chaibasa, Tribal Research & Training Centre, 2002, p. 7.
12. Banerjee, A.K., *West Bengal District Gazetteers, Bankura,* Calcutta, Bengal Government Press, 1968, p. 170.
13. Ibid., p. 170.
14. Hembrom, T., *The Santals,* Calcutta, Punthi Pustak, 1996, p. 82-87.
15. Gadgil, Madhav and V.D. Vartak, 'The Sacred Use of Nature', in Ramachandra Guha (ed.), *Social Ecology,* New Delhi, Oxford University Press, 1994, p. 88.
16. Ibid., p. 85.
17. Quoted from Ibid., p. 85.
18. Ibid., p. 87.
19. Das, A.K., U.K. Roy and S.K. Basu, *To be with Santals,* Calcutta, SC & ST Department, Government of West Bengal, 1977, p. 49.
20. Ibid., p. 59.
21. Mukherjee, Charulal, op. cit., 1962, p. 232.
22. Ibid., p. 271.
23. Bodding, P.O., *The Santals and Disease,* Calcutta, Royal Asiatic Society of Bengal, 1925.
24. Mahapatra, Sitakant, *Modernization and Ritual,* New Delhi, Oxford University Press, 1986, p. 92.
25. Ibid., p. 91.
26. Ibid., p. 91.
27. Chadhuri, A.B., *Witch Killings Amongst Santals,* New Delhi, Asia Publishing House, 1984, p. 10.

28. Bhattacharya, Pradip., *Witchcraft Among the Santals*, Calcutta, Liberal Association for Movement of People (LAMP), 1994, p. 10.
29. Ibid., p. 10.
30. Sinha, Shashank S., 'Adivasis, Gender and the Evil Eye: The Construction(s) of Witches in Colonial Chotanagpur' in Biswamoy Pati (ed.), *Adivasis in Colonial India*, New Delhi, Orient Blackswan, 2013, p. 117.
31. Hardiman, David, 'Knowledge of the Bhils and their Systems of Healing' in Biswamoy Pati (ed.), *Adivasis in Colonial India*, New Delhi, Orient Blackswan, 2013, pp. 312-313.

9

Traversing Mediums of Environmental Discourse: Pursuance for Panacea

Reep Pandi Lepcha

> The age of an ever increasing population is over. The age of city outspread is towards the end too. We are now in an age during which we have to rebuild our country that is moth-eaten and fragmented by over development. It is an age in which we have to rebuild it for human and natural life forms to live comfortably in.
>
> — *Hayao Miyazaki*

Miyazaki apart from co-founding Studio Ghibli in Japan is an environmental activist. The above quote was addressing the efforts of Hirabari Environment Protection Association, connected to the conservation of a forest in Nagoya and aptly describes the various phases of development world-wide. The grim outcome of development, that of disappearing natural diversity serves as collateral and there needs to be a universal redressal to the problem. Though popular media has effectively portrayed apocalyptic situations using varied mediums to highlight environmental discourses, none may have been as successful as Miyazaki when it comes to animations. Miyazaki's productions reverberate of a plethora of ideas that foreground environmental issues and taps into his imagination to give a glimpse of the futuristic possibilities[1]. The first half of the chapter will hence deal with the medium of films and then move to oral tradition or folklores and explore the environmental discourses governing instances of interface between man and nature/ environment; where we are simultaneously confronted with spatial and temporal occurrences that are tied to human choices, basically our actions or inactions.

Before proceeding further, it is important to deliberate on the two terms: "nature" and "environment". My understanding of these terms is meant to explicate my position by highlighting various issues through this chapter. I believe that nature reflects the attributes of the physical world where both living and non-living form a part of a phenomenon, while environment deals more with the effects of conscious human presence on their natural surroundings. Such approaches bring home the simple truth that the human race is plagued by issues which though appear parochial are actually universal and when it concerns conservation or preservation, nations are struggling to find a foothold. Approaches to achieving this goal may be varied, controversial and even contradictory to the discourses governing them. One cannot deny that past experiences play an integral part in informing such attempts.

Locating Important Interfaces: Sites of Contest

Focusing on *Princess Mononoke* and *My Neighbour Totoro,* I will comment on the preoccupation of these animations with the nature-environment interface. *Mononoke* is not an everyday children's animation, it borders around violent portrayals of mistreatment of nature by mankind and the retaliation meted out by nature and its creatures. *Totoro,* on the other hand, exemplifies the harmonious human existence in a 'satoyama'[2], which is encompassed within the larger framework of nature.

There are several important interfaces portrayed in *Mononoke* and it begins with a grim narration:

> In ancient times, the land lay covered in forests, where from ages long past dwelt the spirits of the gods. Back then man and beast lived in harmony, but as time went by, most of the great forests were destroyed. Those that remained were guarded by gigantic beasts, who owe their allegiance to the great forest spirit. For those were the days of gods and of demons.

The consequences following the breach of harmony between man and nature are established from the onset. Miyazaki takes the opportunity to portray the greed of man, which reduces its surroundings to waste; as the movie progresses we see how ambitions of emperors bring about death, destruction and genocide[3] and how industry leads to deforestation. The movie revolves around a powerful curse that consumes anybody who comes in contact. The plot progress depends on the symbolic depiction of the curse and therein also lie the environmental discourses. Miyazaki employs this curse to engage with events which reflect on cause and effect patterns that govern basic existence. Ashitaka of the Emishi tribe has the curse passed on to him by a dying forest spirit Naga. 'Contaminated', Ashitaka embarks on a journey to locate the source of the curse and also to cure it. Ashitaka metaphorically becomes a site of contest and struggle in the movie. A suspicious looking monk befriends Ashitaka and prudently comments:

> ...but now everything is destroyed either by flood, landslide or fire. These days there are angry ghosts all around us. Dead from war, sickness, starvation and nobody cares. So you say you are cursed, so what? So is the whole damned world.

Natural calamities, one can safely gauge have nothing 'natural' left about them. It has become a vociferous reaction triggered by human activity. Hence, the curse traversing cast, creed and kind is a negative depiction of the interface. Ashitaka meets Lady Eboshi, the owner of Iron Town—actively engaged in mining of iron ore and weaponry; she stands unafraid of god, demons or spirits and shows no hesitation in destroying forests. Eboshi undermines discourses which equate women to nature as she directly exploits nature's resources and challenges the popular notion that ecological crises are inevitably an effect of patriarchal culture. Sure enough she is the source of the curse.

The title character Mononoke is raised by a wolf Moro—a guardian spirit of the forest. The concept of feral children is fairly common in literature and history; Kipling's Mowgli[4] and figures like 'Remus and Romulus' provide an example. Mononoke identifies herself more to a wolf than a human and finds it important to protect the forest from all harmful intrusions. Other spirits consider Mononoke with mistrust, which is not surprising as humans resulted in their hardships. Mononoke shows immovable faith in the Spirit; living at close quarters with nature she knows the importance of the forest and the spirits guarding them. The fragile balance of nature should not be disturbed and Mononoke successfully manages to convey this to the viewers.

Yet another example of such interfaces is the great forest Spirit. The physical description given of the forest Spirit by one of Eboshi's injured men: 'a real monster, like a huge enormous deer, except they say it has a human face sometimes'. Miyazaki integrates all things, even human attributes, while moulding his Spirit god. The body of the Spirit becomes a site of dispute as the monk—now addressed as Gonza—along with Eboshi conspires to decapitate it for an emperor who wants to gain access to the head's fabled elixir properties. The exploitative greed is inherent in anything remotely human. Miyazaki intentionally makes the Spirit eco-cosmic (borrowing Knight's term) energy source. Decapitating the Spirit results in 'kodamas'[5] falling from trees and the forest starts dying. The loss of the head signifies a loss of intelligence or even severing humanity from nature. The body of the Spirit turns into a flood like entity engulfing anything in its way[6] suggesting its chastising capability. Miyazaki with the help of rich visuals suggests that the loss of Spirit is irreparable, but one must trust the cyclical nature of life. His story ends with a message of renewal.

Thus characters namely Ashitaka, Princess Mononoke and the Spirit metaphorically portray sites of human-nature interface. Scholars mention that Miyazaki never believes in polarising elements, he always leaves ideas enmeshed and such characters are proof of his attributes.

My Neighbour Totoro (1988) is uncomplicated compared to *Princess Mononoke*. *Totoro* is about adaptation and peaceful co-existence of man with nature. Totoro is a woodland spirit and his appearance is a prototype of the forest spirit even in terms of mannerisms. His giant stature and his wide-rounded eyes is Miyazaki's engagement with symbolically exploring all-encompassing vision, layered with innocence. Peculiarly, Totoro and his companions are only visible to children. Miyazaki intentionally deprives the adults with the power to see a spirit, as 'innocence' of children is a powerful tool for understanding nature, much like Ashitaka's goal to 'see with eyes unclouded'. A child's psychology can be spontaneously simple and complicated, but the process by which it absorbs information in a 'matter-of-fact' manner, is charmingly portrayed. Adults approach information in a cautiously, moreover their vested interests corrupt the process of seeking solution.

A 'satoyama' is an ingenious way to protect natural diversity and the movie endorses the representation of this aspect. The proximity of human-to-nature is buffered by the farming community[7]; this constructed environment eases the sense of direct intrusion and absence of threat supplements this idyllic condition. The parallel worlds of nature spirits and humans coexist without interference or aggression from either quarter in *Totoro*. This feat which is readily available in fiction is utopic in today's reality. It has become a constant struggle to save forest-land and diversity and to resist concrete jungles from mushrooming[8].

Princess Mononoke and *My Neighbour Totoro* also exist as books. A special publication titled *The Art of Princess Mononoke: A film by Hayao Miyazaki*, a Media Art book makes an interesting companion book to the animation. A book review revels on the art techniques used in the anime:

> ...the forest in "Princess Mononoke" is as much a place of darkness as it is of beauty. Bright green dapples the upper reaches of the frame, while the foreground is textured with ominous grays and browns. Not wreathed in shadow—these are places light never penetrates to begin with. Rather, shadow is their essence, and humans can never be anything but intruders.

Miyazaki an ecological activist harbours this sentiment in his animations, his stories and directions are never there by chance, it is always present with the intention of exposing the masses to truth through fiction and for providing brief epiphanic escapes.

Salvaging the Storehouse of Natural Past

Shifting the discussion from animations, I will delve into a regional yet universal content of folklore that deals with projections of environmental history and their socio-cultural importance in negotiating contemporary natural crises with the help of Lepcha folktales.

Folklore though dismissed frequently as ramblings of the common-folk never ceased to fascinate people who read them closely. Narrations of folklores have survived through time continuum, if we look into the discipline of 'folklore studies' particularly in the Indian context, it is fairly new compared to other regions. It is common knowledge that folklores were initially collected by British anthropologists in its first phase and were primarily used to acquire a deeper understanding of the people that inhabited the colonies. Where documented or written history failed, mythology and folktales were often treated as resource to fill the voids of history. There is an ongoing debate regarding the authenticity of the oral narratives given their nebulous quality and this goes against the grain of what history strives to achieve—a certain sense of stability. Yet, there is no arguing that folklore tries to bridge a gap left by other disciplines and provides a periscopic vent to human imagination. History is obsessed with chronology and when we come to a phase in human evolution, where hunting morphs into herding and gathering to agriculture, as noted by Boas[9]; there may be no proper explanation but a possible exposition of this interface lies in folktales.

One popular sub-genre within folktales is the creation myth. The Róngkups/Lepchas, the autochthonous tribe of Sikkim have folktales including this sub-genre. The creation myth is a vista and their inception is always explained through supernatural occurring, far removed from scientific explanations. Indigenous civilisations in fact assume man to be the last and the lowest form of life and scholars like Salleh rightly point out that indigenous groups are indeed correct in assuming this "genuine humility about our human dwelling in nature". The problem arises when existing discourses undermine this humility to establish intellectual superiority resulting in human-nature coercion. This section of the chapter, will hence layout a reading of the environmental past as depicted in folktales and move on to contemporary history and environmental scenarios.

Folktales: Discourses on Environmental Safeguarding

Nye-Mayel Lyang translates into 'Our paradisiacal place' and is the Lepcha nomenclature for the 22nd state of India, Sikkim. There is general acceptance among the populace that *Kongchen-chyu* or Mt. Kanchendzonga is the protector deity of the region; people still practise religious ceremonies to pay their respects to this guardian deity. This custom and belief is stemmed from the Lepcha folktale where *Itbu-mu*/Creator-mother, after creating the world, raised the mountain and designated it the brother of mankind, beckoning him to stand as protector to the land she had created. The folktale also speaks about *Itbu-mu* taking two handfuls of snow from the peak and shaping them as progenitors[10] of Lepchas. This folktale was narrated by Ren[11] Namgyal Lepcha, a resident of Passingdang[12], but the tale survives in many versions. The folktale further narrates the story of six brothers who wanted to dedicate their lives protecting *Konchen-chyu* and told their only sister about their plans. The sister bid goodbye to her brothers promising them that if she bore sons, she would ensure that they worship *Kongchen-chyu* and her brothers. After marrying, the girl was blessed with a son, but she forgot her promise. *Konchen-chyu* feeling neglected sent a *paril-bu*, a huge python to coil itself at the foot of the mountain, this action threatened to flood the region. The son of this lady went to the python and prayed for mercy and simultaneously offered prayers to *Kongchen-chyu*. The fulfilment of the promise subdued the wrath of the protector and the son became the first of the *bongthings* or shamans that belong to the clan of *Kongchen-chyu* worshippers. The shamans usually narrate their history during a ritual in the forms of this oral remembrance. This narrative tale was also recorded and translated by Halfden Siiger, a theologist, on one such ritualistic occasion. Mazumdar (2011) reported that the recording and its translation is still preserved in a museum in Denmark. The significance of this particular clan for Lepchas is of immense importance. Ren Samdup Tasho Lepcha, a *bongthing* claimed lineage to this clan and was given the duty of annually carrying out the rituals which he sincerely executed for fifty years, he breathed his last at the age of 83 on October 29, 2011, but he never named his successor.[13] As a result there are no more *bongthings* from this clan to carry out one of the most important rituals. There is mass grievance among the Lepchas that centuries-old ritual meant to safeguard the region has been brought to a halt and with it an important section of an ill-documented history of the Lepchas is lost. A posthumous felicitation was carried out by the *Tshuklakhang* Trust, which was founded to look after the religious matters of the state when *Chogyal*[14] Wangchuk Namgyal renounced his throne. This initiative highlights how the ritual was accepted into the folds of Buddhism and how generations of *Chogyals* carried it out with the help of the Lepcha shamans and named the festival '*Pang Labsol*'. Indigenous belief states that *Nye-Maluk-Lyang*[15] or the paradise on earth lies somewhere in the mountainous range and after death, the spirits of the Lepchas are believed to reside in this holy region amongst their ancestors.

This tale is inclusive of not just the traditional customs and beliefs of the indigenous people, but it also extrapolates on the widely accepted history of the indigenous community. A history which narrates a time when mountains stood to protect the race and in turn was held sacred due to faith sustained through mutual respect. Even *Chogyals* monitored the movement of mountaineers and permits were usually never issued to climb the face of this peak.[16] The climbing of the summit was considered to be a sacrilegious offence and people feared the wrath of deities. A British expedition which finally made an attempt in 1955 just stopped short of the peak, out of respect for the Lepcha belief and similar expeditions to the mountain followed their suit. Such incidents integrate concerns of nature and one's environment, with the help of customs and rituals which psychologically bind people to uphold beliefs. Though common sense would dismiss such tales as archaic or superstitious,[17] it is important to draw attention to the fact that it is to their credit that people in the region managed to safeguard their environment from any untoward developmental damage. In the absence of an affinity to the cultural and environmental heritage quotient, the protection of natural spaces becomes difficult.

I would now like to discuss in a similar context the story of two rivers Teesta[18] and Rangeet. Lepcha mythology states these two rivers as lovers. One day the two rivers planned a race and after deciding the rendezvous point, each chose a guide each. Teesta chose a snake, whereas Rangeet chose a bird, *toot-pho* for a guide. When the race ensued, Teesta guided by a slithering snake carved a smooth journey to their destination. The bird which was guiding Rangeet, kept fleeting in the direction of crumbs and worms, as a result Teesta reached the destination earlier than Rangeet. When Rangeet saw Teesta patiently awaiting his arrival, his fury knew no bounds and he started receding in the direction he had travelled; this resulted in flooding. Alarmed Teesta bid Rangeet to calm his fury for his actions would be disastrous for the human race. To subdue his anger, Teesta bid her love to flow above her signifying Teesta's willing submission to defeat for the sake of saving lives.[19] The confluence of the rivers is at Peshok, a holy site, where both rivers are offered prayers usually by the newly-weds belonging to the indigenous tribe; reinstating their faith in the river gods and their love.

I chose this tale because the two rivers which have been celebrated in the past are now under threat due to many hydro-power projects. These hydro developmental projects have been planned, even for areas like Dzongu, in North Sikkim. Dzongu is protected under Article 371F of the Indian Constitution as the special reserve for Lepchas and had been declared a protected site since 1956, when Tashi Namgyal, the *Chogyal* of Sikkim brought out an official notification, issued by the Home Department, Government of Sikkim. Moreover, the area already falls under the Kanchendzonga Biosphere reserve, a biodiversity hot-spot. There was a huge outcry from the people of the indigenous community[20] when the projects were announced as it threatened to run their sacred rivers dry.

Similarly, hydro power projects were announced in 1990 with the Rathongchu Hydro Power Projects, but it met with remarkable resistance from strange quarters. The Rathongchu power project threatened the religious heritage of the people and affected the sacred festival of '*Bumchu*'[21]. The water which is used to annually fill the vase is taken from Rathong Chu (river), which the projects threatened and so monks and spiritual leaders unitedly protested as it violated many aspects of life in Sikkim, needless to say the government reverted its decision. Prior attempts of damming the river have been mentioned in the imperial government records, but they were plans for constructing small-scale dams. The Sikkim Durbar in a correspondence file on the 'Teesta Dam Scheme' found in the External Affairs Department files in 1946, mentions how A.N. Khosla a prominent Indian engineer, has omitted the mention of: 'The possible effect on the hillsides especially on the shalely soils as a result of seepage of the reservoir water and its subsidence from time to time' which apparently had been discussed at a conference. The same document also mentions how Khosla had assured that the subsidence would be: 'So low and imperceptible that the hillsides will not be affected. If however landslips occur as a result of the seepage of water on the hillsides the Teesta Dam Project should be responsible for the damages and the costs involved for maintaining the stability of the hillside'. It indeed came as a surprise that such plans of hydro-power projects were underway as early as 1946. Even a geologist like F.A. Nickell was appointed to compile a report of the dam sites. Nickell addressing the issue of seismicity of the region writes:

> Tista Canyon lies in the seismically active region of the eastern Himalaya. Several major earthquakes have strongly affected the district and it is quite likely that additional disturbances will occur. A drawing in Mr. Auden's report on the Coronation Dam Site (January 1946) illustrates successive earthquakes embracing the area within isoseismals 6-8. While the epicentre of disturbances are far removed and shocks have not been translated into ground displacement locally, it is obvious that design of any dam must include a substantial factor for protection against earthquake, at least one quarter gravity. (Nickell, 1946, p. 4-5).

Nickell clearly voices his concern that dams can be built if it is constructed to withstand an earthquake and should not be higher than 150-200 feet. The projects that have been planned for the two rivers are more than twenty in number and ranging from small, large and mega hydro power projects. Sikkim has a history of seismic activity since it falls in the Himalayan fold region; when such an unstable land is made privy to tunnelling and frequent blasting—required for the construction of hydro projects—it takes a heavy toll. On September 18, 2011, the state witnessed an earthquake measuring as high as 6.9 on the Richter scale. Massive damage to lives and property was reported and it came as no surprise that the epicentre of the quake was traced to North Sikkim, which is a site for as many as seven hydro power projects. There were also many things that went unreported like the number of wildlife casualties and the ecological damage, though this may appear a high-ended sarcasm, it nevertheless rings of truth.

Sikkim is one of the smallest states in India, with a population just over six lakhs and the power demand of the state was slated to around 83 megawatts/MW in the year 2011-12, with an expected increase to 150MW in the next ten years and was reported in Annexure III of the 17th Power Survey of India. The hydro power projects are aiming to generate about 5,000MW by the year 2017, but will compromise heavily on natural life and environment. My experience with hydro power constructions is mostly limited to my observations and it has been far from pleasant. These projects immensely damage the natural course of the river which leads to drought, heavy loss of biodiversity, climate change and hamper agricultural activities. These are a few negative impacts, but are tied directly to environment and nature.

The tales discussed here are drawn from the past, whether people take them to be historical or mythical is of little consequence; what is important is locating the action which mandates a collective understanding of current contexts of environmental security, which the indigenous people have successfully identified and prudently tried to sort out. It is paramount to give precedence to similar environmental movements in order to learn and re-connect with nature; to give nature its due.

Conclusion

As mentioned earlier there is nothing 'natural' left in 'natural calamities'; the frequency of floods, earthquakes and landslides have increased and unchecked developmental projects carried out on a massive scale—with all the shady governmental clearances in place—is a ticking disaster set off by man. It would be foolhardy to shift the blame to nature. Materialistic mankind reduces everything to 'resource' and even though mankind is aware of nature's finite disposition, it has not stopped us from embarking on a fatalistic approach. For these reasons, Miyazaki's futuristic propositions sadly become prophetic. The apocalyptic ideas which litter various forms of media, be it theology, literature, films, science or even parts of our oral tradition, induces it to become less of a figment and moves closer to resembling reality. Human action and inaction are equally responsible for the predicament that we are currently facing. Conservation and preservation scenarios have arisen mainly due to the skewered orientation of human actions towards nature. If the inaction towards uninhibited approach to exploitation had an early start, one can assume that we would have been in a better position than how we are currently placed. The gravity of the situation can be gauged with the help of a popular website—Conservation International[22] which recently launched a campaign called 'Nature is Speaking' on October 6, 2014. Hollywood's well known actors and actresses leant their voices to the various elements of nature and they had a very explicit message to share: 'Nature does not need people. People need Nature.'[23] Though the organisation has sported controversies, nevertheless, they have managed to make an impact. The entire series of 'Nature is Speaking' has eerie facts captured by the voice of artists. Directors like Miyazaki also invoke a sense of nostalgia by portraying nature in its pristine state; using reminiscence of ancient cultural and historical past and metaphorically projecting the visualisation of our future—all to evoke a sense of responsibility in our day-to-day interface with our natural surroundings, where we stand to make a difference and all within our reach. Folktales, an oral medium plays a similar role, it gives us a sense of belonging and identity which we tend to fiercely protect and when tales are connected to nature or contextual environmental history, it affects the folds of discourses which focus on safeguarding of nature, simultaneously giving impetus to environmental movements. Though it may appear tempting to presume that distancing ourselves from our cultural or religious heritage, we bring impending doom, but as scholars we should know better. Evolution is unavoidable for all spheres of life hence change of all forms is inevitable. The panacea has always been available to mankind and it has always been within reach, the fact of the matter lies in simple truth that nobody is willing to take the bitter draught or be a part of a rude awakening.

NOTES

1. *Nausicaa of the Valley of the Wind* (1984) is a perfect example; it begins after the industrial revolution when forests have become toxic and pose threat to humans.
2. A 'satoyama' is an interesting cultural practice in Japan; it forms a buffer-zone between man and nature. Hiromi Kobori and Richard B. Primack discuss the concept of 'satoyama' extensively in their article 'Participatory Conservation Approaches for *Satoyama*'(2003).
3. Emishi is an indigenous tribe in the movie and are victims of displacement and imperial expansion. Their situation paints a realistic picture about displacements that occur in the wake of developmental endeavours.
4. Mononoke is a mirror impression of Mowgli and exhibits Miyazaki's preoccupation with the female protagonist.
5. According to Japanese mythology, *kodamas* are the spirits of the tree—similar to dryads of Greek mythology.
6. Miyazaki turns it into his 'flood-episode', an idea which has been explored in various mythologies like the *Gilgamesh* epic; or the '*Tendong*' flood in the case of Lepchas. The flood always signifies cleansing and it is no different in *Mononoke.*

7. Miyazaki admits that farming is less ecologically productive as compared to a forest, yet it is a better option than total concretisation.
8. It is important to mention that even satoyamas are facing survival challenges.
9. Boas in *Primitive Man* uses the concept to explicate on the theory of biological evolution.
10. They were *Nuzong-Nyu* and *Fhudong-thing*, who were given different paths to reach *Nye-Maluk-Lyang* as they were not intended to be a couple.
11. 'Ren' is an honorific term in the Lepcha.
12. *Passingdang* in North Sikkim; the story was narrated during my field visit in October 2013.
13. Though he has a son, he is not keen to follow in his father's footsteps.
14. *Chogyals*/the Dharma Rajas came from Tibet and ushered Buddhism into the region.
15. *Nye- Maluk-Lyang* in Lepcha mythology is a specific region hidden near *Kongchen-chyu*.
16. A document housed in the National Archives in Delhi under the section of External Affairs Department and dated 1939 mulls on this issue.
17. Many scholars including Murphy have spoken about 'nature' and 'tradition' equated with regressive thinking, a Third-World 'condition' which needs to be replaced by industry of the First-World; I definitely do not agree with such polarity.
18. Teesta is also known by the name *Rangyoo*.
19. Though the tale encourages an eco-feministic reading, it would be a digression at this point.
20. A.C.T. or the Affected Citizens of Teesta was formed and were relentless in their effort to save the rivers.
21. *Bumchu:* 'vase of water'—each year the water mark in the vase is assessed by high monks and on its basis environmental prophecies are made for the year.
22. C.I. was founded in 1987; a non-profit organisation which is dedicated to efforts of saving, conserving and preserving nature.
23. This 'post- postmodern' (Murphy, 2008) world though appealing is in tune with the idea of earth evolving without human beings.

REFERENCES

1. Adhikari, Biraj, *Sikkim: The Wounds of History*, Siliguri, Impact Press, 2010.

2. Bhasin,Veena, *Ecology, Culture and Change: Tribals of Sikkim Himalayas,* New Delhi, Inter-India Publications, 1989.
3. Bhutia, Doma T. (ed.), *Independent People's Tribunal on Dams, Environment and Displacement,* Delhi, Human Rights Law Network, 2012.
4. Boas, Franz, *The Mind of Primitive Man,* Macmillan,1911.
5. Clements, Jonathan and Helen McCarthy, *The Anime Encyclopedia: A Guide to Japanese Animation Since 1917,* Berkeley, Stone Bridge Press, 2006.
6. Clifford, James and George Marcus (eds.) *Writing Culture: The Poetics and Politics of Ethnograpy,* University of California Press, 1986.
7. Conservation International. Nature is Speaking. [online] October 6th. Available from: http://natureisspeaking.org/. [Accessed: October 19, 2014].
8. Lahiri, Souparna, Hydro Power Projects in Sikkim: A Story of Violation, Coercion and Suppression. In Bhuita, T. Doma (ed.) *Independent People's Tribunal on Dams, Environment & Displacement,* Delhi, Human Rights Law Network, 2012.
9. Martin, Ian, A deeper look at Hayao Miyazaki's nature, *The Japan Times.* [Online] August 2, 2014. Available from: http://www.japantimes.co.jp/culture/2014/08/02/books/book-reviews/deeper-look-hayao-miyazakis-nature/#.VFictzSUd40. [Accessed: October, 2].
10. Mazumdar, Jaideep, Peak Without A Priest, *The Times of India Delhi.* [online] November 6, 2011. p. 21. Available from: http://epaper timesofindia.com/Repository/ml.asp?Ref=Q0FQLzIw MTEvMTEvMDYjQ XIwMjEwMQ==. [Accessed: October 22, 2014].
11. Murphy, Amy, The Future Tradition of Nature. *Traditional Dwellings and Settlements Review.* [Online] Jstor. Vol. 20(1), p. 37. Published by International Association for the Study of Traditional Environments (IASTE), 2008. Available from: http://www.jstor.org/stable/41758583. [Accessed: October 13, 2014].
12. GhibliWorld.com. *Miyazaki and The Environment-Part-I* (10th of October). [Online] Available from: *http://*www.ghibli world.com/news.html#1010 [Accessed: October 18, 2014].
13. Government of India, External Affairs Department, File No. 9(42)-G/37. National Archives, 1939.
14. Government of India, External Affairs Department, 'Teesta Dam Scheme', File No. 254-CA/46. National Archives, 1964.

15. Government of Sikkim, Cultural Affairs and Heritage Department, 2009-2010. [Online] Available from: http://www.sikkimculture.gov.in/Cultural%20Festivals/Pang%20Lhabsol.aspx. [Accessed: October 29, 2014].
16. Guillen, Michael, An On-Stage Conversation with Hayao Miyazaki, 2009. [Online] 31st July. Available from: http://www.ghibliworld.com/news.html#3107_02 [Accessed: October 10, 2014].
17. Hendrix, Grady, From Nuclear Nightmare to Networked Nirvana: Futuristic Utopianism in Japanese SF Films of the 2000s. *World Literature Today*, Vol. 84, No. 3 (May/June 2010), pp. 55-57. Board of Regents of the University of Oklahoma. [Online] Available from: http://www.jstor.org/stable/27871088. [Accessed: October 13, 2014].
18. Inaga, Shigemi, Miyazaki Hayao's Epic Comic Series: Nausicaä in the Valley of the Wind: An Attempt at Interpretation, *Japan Review*, No. 11 (1999), pp. 113-127, International Research Centre for Japanese Studies, National Institute for the Humanities. [Online] Available from: http://www.jstor.org/stable/25791038. [Accessed: October 13, 2014].
19. Jigme, N. Kazi (Blog). http://jigmenkazisikkim.blogspot.in/2013_04_01_archive.html. [Accessed: October 29, 2014].
20. Knight, John, A Tale of Two Forests: Reforestation Discourse in Japan and Beyond, *The Journal of the Royal Anthropological Institute*, Vol. 3, No. 4 (December, 1997), pp. 711-730. Published by Royal Anthropological Institute of Great Britain and Ireland. [Online] Available from: http://www.jstor.org/stable/3034035. [Accessed: October 5, 2014].
21. Kobori, Hiromi and Richard B. Primack, Participatory Conservation Approaches for Satoyama, the Traditional Forest and Agricultural Landscape of Japan. *Ambio*, Vol. 32, No. 4 (June, 2003), pp. 307-311. Published by Springer. [Online] Available from: http://www.jstor.org/stable/4315386. [Accessed: November 28, 2014].
22. Morrison, Tim, Hayao Miyazaki: An Era of High-tech Wizardry and Anime–Auteur Makes Magic the Old Way, 2011. *Time Asia*. [0nline] 23rd June. Available from: http://web.archive.org/web/20110623060452/http://www.time.com/time/asia/2006/heroes/at_miyazaki.html [Accessed on: October 11, 2014].
23. Plumgood, Val, *Environmental Culture: The Ecological Crises of Reason*, London & New York, Routledge, 2002.
24. *Princess Mononoke*. Animated Film. Directed by Hayao Miyazaki.

[avi] Tokyo, Studio, Ghibli, 1997.
25. Ray, Arundhati, Mortal Call Them Rivers, 2011, *The Hindu*. [Online] 8th July. Available from: http://www.thehindu.com/2001/07/08/stories/1308106f.htm [Accessed: October 8, 2014]
26. Rose, Steve, My Neighbour Totoro- review, *The Guardian*. [Online] 23rd May. Available from: http://www.theguardian.com/film/2013/may/23/my-neighbour-totoro-review. [Accessed: October 11, 2014].
27. Salleh, Ariel, *Ecofeminism As Politics: Nature, Marx and the Postmodernism,* London & New York, Zed Books Ltd, 1997.
28. Santos, Carlo, Review—My Neighbour Totoro, Novel. [Online] 20th October. Available from: http://www.animenewsnetwork.com/review/my-neighbor-totoro/novel [Accessed: October 10, 2014].
29. 'Satyagraha', *Affected Citizens of Teesta (ACT)*. [Online] Available from: http://www.actsikkim.com/satyagraha.html . [Accessed December 10, 2013]
30. Schilling, Mark, An Audience with Miyazaki, Japan's Animation King, *The Japan Times*. [Online] December 4, 2008. Available from: http://www.japantimes.co.jp/culture/2008/12/04/films/an-audience-with-miyazaki-japans-animation-king/#.VFiZfzSUd41. [Accessed: October 2, 2014].
31. Sustainable Brands, Nature is speaking in new, star studded campaign...and she is not amused. [Online] 6th October. Available from: http://www.sustainablebrands.com/news_and_views/marketing_comms/sustainable_brands/nature_speaking_new_star-studded_campaign_she_not_ [Accessed on: October 19, 2014]
32. Tallman, Dave, Interview with Hayao Miyazaki- getting facts about his retirement. [Online] 11th February. Available from: http://web.archive.org/web/20010211030138/www.acsys.com/~tallman/miya_e.html [Accessed: October 2, 2014].
33. *The Gazetteer of Sikhim,* With an introduction by H.H. Risley (ed.) in the Bengal Government Secretariat, Calcutta, Bengal Secretariat Press, 1894.
34. *The Telegraph,* Samdup Tasho. [Online] 9th November. Available from: http://www.telegraph.co.uk/news/obituaries/religion-obituaries/8879824/Samdup-Taso.html#disqus_thread [Accessed: October 29, 2014].

10

Understanding the Relation Between Religion and Environment of the Ao-Nagas Through the Ritual Process

Resenmenla Longchar

Like any other tribal societies of India, the Nagas[1] traditionally consider themselves as part and parcel of nature are animistic[2] in their religious behaviour. The Ao-Nagas[3] deify the elements of nature and worship them to realise their wishes. They are also polytheistic[4] and venerate several benevolent and malevolent gods and spirits, in different names for different purposes. They believed that their lives are regulated by earth, heaven and spirits. They opine that the earth takes care of sustenance, the heaven takes care for life and death and the spirits take the responsibility of controlling every phenomenon in nature. Traditional Nagas believe in supernatural powers. In their worldview these powers exist behind high mountains, in flooded rivers, big trees, stones and in epidemics that threat the populace. The traditional Nagas conduct animal sacrifices by offering cows, pigs, chicken, birds, and items like food, drink, clothes, etc. to appease their pantheon. The Nagas firmly believe in the existence of a Supreme Being, a benevolent god that creates everything for the good and welfare of humankind in the universe. This chapter will examine the different gods (*tsungrems*) associated with the environments of the Ao-Nagas and also see one of the ritual processes of a major ceremony (*among*) called *Lijabamong*, observed by the people in order to balance the nature from disequilibrium. It will further explain how the Ao-Nagas in particular till date retain their traditional beliefs and practices, symbolically to endure their cultural continuities and thus establish past-present-future continuum of their societal values and norms.

Religion is inseparably articulated with the socio-cultural life of the Ao-Nagas. According to Panger Imchen[5], *An Ao cannot conceive of a world apart from religion. The whole universe is sacred and filled with gods…Religion possesses ideas and values that are the guiding principles of one's behaviour*. The religious beliefs and practices of the Ao-Nagas are well-established and organised. The Ao respect and fear their gods (*tsungrem*) and seek blessings, protection, security and well-being. They also believed that the causes of troubles and suffering which befall in a person's life or family and the inhabitation are attributed to the action of the evil spirits. So they performed a system of ceremonies by offering sacrifices to keep these deities and spirits in good humour. J.P. Mill[6] describes the Ao-Naga's religion as "not a moral code…[but]… a system of ceremonies… [to appease]… the deities around him who… are always ready to blight his crops and bring illness upon him and his family".

The domain of religion is highly pervasive as it represents not only the cultural beliefs and practices including moral codes, rituals and spiritual ideologies but also mythology that speaks about the creation, nature and purpose of the universe and the role of a god, gods or other superhuman agencies therein. Further, the origination of the user communities of the particular religious ideologies is linked with their respective pantheon. In other words, the devotees are being linked with gods through ritual observances and practices prescribed in the belief system. Thus the religion establishes an identity with its followers and vice versa. As mentioned above, the polytheistic dimension of the Ao-Naga religion gets expression in the functioning of gods and spirits in hierarchical order. The following three tables respectively represent

a) Major pantheon
b) T*sungrems,* the gods associated with nature and environments of the Aos (minor pantheon)

c) Spirits and souls in the Ao-Naga belief system

(These tables are prepared based on the information gathered from folk narratives, personal narratives and exegesis collected in the fieldwork).

Table 1.1: The Major Ao-Naga Pantheon

S. No.	*Name of the God*	*Descriptions*	*Mode of Worship*	*Portfolio*	*Context*
1.	*Lijaba*, creator of the earth.	He stays beneath the earth. He holds the earth between his two hands. He is aware of all happenings and events on earth.	A major ceremony is observed yearly to offer sacrifices and prayers (see *Lijabamong* ritual in the following pages).	He causes natural calamities if the people do not perform the rituals that are prescribed to them. He blesses[7] on one hand and curses/punishes based on the good and bad deeds of the people. The ritual blesses the field after the seeds are sown.	A special day is observed for him in prayer for protection from natural calamities. People observe a 'thanks giving' ceremony (Tsungrem *mong*) before the onset of harvest time.
2.	*Longtitsungba* Lord of Heaven.[8]	He is also called, *Aningtsungba*, *Aning* – heaven, *tsungba*- Chief or Lord.	Sacrificial ceremonies are performed almost every day by one or the other in their respective agricultural fields to obtain plenty of rains. (Domesticated animals like cocks, pigs, eggs, etc, are offered).	The god holds power over the heavenly bodies like the sun, moon and other celestial forces like the rains, storms, lightning, thunder, winds.	People observe *genna* during the times of drought to have a good harvest.
3.	*Tiar/Tiaba*, pre-destiner.	He predicts man's earthly	There is no fixed ritual	He is both giver and	People offer cocks, eggs,

		fortune. He casts spirits of various kinds; some people are not given any spirit so they remain dumb and dull.	but right from birth people offer prayers and sacrifices.	taker of life and futures of the people.	pigs, etc, to ward off sickness or ill fortunes and gain prosperity.
4.	*Meyutsungba,* Lord of Death	He is the god of truth and justice. He judges the deeds of the people when they are alive on earth and punishes them accordingly after they die. *Ongangla,* his wife, assists him to judge people. He remains a silent spectator.	No ceremonies and offerings are given to him because he is the god of righteousness. He has no mercy and a god who is descent. It requires no bargaining.	At the gate of *Meyutsungba* every sin are revealed and disclosed for shame and punishment. He judge right and wrong so he does not know forgiveness.	He gives judgement when meets people on face to face at his place.[9]

Table 1.2: *Tsungrems,* the Gods Associated with Nature and Environments of the Aos

S. No.	*Name of the Deities, Spirits/Souls*	*Descriptions*	*Mode of Worship*	*Portfolio*
1.	*Tekong Tsungrem,* mountain deity; *Tzuba Tsungrem,* well/ spring deity; *Along Tsungrem,* stone deity	It is believed that these deities positively influence their devotees if they properly venerate them.	People offer meat or food items. Devotees are supposed to make mistakes which otherwise is considered as a bad omen.	These *Tsungrems* spirits create havoc on the people through their powers if they are not invoked for their blessings and benevolence.
2.	*Yongpang Tsungrem,* spring deity; *Tzutsung Tsungrem,* deity of lake; Tzuta Tsungrem,	They are believed to reside in bamboo	The illness and suffering happens if the people are captured by the	These are the lesser in the hierarchy of spirits and

	Stagnant and lowland deity; *Mosakni Tsungrem*, deity of indigo; *Thini Tsungrem*, deity of the un-common jungle and certain trees.	groves. *Tsungrems* afflict the physical body with ailments and wounds.	devil deities. During the times of illness, the offerings and sacrifices are being conducted.	deities. They are meant to cause illness and mischiev-ous activities to man.
3.	*Atsu Tsungrem*, water deity	*Ahlachetla* is the water deity and believed to be the most dreadful deity. This deity lives in the rivers, lakes, and stagnant places.	The villagers observe a one day ceremony to offer sacrifices to the deity and clean the common village pond.	A patient attacked by this deity does not survive.
4.	*Kini Tsungrem*, house site deity	There is no specific description of this deity.	This god is propitiated before putting the first spade on the earth while digging the foundation for building a new house to seek i) protection from evil spirits and elements and ii) getting blessings and benevolence from gods.	The clan *patir*, priest performs the ritual by sacrificing a cock and the whole family have a feast.

Aos also believed that the spirits, ghosts and angels could influence their lives ambivalently showering positive and negative affects on them. A human being is believed to have a personal spirit (*Tiyar*) and a soul (*Tanela/Temhila*). It is further deemed that a man has three spirits and three souls; whereas a woman has two spirits and three souls. The soul is the spiritual or immaterial part of a human being or animal, regarded as immortal.[10] Whereas the spirit is the non-physical part of a person that is the seat of emotions and character (the soul). The animists believe that all living and non-living beings possess souls. In other words, spirits are souls that have passed out of their human body, but for some reason have not left this "illusion" and completed their journey back to the supernatural reality.[11] The space given in the Ao-Naga worldview to the spirits and the souls of human life still gets expressed in their death ritual practices like offering food to the dead in the cemetery or near the death bed (after the death). The following table shows the role played by the spirits and souls in a human being.

Table 1.3: Spirits and Souls in the Ao-Nagas Belief System

S.No.	*Role of the Spirits*	*Role of the Souls*
1.	a. *For a man,* the three *tiyar* respectively brings him (i) happiness and good health; (ii) children and prosperity; and (iii) protection. The first two remain at home and the third, the protector follows wherever he goes. b. *For a woman,* one *tiyar* blesses her with a husband and children, while the other protects her from illness and unseen dangers.	It is believed that every person has three souls, *Tanela/Temhila.* One soul is in a person's eyes. When the person dies, this soul gets released from the body and passes to the land of the dead, i.e. the abode of *Meyutsungba.* The second soul lives in the form of a tiger, wild cat, locust or rat which on the death either dies or escapes death or lives elsewhere. The third soul is a hawk. On the death it flies to the land between the dead and the remaining family members.

Traditional Ao-Nagas venerate *Lijaba* (*Li* means land, *jaba* means real), the supreme god (creator of earth). They regard him as the creator and sustainer of the earth/world and with everything 'embedded in'.[12] The community affirms that the earth is the source of life and hence is sacred. They consider the earth as the provider of space, food and other basic resources that meet the needs of people. Symbolically, like any tribal communities, the Ao-Nagas understand the earth to be the spouse of the Supreme Being. The Nagas view the earth and the Supreme Being as inseparable entities. So their belief system and ritual patterns are constructed to appease them in different cultural contexts.

The following myth associates Lijaba with the creation of

the world in the view of Ao-Nagas:

> *Lijaba* is the creator of the earth and the supreme god. He created the earth very beautiful, smooth and plain. When he was still in the process of creating the earth, out of nowhere a water cockroach (*tsü leplo*) scared him by giving false alarm, "Enemies are coming, enemies are coming to destroy the earth with *daos* and spears." Then the water cockroach disappeared. *Lijaba* thought that the enemies are really coming. Out of hurry he roughly created the rest of the Ao land. For this reason, the Aos believe that the land of the Ao is full of mountains and hills and does not have many beautiful plains, valleys and rivers like the Assam region. The land of Assam looks plain and the place where Nagas live looks hilly in nature.[13]

This short myth is still remembered and retold by many people from the community. From the narration, the Aos conclude that from the very beginning of creation there was an evil force whose main intention was to distract and bring confusion. R.C.Tocy Ao[14] interprets the myth: "The water cockroach is not a cockroach but an enemy of *Lijaba*. The forefathers named his enemy as cockroach. *Lijaba* was frightened by the cockroach because of the notion that he might rule the earth. The enemy was there from the beginning before the earth was created. The enemy might be the Assam people because a different story mentions the war between Nagas and the Assam people".

Society and religion are two essential aspects of any community that form an intricate network to connect the people with one another and also with the society and polity on the other. Rituals are the media through which such a network operates successfully. Social rituals shape the cultures that can create a sense of group identity and further develop social bonds. The rituals give an opportunity to the people and communities to express, reinforce and to spread the shared values and beliefs in their respective societies. Throughout the whole year the Ao-Nagas remain busy in celebrating one or the other ritual to regulate their social roles and behaviour. It is because the Ao-Nagas belief system manifested in their ritual ideology and practices which were rooted in their environment and worldview form the undercurrents of their lifestyle patterns.

Ritual Process of *Lijabamong*

The traditional Aos celebrate the *Lijabamong*, in commemoration of the creator, Lijaba and the myth is still being remembered as a metaphor till date. Aos consider *Lijaba* as the giver of good crops, regulator of the rain and sunlight and responsible for occurrence of natural calamities. The following myth perpetuates Lijaba as the provider of sustenance in the worldview of Aos.

> One day Lijaba, the creator of earth decided to travel to different parts of the earth. After travelling for many days, one evening he reached a village. Lijaba went door to door asking for shelter for the night but all the families in the village refused to welcome him. Everyone had different excuses. Eventually he saw a small house at the end of the village so he decided to go there. He found out that two sisters were staying in the house. When he asked for shelter they welcomed him happily though they were very poor. The girls told him, "We have nothing at home so we are not cooking anything." But Lijaba told them, "Place the pot in the hearth and warm the water." The girls obediently did what they were asked to do. Then he started to scratch his knee. From his knee, a grain of rice came out so he put it in the pot. To their surprise the rice filled the pot. Again he told them to boil water. This time when he scratched his forehead, a piece of meat came out so they cooked the meat. The meat filled the pot. They had a hearty meal that evening. After dinner, three of them went and stood outside the house. Lijaba asked them, "Whose field is that?" "They belonged to the family who insulted us" was their reply. Then he started to curse that field, "Let their field never prosper, let their field harvest only tusk." All the fields were cursed by Lijaba because all the villagers insulted the two sisters. Finally he asked them, "Where is your field?" But the sisters were so ashamed to tell him because was just a tiny patch of a rice-field. Finally he asked the two sisters, "Whose field is that, that small field in the corner?" They were feeling shy but replied to Lijaba, "It belongs to us." Then Lijaba blessed their field by saying, "Let that field be harvested non-stop."

In order to balance nature from disequilibrium people observe it as a major ceremony (among) *Lijabamong*. The ritual rests on the belief that Lijaba sends his spirit *(tanula)* in May and June in

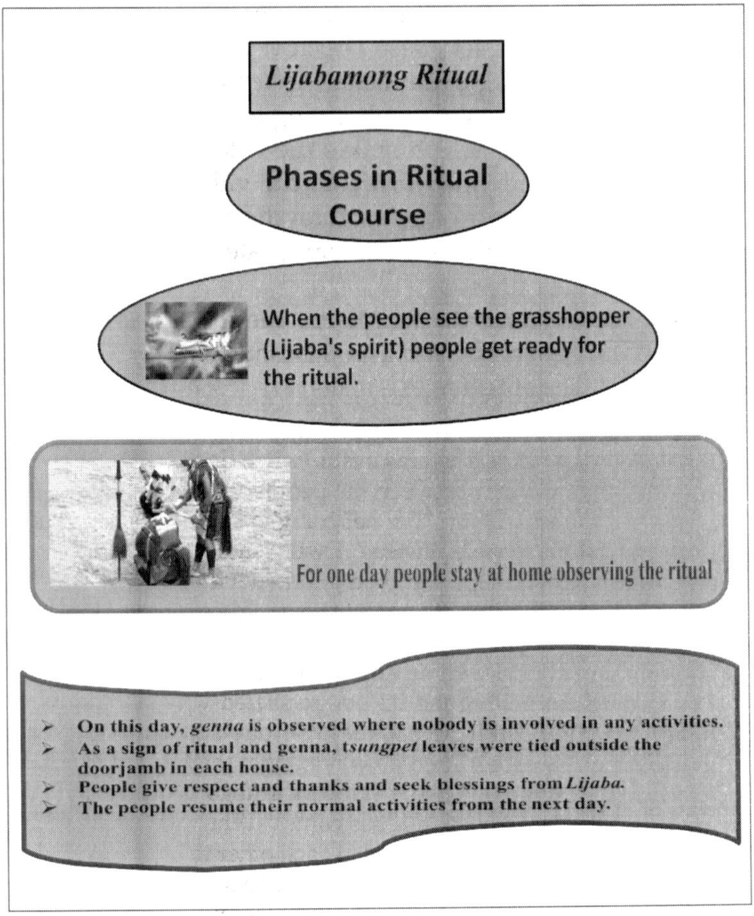

Lijabamong Ritual

Phases in Ritual Course

When the people see the grasshopper (Lijaba's spirit) people get ready for the ritual.

For one day people stay at home observing the ritual

- **On this day, *genna* is observed where nobody is involved in any activities.**
- **As a sign of ritual and genna, *tsungpet* leaves were tied outside the doorjamb in each house.**
- **People give respect and thanks and seek blessings from *Lijaba*.**
- **The people resume their normal activities from the next day.**

Diagram 1.1. Ritual of *Lijabamong*

the guise of *sungkoks* (grasshoppers) to receive thanksgiving from the people in return for his blessings poured on them. On this occasion nobody is allowed to engage in any other activity than this. It is a day of *genna*/prohibition called *anempong* (refers to sanctification and strict restriction).[15] It is an auspicious occasion. Hence the leaves of *Tsungpet*[16] are tied outside onto the doorjamb of each house. It is a 'one day' thanksgiving ritual to Lijaba who showers prosperity on those who worshipped him. The spirit of Lijaba lives on the earth only for a week and later vanishes. Whoever sees the grasshopper in the field informs the village chief or the chief priest. The chief priest then performs the ceremony by killing one rooster (*An tepong*) in the village gate (*sungkum*) as a token of thanksgiving to Lijaba for sending his spirit to the village which makes the village and villagers affluent. From the next day onwards the village resumes its normalcy. The feeling of bliss that the villagers get by performing the ritual makes them rejuvenate their vigour and rigour attends their life core.

The following narrative explains the myth behind the celebration of Lijabamong and also the mode of worship to be performed in this context.

> In olden days, the people worshipped Lijaba as the creator of earth. But nobody saw him. The arasentsür (witch doctor or magician) was the only mediator between the people and Lijaba. One day, Lijaba told the arasentsür, "I'm not going to live any more on this earth amidst the people. Instead, I will send my spirit to bless and punish depending upon their good/evil deeds. Whenever I come people will know. So everyone should celebrate a feast to commemorate my name. One should offer me a perfect, healthy and complete animal without any handicap or scar upon its body. The meat of the animal should not be shared with anyone. The bones too should not be broken". So one summer season a grasshopper appeared. Then people thought that it is the spirit of Lijaba so they uttered, 'Lijabar sungkok aruogo! Lijabar sungkok aruogo! (Lijaba's grasshopper has come)'. When the people saw the grasshopper they announced to each other that Lijaba's spirit had come onto the earth. The entire villagers worshipped and asked for blessings from him. The grasshopper remained with the villagers only for two to three weeks and then disappeared. Ao folk believe that the grasshopper is the spirit of Lijaba and hence venerated it in remembrance of the god Lijaba.[17]

In the Ao-belief system the grasshopper symbolises the spirit of prosperity. The onset of grasshoppers onto the earth depicts full bloom of the grains, trees, vegetables, etc., in the fields. Since it occurs in May and June, it is clear that right after the seed sowing the grasshopper appears. An emergence of the grasshopper shows that the harvest is not far away. The symbolism of the *Tsungpet* leaves shows that the household is in *genna*. No one can visit anyone's house.

In conclusion it has been found out that there are many other gods (*tsungrems*) who have been associated with the environment of the Ao-Nagas and there are various minor or lesser deities and spirits/souls. The deities on the earth are regarded as lesser to *Lijaba* and their respective domains on earth are prescribed by him. The animistic worldview contains both the observed or physical world and the unseen or spirit world. Animists perceive that life is controlled by spiritual powers and live in fear of spiritual powers whose activities must be divined and frequently manipulated. They seek to live in harmony with their world believing that the forces and powers of the world are interconnected. They deify the elements of nature and worship them to realise their wishes. The Aos adore their gods (*tsungrem*) and seek blessings, protection, security and well-being from them through worship. The Aos are also scared of gods because they believe that the spirits may create troubles and sufferings for their families due to the disgrace. So Aos observe rituals and offer sacrifices to appease deities and spirits from causing evil to them. They are god-fearing and believe that *Meyutsungba* would judge the people after death to allocate hell or heaven depending on their deeds. Such spiritual threats existing in the religious thought of the Aos made them embrace a new religion Christianity which also distributed a similar religious message that would bind the god and people together. Inability to bear the cost of expiations in ritual centred Ao-animistic religion, they could easily adapt to Christianity. Even after their conversion to Christianity, the core of their animistic religion still pervades their spiritual ideology. After their conversion to Christianity, the Aos substituted the animal-ritual sacrifice with a special prayer for having bountiful rains.[18] The Ao-Nagas are still connected, rely and identify with the the environment and nature. There are many agricultural festivals celebrated even in the present day that are associated with environment and religion. For instance, *Moatsü* (seed sowing festival which is one of the biggest ceremonies for the Ao-Nagas) is celebrated in the spring season when the villagers have finished with seed sowing. They pray for blessings upon new grains in the field and also for protection of crops throughout the season. This shows that the text and texture of the rituals changed but the spirit of the context remained the same.

REFERENCES

1. Nagas are one among many of the ethnic groups of north-eastern India that geographically share the borders of four countries—China, Myanmar, Bangladesh and Bhutan of Asia. Nagaland, wherein these tribal groups inhabit is geographically situated in the hilly tracts of north-eastern India which emerged as a state on December 1, 1963. Dr. Sarvepalli Radhakrishnan, the then President of India, formally inaugurated it as the 16th state of the Indian Union. The state has now eleven districts, viz. Dimapur, Kohima, Mokokchung, Mon, Phek, Tuensang, Wokha, Zunheboto, Peren, Longleng and Kepheri. The Nagas have their own rich cultural heritage preserved in the form of oral traditions and artefacts. The Nagas claim that they had recorded their history on an animal skin which unfortunately was eaten by a dog. Since then, they say that their history and traditions are being preserved in their memories and disseminated orally in the form of songs, myths, tales and other forms of expressive behaviour, their material culture. The Nagas are distinct from the rest of the Indian tribes not only in their origin, languages and appearance but also in their lifestyle patterns. The Nagas are heterogeneous tribes and belong to Mongoloid and Indo-Burmese stocks. There are as many as seventeen social groups among the Nagas which were further subdivided into several major clans. These cultural groups from the level of a clan to that of a major tribe sustains their distinctiveness in different walks of their tribal lives—traditions, customs, food, religions, social organisation, rituals, political and economic organisation, functioning of customary law and order—and thus protect their respective identities even amidst the changing world's scenario.
2. The genesis of the practice of religion when traced to its roots in primitive tribes and societies is often found to rest in some form or manner of 'animism' (Hokishe Sema, *Emergence of Nagaland: Socio-Economic and Political Transformation and the Future*, New Delhi, Vikas Publishing House, 1986, p. 34). Animism can be defined as the belief either that all natural things and phenomena are alive, or that they possess an innate soul or spirit. http://

www.michaelpnelson.com/Publications_files/Nelson_Animism_EncyWorldEnvHist_2004.pdf, (accessed August 16, 2015).

3. The Ao-Naga is one of the major tribes in Nagaland who had four distinctive dialectic groups viz: *Mongsen, Chungli, Changki* and *Sangpur*. However the major dialects of the Ao-Naga are *Mongsen* and *Chungli*. Though *Mongsen* was the main and poetic mode of expression in the past the dialect *Chungli* had been in use for communication and conversation. It so happened because when American missionaries came into contact with the Aos, they first stayed in Molungyimsen village where the Aos of that region spoke in *Chungli* dialect. Then these people picked up the Chungli dialect for communication. Thus the advent of missionaries around AD 1872 shifted the spoken dialect from *Mongsen* to *Chungli*. Thus the Chungli dialect continues to be used for the mode of communication. The Ao-Naga tribe itself is not homogeneous and is constituted by six major clans which were categorically organised based on the spoken dialect. The *Chungli* group incorporated the *Pongen, Longkumer* and *Jamir* clans and the *Mongsen* group included *Imchen, Walling* and *Longchar* clans.
4. Worshipping or believing in more than one god.
5. Panger Imchen, *Ancient Ao Naga Religion and Culture*, New Delhi, Har Anand Publications, 1993, p. 3.
6. J.P. Mills, *The Ao Nagas*, Kohima, Directorate of Art and Culture, 1926, p. 214.
7. Otsufuba Longkumer, interviewed by Resenmenla Longchar, December 18, 2007, Longkhum village, 73 years old.
8. Longtitsüngba which is also called Aningtsüngba (Aning- heaven; Tsüngba- Chief or Lord)/Lata-zuni Tsungrem (moon-sun god) is custodian of the heavenly elements. He sees that all natural forces get connected with the solar system (Panger Imchen,1993, op. cit., p. 34). The people in general and the individual in particular over the years observe ceremonies and offer sacrifices for plentiful of rain (The Konde of east-central Africa adored Mbamba, a divinity who dwelt with his family in the heights above the sky. The Konde offer prayer and sacrifice to the god who dwells in the sky, especially at times when rain is called for (Mirca Eliade, *The Encyclopedia of Religion*, Vol. 10, New York, Macmillan Publishing Company, 1987) and a special ceremony is performed by the priests for rain during the time of drought. Chickens, pigs and eggs were given at the field altar. The people firmly believe that the god would definitely answer the prayer

requests of his subjects. They further advocate that the god can even reorganise the nature of the celestial bodies for the benefit of the devotees. The following narrative substantiates it. "Once upon a time, the moon was closer to the earth than the sun. So, the moon was warmer than the sun thus causing much heat to the human beings. The people on the earth could no longer tolerate the hot rays of the moon. They complained about the matter to Aningtsüngba, the god of heaven who could regulate the roles of sun, and moon. After listening to them he threw cow dung on the face of the moon to diminish its heat and brightness during the nights. Then the moon felt ashamed with the act and slowly moved away from the earth and the sun. Till today, this story is being narrated by the older people". (Otsufuba Longkumer, December 18, 2007, op. cit.).

9. The tradition holds that there is a place called *Asü Yim/Diphu Yim*, village of the dead (commonly accepted direction by the Aos to which the dead go which is underneath *Wokha* (District Hill, south-east of Longkhum village, an Ao village). A person's soul goes to the eternal home of the souls called *Depuli/Kodakli*. On their way to the land of the dead, the person has to cross a stream called *Longritzü* (lonely river) only then he/she enters the land of *Meyutsüng* (Lord of Judgment). Before reaching the *Longritzü* river (which is believed to be a big river with transparent water), the soul of the person does not know whether he/she is dead or alive. When the dead washes the face, legs and hands it looks pale and sees holes on their palms. They thus realise that they are dead and have to cross the stream never to return. Then they cry bitterly thinking of their loved ones.
10. Soul.http://dictionary.reference.com/browse/soul, (accessed September 17, 2015).
11. www.spiritualhealingenergys.com/terminology.
12. The Rengma-Nagas believed that *Songinyu/Aniza* who lives in the sky and is the father of all living things, as earth is their mother but for the Aos there are no such things as mother. The eastern and the western Rengmas have different opinions on how the earth was shaped. One says it was *aniza,* while the other says it was *Ndü* or *Asükhi*. (J.P. Mills, 1926, op. cit., p. 165)
13. Otsufuba Longkumer, December 18, 2007, op. cit. This narration is also mentioned by J.P. Mills. In his version instead of a water cockroach it is a water-beetle. (J.P. Mills, 1926, op. cit., p. 220)
14. Interviewed by Resenmenla Longchar, June 26, 2009, Yaongyimsen village, 53 years old.

15. According to A.W. Davis, 1891, the word genna is used in two ways: it may mean practically a holiday, i.e. a man will say my village is doing genna today, by which he means that, owing either to the occurrence of a village festival or some such unusual occurrence as an earthquake, eclipse, or burning of a village within sight of his own, his village people are observing a holiday; genna means anything forbidden. (Verrier Elwin, *The Nagas in the 19th Century*, London, Oxford University Press, 1970, p. 514)
16. A kind of shrub, with a strong odour.
17. Otsufuba Longkumer, December 18, 2007, op. cit.
18. Ibid.

11

Forests, Ecology and Traditional Knowledge: A Kuki Woman's Perspective in the Northeast

Ngamjahao Kipgen

Introduction

The northeast region of India consists of diverse ethnic and cultural groups, each with its own traditional cultural systems and survival strategies based on resources available in its immediate ecosystem. The management of their natural resources including land-use, land protection, forest management, and agricultural practices employs a wide array of traditional knowledge systems based on their perception of man-environment (nature-culture) relationship. Most of the land based production in the region is based on traditional knowledge systems. Traditional knowledge plays an important role in developing self-sufficiency and the wise and sustainable management of natural resources. In other words, both technical and social aspects of forest management are treated as part of a single system[1]. This reflects the high value attached by local inhabitants to their forests. The understanding of traditional knowledge and practices in relation to biodiversity resource management is one of the key issues for achieving sustainable development.

In recent development theory and practice, there has been a growing interest in understanding people's knowledge systems[2], where local knowledge is increasingly seen to play a critical role in the context of sustainable resource use and development. The sustainable use of resources requires that management practices and institutions take into account the dynamics of the ecosystem. However, the perspectives and interest of women are often ignored and always remain as a mere footnote. Men who derived their political power (masculinity) from their prowess at war, their wealth and ritual status in the tribal community have traditionally managed village affairs. The politics of resource control and ethnicity have been closely interwoven.This chapter examines the ecological knowledge of women and their position in the Kuki household by focusing on the cultural practices within the traditional milieu. The basic idea of this chapter is to analyse the traditional knowledge and its manifestation in the livelihood patterns—and thereby locates women's position—and seeks to identify the factors impinging on women's ability to claim, control and manage land and resources. The chapter indicates that Kuki women have substantial knowledge of resource and ecosystem dynamics from the individual land-used (jhumming) to that of the forest commons, as reflected in a variety of interrelated management practices embedded in and influenced by institutions at several levels. Therefore, an attempt has been made to unravel some strands in the tangled knot of gender, tribe and community control of resources because of the intense pressures that are fast eroding the landscape. Using a socio-historical approach the chapter discusses women's role in managing resources and provides a comprehensive overview of traditional knowledge and attitudes towards the forest and its resources by taking the case of the Kuki tribals in northeast India. The sources in this study are largely drawn from a multi-sited fieldwork based on interviews, focus group discussions and oral literature collected during 2008-2010. The study is restricted to the hill areas of Manipur inhabited by the Kuki tribes.

Conceptual and Theoretical Framework

Unlike the colonialists, environmental historians of India today no longer see tribals as inferior and unscientific in their natural resource management.[3] Tribals or forest dwellers are accorded its due importance in the new environmental history showing them as doers, masters and shapers of environments rather than as their passive captives in need of external redemption. Earlier works on indigenous knowledge, Fairhead and Leach[4] have linked traditional management practices to nuanced understanding of landscapes and narratives of environmental transformation. However, rigorous historical, ecological and anthropological research combined with detailed field investigation allowed to deconstruct the colonial narratives and convey a different environmental history that also lent support to advocates of localised (traditional) environmental management.

New ecological anthropology[5] undermines the before and after distinction common to environmental history by demonstrating the ways in which human societies and the natural world have reciprocally constructed each other. Therefore, one needs to look at tribal environmental history as a conjuncture of adaptation, cultural and environmental flux. Works by scholars such as Karlsson[6] and Ramakrishnan[7] introduces the relative sustainability model of tribal environmental and natural resources have continued to play a prime role in providing not only a base for development but also in providing food and other requirements. The inroads of modernisation do not deter people's dependence and reliance on these resources. In fact, the diverse extraction activities from nature produced balanced and organic diets and incomes for tribals. Considerable work has been done on the role of state local institutions and communities in the management of natural resources in northeast India.[8] In the northeast, the dominant conservation theme has been that of protecting the ecosystem and wildlife species, though this is now giving way to a broader debate linking conservation to the process of rural development and the survival of agrarian societies in the region. Tribal communities evolved conservation measures prompted by their environmental experience, economic needs and religious beliefs.

Many observers have attempted to dichotomise indigenous

Knowledge (IK) or traditional ecological knowledge (TEK) or at times traditional knowledge (TK) and Western science in terms of their respective ideological underpinnings, substantive content, methods, epistemology, and context.[9] TEK has been defined as "a cumulative body of knowledge and beliefs, evolving through adaptive processes and handed down through generations by cultural transmission, about the relationship of living beings (including humans) with one another and with their environment."[10] Traditional knowledge, most often tightly interwoven with traditional religious beliefs, customs, folklore, land-use practices and community-level decision-making processes, has sustained the cultures, livelihoods, and agricultural resource management systems of local and indigenous communities throughout the world for centuries. According to Seeland and Schmithusen,[11] indigenous knowledge emerges as people's perception and experience in an environment at a given time in a continuous process of observation and interpretation in relation to the locally acknowledged everyday rationalities and transcendental powers. In a traditional society the local context is taken as the universal frame in which knowledge matters. The concept of TEK thus includes—empirical observations by individuals of specific events or phenomena and generalised observations based on personal and shared experience,[12] stories, and oral history. In short, TEK is what people learn from experience, from family and community, and from stories handed down about how to live fully and effectively in their environment.

Forests Use and Kuki Economic Systems

Forests have always been significant sources of livelihood for the tribal populations. As Rappaport[13] argued, "The tribals' use of the materials of the forests rests, on the one hand, on a detailed knowledge of the variety of flora and fauna and on the other hand, on the knowledge of procedures of rituals and technological activity which regulate an ecologically balanced relation with the natural environment." Apart from using the forest resources for sustenance, the tribes also preserved it for posterity[14] and use of forest products by tribes was never at the cost of forest regeneration.[15] The major land and forest use system in Kuki villages is jhum cultivation[16] and gathering of non-timber forest products (NTFPs).'Jhum cultivation was seen in much distaste, as a 'rude system' and certainly a very wasteful method of cultivation,' noted Shakespear[17]. Contrary to this, Francis Buchanan noted that swiddening is not that 'wasteful' and inefficient method compared with the lowland cultivation. He further explains that an ordinary family in the hills can easily raise 100 baskets of rice besides cotton, yams, arum, tobacco and others in proportions. Buchanan even observed that the northeast hills were able to 'maintain many thousand inhabitants in ease and abundance.'[18] Similarly, the jhum system, according to Payn,[19] "(t)he primitive mode of agriculture all over the world and widely practised, even yet, where virgin forest land is abundant, for in such circumstances it is the most economical method, because it produces the largest net return."

A noted ecologist, Ramakrishnan[20] who works extensively in the northeast region pointed out that shifting cultivation constituted the earliest form of agriculture and provided the basic needs of man and placed him in harmony with 'nature'. The practice of shifting cultivation or jhumming for the Kukis is not merely a subsistence agricultural activity, but is closely linked with social life, customs, the polity and religious practice. Studies of jhumming showed that the jhumias (shifting cultivators) are strongly influenced by their customary and cultural traditions.[21] The Kuki experience proves that for the past generations they have not only depended but also sustainably managed the biodiversity that contributes towards their subsistence livelihood needs.

Besides the normal agricultural activities, NTFPs available in the village commons (VCs) also play a very important role and provide basic sources of earning cash for the forest dwellers and revenue for the Forest Department.[22] Being cognisant of the importance of forests to their lives, the Kukis developed norms and conventions, guarded by myths and folklore, which forbade destruction of scarce and vital trees, promoted a culture of sustainable utilisation of trees and animals. For instance, among the Kukis, it is a traditional practice to reserve forests in the immediate surroundings of the village and such forests are never cleared for cultivation purposes but are used as a conveniently accessible source for the collection of materials for domestic requirements. A well-defined season and days for extraction of forest products like bamboo, timber, fruits and leaves are maintained. Such traditional knowledge regulates the extraction of forest produce among the Kukis in the region. Forest resources fulfil a variety of basic needs of the community. An older woman (aged 50) stated, "There are many varieties of non-timber or minor forest products that are used for home consumption and also sold in the local markets.[23] The Kuki people have a rich tradition of medicinal uses and plants, the knowledge being passed from generation to generation through the oral tradition."

Women's Participation in the Economic, Political and Social Life

The most basic division of labour appears to be found on gender. These differences emerge through the combined impact of ascribed gender roles and livelihood patterns. It has been argued that 'for every individual and every family there is a "map" of the appropriate domains of women and men.'[24] These domains are largely determined by culturally ascribed roles and responsibilities, which give women greater responsibility for work within the home, care and nurture, and greater responsibility to men to provide food and shelter through work outside home.For a better understanding of gendered environments it is valid to question the differences in environmental experience by gender and other patterned forms of social dominance. Also, one should study the differences in environmental experience among men and women in agricultural societies as women engage in largely unpaid farm work near homes and villages, which likely leads to difference in experiential knowledge about the environment.[25] As rightly observed by Guha (1989) one of the peculiar characteristics of hill agriculture is the role assigned to women—as no single economic activity can sustain the household thus requires the equal participation of women. There is a popular perception that higher labour force participation could enhance women's ability to bargain for a larger share in the household resources and increase their say in decision-making.And generally, it is assumed that tribal women have a better social status than in caste-based society.[26] Elwin (1969)[27] remarks that tribal women are exactly the same as any other women, with the same position—love, fears, same devotion to the home, to husband and children, the same faults and the same virtues.

While discussing the traditional economic systems and livelihood patterns in the Kuki society, it is pertinent to understand how Kukis perceive work in relation to their social and cultural practices. Work occupies the most important and primary human activity, and a defining force in people's livelihood. Customarily, the exchange of labour is practised in the form of a 'working-guild'—which is a collection of groups of people of the same age cohorts that work together on a rotational basis. Such a rotational working system is called lawm.[28] An elder explains, "The motive behind the formation of lawm is to accomplish the cultivation (jhum) work of each household in a village at the allotted time frame." Such a sphere of exchange of labour is important to the fulfilment of economic obligations, thereby perpetuating a social order. The reciprocal arrangement and exchange of labour makes the household's economic pursuit less burdensome. In traditional societies, such exchange of economic activities can hardly be separated from social and cultural behaviour. The exchange of labour is compensated in kind and not in monetary terms.[29]

Ecological knowledge and skills are sharply differentiated by age and gender. For instance, older women are better informed and can identify varieties of seeds suited to differing soil conditions. The younger generation lacks this skill. With the burden of food production being shifted almost entirely on to older women, and the ecological knowledge of men and educated youths being eroded, the sustainability of resource use is becoming problematic. Men's knowledge about agriculture is on the decline as their traditional role in many jhumming operations is less. However, certain gender roles are firmly established by tradition. Customarily, only men are entitled to wield guns—to hunt and the axe—to slash down the trees in the jhum field. All other tasks involved in the jhumming cycle are either done jointly or by women alone. Women participate in clearing the slashed and burned debris, and they prepare the land for planting. Seed storage is chiefly the woman's responsibility—small quantities such as of maize or beans are stored in dry gourds (locally called *um*), and larger quantities, such as paddy are stored in bamboo baskets (*bem*). Women generally do the sowing of seeds both by broadcasting or dibbling with a small stick or hoe. Wood ash is used for protection from termites. Weeding, which is most arduous and has to be done repeatedly, is almost wholly the women's task, though harvesting is done jointly. An elderly woman said, "Transplantation and weeding is back breaking work and one needs patience to do such work. However, men seldom perform such work." Kuki women of the household are the first to rise—before the crack of dawn—and start the day's work. For Kuki women, daily life is a juggling act as they try to fit in a range of tasks and responsibilities.

Apparently, female labour force participation in work outside the home does not put women in a better position in the context of Kuki society—the women neither have any share in the household nor say in decision-making. Traditionally, both in law and in practice, property inheritance, and especially the inheritance of arable land, was overwhelmingly patrilineal that is inheritance through the male line. In fact, women typically enter the labour force out of economic compulsion. Kuki women have a greater range of responsibilities, from domestic work—within and outside the homestead—to various agricultural activities. Gender disparity measures in my study reveal that men's responsibility for household activities is shrinking while women's workload is increasing, as they take over work traditionally designated as 'male'.

Noting the significance of direct access to land, it is vital to trace women's past and existing rights to land and in Kuki customary law–and identify the factors impinging on women's position and management of resources today. Women's visibility in the economic life of tribal villages and their greater freedom of movement has contributed to the myth of gender equality created by British ethnographers and reinforced by Indian administrators. Critiquing the 'ethnographer's romanticism model', Nongbri[30]articulates that the 'tribal women's greater economic independence and freedom of movement' compared to 'their counterparts in non-tribal societies cannot be disputed', but it is 'naïve to equate this with superior status'. She argues that a 'closer look would show that gender inequality is not alien to tribal societies but it is obscured by their poor economic conditions which forces men and women to cooperate and share in joint economic activities'. The Kuki women bear almost the entire responsibility for food production, but they have few rights in the deeply patriarchal society. Women's subordinate status in legally binding tribal customs is succinctly summed up in the Kuki adage: 'Wives and old bamboo fences need to be changed'; 'the words of women and the horns of the female mithun (bos frontalis) are useless'; 'the speeches made by women are like the chirping of birds at night'; 'it is thought that the wisdom of women was up to the neck, but it reached only up to the knee'.

It is true for the Kukis that political and social life is inseparable. The restricting factors of women's low participation in the formal forums—include the traditional exclusion of women from village assemblies and councils, known to be 'male spaces'. In all these male gatherings men's power and control at home, in the village, community and wider society, is defended and continually legitimated. This masculinisation of space means an access to and control over resources of various kinds, material, socio-cultural, political and ideological. Kuki society is deeply patriarchal—the father is the head of the family and only male members of the household can inherit ancestral property (read as agricultural land). A man is the legal head—right of ownership and legal guardian of children are accorded to him—a right denied to women. There is no codified law granting the women any legal rights. If there is no male in the household, the property goes to the nearest male member among the clan members. Consequently divorce becomes easier for him as a divorced woman cannot make any claims to her husband's property, nor her children.[31] No female can inherit the family landed property. This customary practice still continues in Kuki society even today.

Traditional Ecological Wisdom of the Kuki Women

The relationship of women and men to the environment has been extensively debated. Some early ecofeminist writers celebrated the identification of women with nature as an ontological reality.[32] Seeking to topple the negative association of women with nature, they erroneously accepted the biologising of the personality traits that patriarchal society assigns to women, claiming these connections to be positive with such constructs as Shiva's 'feminine principle'.[33] Carolyn Merchant[34], one of the earliest ecofeminist thinkers to investigate the historical lineage of the women–nature linkage contends that pre-16th-century societies in the West were built around integrated and closely knit social ties based on an embodied connection between nature and humans. Shiva (1988) similarly attempts to explore the historical origins of modern 'reductionist science'—the violation of indigenous knowledge systems in the name of the Western form of development has contributed to a disjuncture between women and environment.

Women being providers of vital basic needs (fuelwood, food, medicinal and other non-timber products) are regular visitors to the forests. This gives them their knowledge of the phenological cycle of the forest. Group gathering of fuelwood, food-greens, mushrooms and medicinal products assures cohesiveness in the community, exchange and inter-generational transfer of knowledge. Women know better than men the niches occupied by different species and forest communities, because women to meet daily subsistence needs collect most of the varieties.The women's experience and knowledge of food plants, food culture, and food preparation allow them to evolve a food system based on the resources of the habitat, making judicious use of the resources. Women's connections with land and forest resources are related to their subsistence use. Traditional knowledge is an integral part of the traditional village ecosystem. This includes knowledge about ecosystem functions, regenerative processes, the phenological cycle (the various observable stages of growth) of the forests, other areas and their multiple uses. Each zone of landscape is aligned ecologically with every other and functionally linked with the community or the village hamlet through the occupations that both men and women undertake to fulfil their social responsibilities towards reproduction, production and community life.

So far, I have delved into some of the debates and differing perspectives on women—the economic role (land and forest use), and their social and political participation. Divergent from the above discussion, this section reflects on the *chang-ai* ceremony, which delineates the significant position women held in Kuki traditional society.

Chang-Ai Ceremony

Women's intervention in the socio-cultural sphere is not a new concept among the Kukis, but almost on every occasion—women's participation is acknowledged and respected in the past. Here I will highlight the ceremony of chang-ai[35] wherein women play a significant role in the community space. It would not be a mistake to say that Chang-ai is the only known ceremony in which a Kuki woman plays a prominent role. It is a ceremony performed by a woman who has harvested paddy beyond her family's requirements—she expresses her gratitude to Pathien (Supreme God) for the bountiful harvest. So when a person amassed abundant grain for consecutive years, she is considered fulfilling her duty—thus entitled to perform chang-ai.[36] This is accompanied with a community feast—usually the entire village and extended clans are invited to grace the occasion. The chang-ai ceremony is harmonised with merriment such as singing, feasting and drinking. Some of the songs sung during the occasion are given here (narrated by a former village priest):

> *Jacha'ng thang kadei luot, Gam vengke bang*
> *Setlei thaini vuongie, Sum tinthang kadei luot*
> *Kalhaw lamma, Kavai ngeitil ngawnnie*
> (Free translation)
> Seeking wealth and prosperity in grain
> I labour and till the soil all day long like a quail seeking riches in wealth and money
> I urge my offspring on to the fields

When the ceremony comes to an end, the women who performed the 'chang ai' are publicly conferred the coveted title 'thansuo' and are honoured with highly rated traditional cloth 'thangnang-puon' (dark blue in colour with embroidery at the two ends in red and white cotton of special design). A respondent (a woman aged about 76 years) in Kotlen village stated, "This auspicious occasion [chang-ai] used to be celebrated with pomp and grandeur by slaughtering mithuns and pigs for the public feast, because from that day onwards the performer and her family would be accorded the privilege to enter 'peogal', meaning the land of eternal bliss after death". The person who performed chang-ai ceremonies is believed to have earned uninterrupted passage to heaven. According to the Kuki mythology, it is believed that a certain female devil called *kulsamnu* dwells on a path leading to 'mithikhuo' (village of the death) who harasses everyone passing through. But she dare not touch the souls of those who have performed such a ceremony. Thus the celebrations are not mere show of extravaganza or wealth or skill but a preparation to enter a different mode of existence, and also a celebration through which the individuals would overcome a 'difficult passage'. Such persons when they die their bodies are accorded honourable disposal different from ordinary mortals.

As discussed above, the ceremonies and rituals illustrate that nature, culture and production of life are inseparable domains among the Kukis. Tradition and wisdom, which are properties of the communities' specific to their ecosystems, have evolved through human-nature interactions. The connections between gender and ecological sustainability have been analysed in this chapter, referring to the status 'ascribed' to men and women within their ecosystems or habitats. Ecological sustainability over a period is also related to the interactions between the human occupants and the habitat. The roles that men and women play in a given ecosystem are central to ecological sustainability, irrespective of whether they work for cash, kind or for restoration, and the measures used to evaluate the social impacts on the ecosystem have serious implications on sustainability.

Conclusion

With the deepening ecological crisis it is of tremendous research interest to see what social factors are contributing to such degradation. In this chapter, the 'place' of gender is re-examined in the light of the necessity of integrating the social and community-linked processes to achieve sustainability. Ecological sustainability is linked with the sustainability of the landscape. The women's observations on ecosystem functions have become essential elements in conservation. Gender differentiation has permitted greater diversity creating distinctive spaces for men and women to occupy and to sustain the ecological balance of the landscape. On the other hand, the gender-differentiation also reveals the patriarchal relations that have hindered women's potential contribution to modern ecosystem management and the entry of extension services to enhance traditional practices.The traditional knowledge of ecological sustainability is an integral part of the community, where sharing, collective action and customary practices are respected. Women, who are 'knowers' of the ecosystem, and the use of its resources for subsistence, express a committed interest to sustain the ecosystem for the future. Finding solutions to socially established inequalities are priority concerns of women because their ecosystem-based activities suffer from imbalances in the system. From a gendered perspective, key elements of ecological sustainability are regeneration and replenishment. Women's traditional knowledge and experience allows them to deal with resources in a very selective manner, and to handle different crops, fields, and soils differently.

Women assumed a distinctive role and participate in a 'basket' of economic activities ranging from cultivation, preservation of seeds, and market activity of the produce, apart from the day-to-day activity of nurturing the family. As the sole custodians of traditional knowledge systems, they have acquired an intuitive sense about the protection of their immediate environment. There is thus a great need to connect the vast resources on women's indigenous culture and contextualise women's cultural resources and inherent capacities of knowledge making and preserving traditional knowledge systems. Bina Agarwal (2001) rightly argues that women are structurally compelled to spend additional time and energy in order to preserve forest diversity because of the ways that patriarchal divisions of labour and systems of land ownership deny their rights. In general, women tend to lack decision-making power over the allocation of resources within families and communities, though the gender division of labour makes them disproportionately responsible for securing everyday subsistence requirements. As a result, they have little choice but to rely on the availability and diversity of common resources. To put in a nutshell, women's primary concern is in the availability of fuelwood and foodgrains throughout the year, preventing prolonged scarcities. It is their interest in securing subsistence needs rather than in getting commercial opportunities, and their experience within the ecosystem that has enabled them to become conservationists in their own habitats.

References

1. Fisher, R.J., (eds.), 'The Management of Forest Resources in Rural Development: A Case Study of Sindu Palchok and Kabhre Palanchok Districts of Nepal', *Discussion Paper No. 1, Mountain*

Populations and Institutions, International Centre for Integrated Mountain Development, Kathmandu, 1989.

2. Agrawal, A., 'Dismantling the Divide between Indigenous and Scientific Knowledge', *Development and Change*, 26 (3): 413-439, 1995.
3. Guha, R., *The Unquiet Woods: Ecological Change and Peasant Resistance in the Himalaya*, University of California Press, Berkeley, 1990; G. Cederlof and K. Sivaramakrishnan, *Ecological Nationalisms: Nature, Livelihoods and Identities in South Asia*, Permanent Black, Delhi, 2005.
4. Fairhead, J. and M. Leach, *Misreading the African Landscape: Society and Ecology in a Forest-Savanna Mosaic*, Cambridge University Press, Cambridge, 1996.
5. Conklin, H.C., 'The Study of Shifting Cultivation', *Current Anthropology*, 2 (1): 27- 61, 1961; Ellen (eds.), *Indigenous Environmental Knowledge and its Transformations: Critical Anthropological Perspectives*. Harwood Academic Publishers, UK, 2005; P. Sillitoe, A. Bicker and J. Pottier, (eds.), *Participating in Development: Approaches to Indigenous Knowledge*, Routledge, London and New York, 2002.
6. Karlsson, B.G., *Contested Belonging: An Indigenous People's Struggle for Forest and Identity in Sub-Himalayan Bengal*, Curzon Press, UK, 2000.
7. Ramakrishnan, P.S., *Mountain Biodiversity, Land Use Dynamics, and Traditional Ecological Knowledge*, Oxford University Press, 2000.
8. Fernandes,W., 'Forests and Tribals: Informal Economy Dependence and Management Traditions', in Mrinal Miri (ed.), *Continuity and Change in Tribal Society*, Indian Institute of Advanced Study, Shimla, 1993; Nongbri, Tiplut, 'Gender Issues and Tribal Development', in Bhupinder Singh (ed.), *Antiquity to Modernity in Tribal India* (Vol. II: Tribal Self-Management in North Eastern India), Inter India Publications, New Delhi, 1998, pp. 221-43.
9. Johnson, M. (ed.), *Lore: Capturing Traditional Environmental Knowledge*, Dene Cultural Institute and International Development Research Centre, Ottawa, 1992; F. Berkes, *Sacred Ecology: Traditional Ecological Knowledge and Management Systems*, Taylor & Francis, UK, 1999.
10. Berkes, F., *Sacred Ecology: Traditional Ecological Knowledge and Management Systems*, Taylor & Francis, UK, 1999.
11. Seeland, K. and F. Schmithusen (eds.), 'Local Knowledge of Forests and Forest Uses Among Tribal Communities in India',

Proceedings of an International Seminar Jointly, 1997.

12. Since, TEK is based on direct observation, it can be unique to the individual and is likely to be specialised by gender—for example, where men harvest and women process food, they observe different things and by age and experience.
13. Rappaport, R.A., *Ecology, Meaning, and Religion*, California North Atlantic Books, Richmon, 1979.
14. Fernandes,W., 'Forests and Tribals: Informal Economy Dependence and Management Traditions', in Mrinal Miri (ed.), *Continuity and Change in Tribal Society*, Indian Institute of Advanced Study, Shimla, 1993.
15. Dasgupta, B., 'India's Tribal Population: An Overview', *Journal of the Indian Anthropological Society*, 32 (2), 1997, p. 195.
16. Shifting cultivation is a process involving slashing and burning of forests. The burnt area is used for cultivation for a year and the group moves to another site in the subsequent year. Eventually, the cultivation shifts back to the old site when the area is fully re-vegetated. Sedentary terraced cultivation is also practised in Kuki society but it is confined to the foothill ranges and to narrow riverbanks and valleys.
17. Shakespear, J., *The Lushei Kuki Clans*, 2 Parts, Macmillan & Co. Ltd., London,1912, pp. 31-33.
18. Schendel, W.V. (ed.), *Francis Buchanan in Southeast Bengal (1798): His Journey to Chittagong, the Chittagong Hill Tracts, Noakhali and Comilla*, University Press Limited, Dhaka, 1992, p. 133.
19. Hodson, T.C., *The Nagas of Manipur*, Low Price Publications, Delhi, 1911, p. 15.
20. Ramakrishnan, P.S., *Shifting Agriculture and Sustainable Development of North-eastern India*. Unesco-MAB Series, Paris Parthenon, Oxford University Press, New Delhi, 1992.
21. Saha, N., 'Customs and Economy', in S.M. Dubey (ed.), *North-East India: A Sociological Study*, Rawat Publications, Delhi, 1978.
22. Burman, J.J. Roy, 'Community Participation in Indian Forestry', *Journal of the Indian Anthropological Society*, 32(2), 1997, p. 175.
23. Plants collected from the forest include secondary staple foods, vegetables, fruits, flowers, seeds, tubers, mushrooms, and bamboo shoots besides many medicinal plants, fibres and weaving materials. Thus, a wide variety of wild plants, animals and insects serve as dietary supplements as well as medicines.
24. World Bank, *Gender and Poverty in India*, The World Bank, Washington DC, 1991, p. 3.
25. Agarwal, B., 'The Gender and Environment Debate: Lessons from

India', *Feminist Studies*, 18(I), 1992, pp. 119-158.

26. In tribal society, the status of women is generally measured in her 'freedom of choice', types of taboos, role in the family and clan, role in household work and customary status.
27. Elwin, V., *The Nagas in the Nineteenth Century*, Oxford University Press, London, 1969.
28. The word *Lawm* signifies an informal labour organisation in an agrarian village life of the Kukis. It is an organisation which is concerned chiefly with the economic aspect and it imparts a sense of duty and dignity to the individual members. See also, Kipgen, Ngamjahao 2008. "Significance and Relevance of 'LAWM' in the Contemporary Kuki Society". Available at<http://kukiforum.com/2008/11/significance-of-lawm-in-the-contemporary-kuki-society/>.
29. However, of late with the external intervention of schemes (such as MNREGA) has ushered in the concept of wage labour to some extent to disrupt the cultural interaction and its value system.
30. Nongbri, T., 'Gender Issues and Tribal Development', in Bhupinder Singh (ed.), *Antiquity to Modernity in Tribal India* (Vol. II: Tribal Self-Management in North-Eastern India), Inter India Publications, New Delhi, 1998, p. 223.
31. Recently, the Mizoram Assembly passed the Mizo Marriage, Divorce and Inheritance of Property Bill 2014 which gave the right to the share of family property to the wife in the strictly patriarchal society. Empowerment will continue to remain a far cry unless a codified law, which entitles her to property, custody of children and maintenance rights for children, is granted to her even after she is divorced.
32. Griffin, S., *Woman and Nature: The Roaring Inside Her*, Harper & Row, 1978; Vandana Shiva, *Staying Alive: Women, Ecology and Development*, Zed Books, London, 1988.
33. Shiva, V., *Staying Alive: Women, Ecology and Development*, Zed Books, London, 1988; Janet Biehl, *Finding Our Way*, Black Rose Books, 1991.
34. Merchant, C., *The Death of Nature: Women, Ecology and the Scientific Revolution*. HarperCollins, New York, 1980.
35. *Chang* is 'paddy' and *ai* is seen as 'victory', thus *chang-ai* is thanks giving for the victory over the soul of paddy.
36. Gangte, T.S., *The Kukis of Manipur: A Historical Analysis*, Gyan Publishing House, Delhi, 1993, p. 185.

SECTION-IV

SCIENCE & TECHNOLOGY AND MEDICINE

12

Change, Cosmology, and Time in Innovation: The Idea of Non-Obsolescence in Shifting Cultivation

Abhinandan Saikia

Innovations are cornerstones of almost all socio-economic processes. It can be assumed to be present in all societies and all spheres of human activities. However, on many occasions, traditional non-market societies are characterised as inert, lacking innovative capacity. Mostly, the presence of common property rights system, which, allegedly, runs counter to the logic of valuing private gains, has been identified as a key reason deterring innovative change in these societies. The chapter argues that the reason for terming these societies as 'inert' lies in the inability to understand the differences in time belief that exist between modern (Western) capitalist societies and many pre-capitalist societies of Asia, Africa and Latin America. Some empirical observations from the shifting cultivating communities of Nagaland have been carried for the study. The chapter has six sections and Section I discusses the key features of the innovation theories. Since innovation is intricately linked with science, which also is a rather modern concept, we need to understand the nature of 'science' in non-market societies to cast light on their innovative behaviour. Section II discusses the notion of science in non-market societies where an attempt is made to blur the distinction between 'indigenous science' and 'modern science'. Section III discusses the various belief systems associated with time, and their manifestations in social processes. Section IV discusses the various religious and cultural characteristics, which are reflections of the time belief of shifting cultivators of Nagaland. Section V analyses our findings, and finally Section VI makes the concluding remarks.

I. Key Characteristics of Innovation Theories

What perhaps distinguishes innovative changes from other changes is that the former is exclusively directed towards economic use. Joseph Schumpeter (1934) offered a first systematic account of innovative processes, albeit in the context of a modern capitalist system. Some key features of the Schumpeterian theory of innovation can be listed as:

a) Innovation represents major advancements, and follows breakthroughs in the fundamental body of scientific knowledge (namely, invention).
b) Innovations are outcomes of the efforts of individual entrepreneurs or business organisations. Indeed, recognising this individual effort lies at the core of the system of intellectual property rights.
c) Dates of innovations are clearly identified (Rosenberg 1976). It may be noted that innovators in modern societies have to establish dates of innovations clearly in order to get patents.
d) Dimensions of innovation are: new products, new processes, new channels of distribution of products, new kinds of organising production, and new sources of raw materials.
e) Innovations replace older technology. So a continuous flow of innovations implies a continuous flow of technological obsolescence.[1]

Later researches in development economics have broadened the ambit of innovative activities by including minor innovations (Rosenberg 1976, Lall 1987). The sociological-anthropological literatures have also broadened the scope of innovation by replacing 'economic use' by 'practical application' as a key feature of innovations (Rogers 1995). All such ideas enable us to analyse innovative changes in contexts, where direct economic value of innovations are not measurable (e.g. in non-market societies), or in contexts which do not involve market transactions.

However, non-market societies have often been characterised as static and lacking creativity needed to deliver innovative changes (Hagen 1962, 1963). New theories, however, admit that creativity is a universal phenomenon and everyday feature of human beings in order to improvise, and adapt in a changing environment.[2] Studies on creativity and innovation of non-market societies, however, remain few and far between.

From the institutional point of view, many of these societies are characterised by existence of common property rights system, and absence of private property rights. Prevalence of the common property system is often assumed to discourage individual aspirations (De Sotto 2000). However, the extensive body of research pioneered by Elinor Ostrom (2000) show that various individualistic aspirations are often incorporated within the broad structure of the common property system in the form of bundle rights. At the same time, the literature on indigenous science points out that the body of indigenous knowledge of non-market societies also grows over time, suggesting the presence of innovative activities in these societies. The chapter argues that more than the differences in property rights regime or form of exchange what distinguishes non-market societies from modern market societies is difference in time belief. While modern market societies believe, primarily, in a linear version of time, non-market societies believe in a spiral notion of time which mixes cyclical notion with linear notion of time.[3]

II. 'Science' in Non-Market Indigenous Societies

Since innovation, in its most over simplified version, refers to expansion of scientific and technical knowledge, it may not be completely out of place to examine the characteristics of such knowledge systems in the context of non-market societies. There is, often, unanimity that scientific knowledge is "public knowledge" (Merton 1942, Ziman 1967).[4] Scientific knowledge is generally considered universal in at least three senses. First, scientific laws are logically, spatially, and temporally universal. Second, scientific knowledge can be applied anywhere in the universe. Third, Western science-based technology has a geographic universality of applicability. Any society can use it in any environment.

On the other hand, indigenous knowledge system is culture-specific and gives an identity to a community.[5] Such culture specificity has often, allegedly made this knowledge system 'weak' in its scientific contents. Ogawa, however, proposes that every culture has its own science and refers to the science in a given culture as its "indigenous science" (Ogawa 1995, Elkana 1981). The term 'indigenous', refers to systems that are generated by internal initiatives within a local community (Fisher 1989). Indigenous science is sometimes referred to as ethno science or native science, and it has been described as the study of systems of knowledge developed by a given culture to classify the objects, activities, and events of its surrounding universe (Hardesty 1977). In other words, it interprets, through a cultural lens, how the local world works.[6]

The science in these systems grows by running experiments in the natural world, without controlling for any factors. In other words, native or indigenous science, arguably, relies on total involvement of the person along with the surrounding environment. Gadgil and Berkes (1991) characterised these communities as "I-Thou", where there is an intricate relationship between human being and nature, and both relate to the same clock.[7] The 'data' in the process of experimentation in these societies often reflect the lifetime experiences of a family or a clan.[8] Because of this high reliance on the oral archival system, elders are given importance in the social hierarchy and considered as custodians of the knowledge system. The goals of such experiments are, presumably, to achieve peace of mind, and not any material gains.[9]

The picture however started changing after the dawn of the post-modernist era.[10] To be precise, Science and Technology Studies (STS) have taken a critical look at some of the key dimensions of science especially in the areas concerning localness or universality of science, and on the importance of observation science. According to STS, modern science is a form of local knowledge, where scientific knowledge gets localised in the laboratory. Effects are created through artificial conditions, especially in case of bio-labs, where micro-organisms are studied in an *unnatural* way (Hacking 1983). In the opinion of these scholars, the claim of universality of modern science is a product of these local conditions of laboratories (in various places) and transportation of these local results.[11] The perceived differences between scientific thoughts and actions of modern and indigenous societies are thus superficial at best. As a result, the conventional view to describe indigenous societies as inert, lacking innovative capacity falls apart. It is in this context, the differences in time belief hold the key to a proper understanding of innovative behaviour of these societies.

III. Time Belief

That belief, reasoned or blind faith, shapes human behaviour is not a mystery.[12] However, the role of time belief on human socio-economic behaviour has remained largely unexplored. In a rather oversimplified manner, one may argue that cyclical time belief refers to endless repetition of pasts in future. However, it is worth pointing out that the cyclical notion of time, which refers to repetition of pattern only, is different from 'super-cyclic' notion of time. The latter refers to repetition of patterns as well as forms. For Raju (2003) the super-cyclical notion is a misinterpretation of the cyclical notion of time, constructed in the 4th century AD. It seems this (mis) interpretation has importantly shaped the conclusion of many anthropological studies seeking to analyse the implications of time belief for social processes in non-market societies. Many such studies arrive at the conclusion that non-market societies generally indulge in endless repetition of past activities without any change.[13] An incident reported in Scaglion (1999) provides an important insight in this regard.

When Richard Scaglion was doing his field visit in Nelgium with

> the Abelam people, he was given a local name by the Abelam people. Since, names and identity have great significance for the Abelam people, the villagers named him 'Urukwaapwi' which means somebody who flies like a bird. Originally, the name had belonged to a warrior of great renown, whose enemies, unable to kill him, had claimed that when they tried to trap him, he "flew away like a bird". Interestingly, the author was given the name because he had arrived in Papua New Guinea by airplane!

Although Scaglion (ibid.) explains this phenomenon as repetition of the past, this chapter construes a different interpretation. For the author, this incident offers crucial insights into the way these communities accept and recognise change. Two things are noteworthy: first, they incorporated a new individual of non-native origin into their system, and they showed their receptive attitude to modern technologies like aeroplanes. Therefore, it will be counter intuitive to assume that these societies do not incorporate novelty. Rather, they perhaps incorporate novelty by assimilating them into their existing broad social structure. This is evident from the fact that they incorporated the novel individual by giving him a native name.[14] Secondly, they accepted the idea of the aeroplane by comparing it with a bird, once again an attempt to assimilate novelty (here aeroplane) into the system by comparing it with things and patterns they are familiar with. Indeed, in religious history, Eliade (1954) argues that traditional societies have also evolved with time implying that they are also not devoid of creativity. He further argues that creativity or doing new things to them means associating that activity with some mythological events (known or familiar patterns).[15]

III.a. Time Belief, Traditional Societies and Innovation: A Literature Review

There are two key building blocks of belief in time (Raju 2003). They are:

(a) Origin of the Universe, and

(b) Existence of Soul.

Belief in linear time supports the hypothesis that

(c) There is a specific date of the creation of the present Universe (as a consequence they support the theory of Big Bang), and

(d) Souls, even if they exist, do not incarnate after the present human life.

Indeed, a clearly defined past, present and future is a key to understand the course of modern Western civilisation. St. Augustine, a key propagator of linear time belief, asserted that *"civilisation is progressing, and we remember who performed this deed or developed that technique"* (Hawking 1988: 8). Interestingly, it is to be noted that the theories of innovation, especially in the Schumpeterian tradition, also see innovation as 'progress', where older technologies are made obsolete by newer, more efficient or economically more useful technologies (Rosenberg 1982). Firms or individuals who create innovations are also identifiable, and are given the due credits (e.g. patent protection) for making those innovations.

In contrast, belief in cyclical notion of time assumes that:

(a) Either the Universe is eternal (leading to the belief that time has no beginning or end), or there is continuous creation and destruction of the Universe taking place giving rise to cyclicality in time (Davies 1992, Raju 2003).

(b) Human beings have souls. Souls are immortal (eternal) and they only change form.

It is generally believed that all pre-Christian religions believed in the concepts of re-birth and souls. In fact, soul has been the fundamental concept of the tribal religions all over the world (Eliade 1954).

They believe that every object has a soul. The myth, which teaches that the Supreme Being works and reveals mysteries through creation, is the base of animism. According to M.M. Thomas (1969: 449), the worldview of the tribal religion is that, *"there is the sense of spiritual continuum within which the dead and the living natural objects, spirits and gods, the individual, the clan, the tribe, animals, plants, minerals and man form an unbroken hierarchical unity of spiritual force. The self of man is not an individual self, but an extended universal self present and actively participating in all the parts of totality"* (chapter's emphasis).

However, their notion of time is not uniform. While in ancient Indian philosophy and in the context of Mayan civilisation, cyclicality of time is explicitly referred to, there are not many studies to this effect for the tribes in Africa. The existing studies on Africa, however, note that the existence of past, present and future is blurred for the native Africans. Especially, future is embodied in the present. Anything that does not exist in the present is not to be concerned with. On the other hand, any event that exists in the present will have expected consequences in future. The future can be supported by present action, but cannot be controlled or altered.[16] Nevertheless, these societies seem to have continued with their faith in re-birth, a central pillar of cyclical time belief, despite being under the influence of Christianity and Islam for a long time (Besterman 1930). Also, unlike the Christian belief, African societies do not believe in creation of the Universe in a particular moment of time.[17] For them, creation is a continuous process, where "god created semi-human creatures, which with time became human. This process of creation is still continuing (Ayanga 2007). For these societies, Eliade (1954) argues, cosmic change and social behaviour are inter-related. In fact, the various phases of lunar cycle influence social behaviour in a major way in pre-capitalist societies (ibid: 86). As Eliade explains, "*the moon reveals the eternal return*", and lunar myths form the "*first coherent theories of death and resurrection, fertility and regeneration.*"[18] Eliade (ibid.) found a strong role of festivals in these societies. Their life cycles seem to revolve around these festivals, which reflect creation, destruction and new creation. For Eliade, these festivals reveal the desire of these societies live in the 'a temporal instant of the beginnings'—a way to refuse to become historical (and obsolete in the present). In fact, Eliade argues that all societies believing in cyclical time mark a 'refusal of history' in varied ways (ibid: 117).

The chapter argues that innovations in societies having cyclical time belief would have implications for the dimensions of (i) technological obsolescence, (ii) identification of innovators and (iii) specification of the date of innovation.

Before, however, analysing the empirical findings, a brief profile of the shifting cultivators of Nagaland is given below.

IV. Shifting Cultivators of Nagaland

Shifting cultivation is perhaps the oldest agricultural practice to have survived the savagery of time. Locally, it is known as *Jhum*. Scholars have highlighted the diversity in the practice of shifting cultivation across regions to drive home the point that the system is far from being static, as is commonly understood in the arena of policy making, and it has a capacity to adapt with changes in physical and human environments (Darlong 2004, Tiwari 2003). Some recent studies, especially by the noted researcher P.S. Ramakrishnan (2003), have explored the role of traditional ecological knowledge behind the diversity in the practice of *jhum*. Indeed, inter-regional diversity in the practice of shifting cultivation can be taken as a proxy for innovativeness (Kerkhoff and Sharma 2006).

Regarding Nagaland, which is one of the states in India, the majority of the land is earmarked as *jhum* land where community ownership is mostly prevalent and regulated by the Village Council. However, individuals/families enjoy temporary rights of exclusion, withdrawal and management of these lands during the period of shifting cultivation (Ostrom 2000). Economic theory predicts that individuals will undertake efforts to improve properties when such rights exist. This is because individuals can exclude others from free riding on his/her effort. During the study, however, the problems of free riding are found to be of less concern. In contrast to 'modern' society, here, individuals often seem to reveal their innovative efforts voluntarily to others in the meetings of their respective Village Councils. This phenomenon perhaps justifies the position of Christopher Alexander (1964) that change in traditional societies are often carried out with an '*unselfconscious*' attitude.

Currently, almost all the people of Nagaland are Christian by faith. Christianity came to north-east India with the arrival of the Western Christian missionaries and establishment of the British rule. However, they did have a tribal religion before the missionaries had arrived (Singh 2008). Their traditional tribal religion is basically a community religion, where individual life and community life is inseparable from each other. The rituals and religious practices, which developed among the different Naga tribes, are all based on the faith of animism, which believes in the centrality of the idea of the soul or spirit. All the tribes had their own religious myths, which contained their religious scriptures and creeds. The animism shaped their understanding of the environment, the universe as well as their social and cultural lives. The interrelation of all cultural components in a holistic way is a manifestation of such belief.

The Naga people believed in a power, which, according to them, is superior to all and determines all actions. The omnipotence and omnipresence of this power is reflected through various agencies and means such as trees, stones, ponds, and mountains. In fact, the ancient Nagas believed their origin to be in the stones or mountains and tree roots. Many of these beliefs are visible among the Nagas even today. During the ceremonial festivals, they still practise many of the rituals of their ancient religion.[19] It clearly indicates that the ancient Nagas believed in *continuation of souls* in various forms. They also had the idea of salvation or deliverance, for which one had to live a life of purity and prudence.

An education system was also in place to reinforce this system of belief. Being a traditional and primitive society, the written form of any script was unknown to the Naga people. Before the advent of missionaries, the mode of education was centred on the '*Morung*'.[20] This institution served Naga society for centuries and incorporated in its functioning various tribal values, life-centric learning and exposure to customary practices and experiences. Here, young men and women grew up under the supervision of the community elders.[21] The youth, through community living and working together, also got to know each other in a natural way and forged relationships that extended from the personal to the social domain.[22]

The long history of *Morung* and its role however have had a deep impact on the village community, especially on the elders. These elders generally become the Village Council members. Their decision is influenced mostly by the lessons they learnt in *Morung* during their childhood. Due to the presence of their authority, often the decisions made in the Village Council are based on the well-being of values and customs associated with the community. One can get the impression on how any new or innovative idea gets oriented when it comes in touch with the Village Council.[23]

Jhum cultivators in Nagaland generally practise either dibbling and/or broadcast methods of sowing and mixed cropping. In a mixed cropping system, crops are sown in irregular fashion or random planting. There are no definite crop mixtures. Every cultivating family follows their own system of crop combination according to his family requirements and Naga *jhum* farmers normally grow as many crops as possible, the upper limit being decided by the community. Before the commencement of sowing, the village priest would be invited to initiate the formal sowing on any day after the tenth day following the new moon. In case of a village like Sungratsu (Mokokchung district), sowing is done in February-March-April following the lunar calendar. Generally sowing takes place after the five days of full moon/new moon.

The importance of this calendar is so prime that farmers avoid making changes in the variety of crops in a particular season, fearing any distortion in the chemistry between the moon and the crop. There is a distinct socio-cultural link here. Such connections between cosmological objects and social behaviour have also been found in shifting cultivation practised elsewhere in the world, like in the case of Philippines. It may be worth reiterating here that cosmology is an integral component of indigenous science. Another distinguishing feature of this calendar is the relationship between various stages of cultivation and festivals. Almost all phases of the cultivation cycle are attached to a particular type of festivals—a key feature of societies believing in the cyclical notion of time.

V. The Innovation Dynamics of Shifting Cultivators: An Analysis

During the fieldwork, the community (practising *jhum*) showed a tendency to under report changes that have taken place in their crop variety, method, tools and organisation of cultivation in the first instance. Also, they never gave a cause-and-effect relationship in terms of specific reasons of change, and dates of change. However, the presence of novelty was there, to observe. While tracing the dates of innovations in *jhum* cultivation, the study found some *imprecise* responses, ranging from "recently", "when I was a kid" to "when my father was a farmer"! All these instances perhaps bear testimony to the fact that the concept of time is strongly intertwined with events. To know it further, an analysis is done on the time belief and its implications on their innovative behaviour.[24]

The study examines some cases of innovations to understand the dimensions of (i) obsolescence, (ii) date, and (iii) role of individuals in the innovation processes.

V.a. Seed Variety

Generating new products is an integral part of innovation. In farming communities, in general, production of new crop variety is a well-recognised innovative activity. Instances of generating seed diversity are also present in the sample villages. New seed varieties are generated through various means. Often, village women collect the mature seeds for future storage during the time of harvesting. Seeds are also exchanged between neighbouring villages. Travellers from outside the region too have played an important role in introducing new crops and varieties in the villages. For instance, locally found chow-chow and passion fruits may not have originated in Nagaland. It is presumed that exotic seeds of these crops were brought by the travellers. Finally, government programmes also play an important role in bringing new crops into the *jhum* field.

An interesting aspect of their attitude to crop variety is their judicious use of seeds according to specific climatic conditions. If in the past, some varieties had produced satisfactory yields under some specific climatic conditions, it is stored for future uses. The chapter argues that such behaviour reflects the belief in the cyclical notion of time, where specific climatic conditions experienced in the past are also perceived to be repeatable in *future*. As a result, they think it judicious to store these varieties, even when they add new varieties in their granary. A situation is therefore observed where new technologies do not necessarily make the older technologies obsolete. Such preservation of different varieties thus reflect their belief in cyclical time where they 'remember the future', as a recurrence of past! Also, these new seeds are distributed within the community members without any compulsory exchange obligations.

Generally, the names of people who introduced these changes are also not identifiable. In one case the respondent recalled naming a paddy variety as *Mangtang Chak* (meaning 'Dream paddy') since a villager saw in his dream the existence of such a variety in the Chakhesang area (Phek district). According to the respondent, the villager then went to Chakhesang to search for this seed variety. But the name of the villager is not considered while naming this seed variety. In some cases, names were also given looking at the place from where these seeds are brought. The examples include 'Shillong rice' brought from Shillong, Meghalaya. Again it seems too *unimportant* for them to note who brought the seeds. In one case, however, the names of the seed bear the name of the person who used it first. For instance, the rice variety named *Taka Nungshi* was named after a villager in Changki village (Mokukchung district), who created this rice through a selection procedure in his field.

V. b. Tools

Evidences of innovation are also present in the tools used for *jhum*. Tools used for cutting the vegetation are *dao* (machete) and sickle. Henhoe is used for cleaning the soil debris before planting seeds in soil. Racks are used to properly mix flying ash with the soil after a field is burnt. Dibbling sticks made of bamboo are used for sowing. Various types of such local baskets are used to carry seeds, agricultural products, firewood, and other non-timber forest products (NTFPs). In recent years, the farmer also use a spade, which is a recent addition to the category of tools used in *jhum*. Almost every tool has a local name according to the tribal dialect spoken in the respective districts. Prima facie, changes or modifications in the tools appear rare. In every discussion, farmers would, in the beginning, not even be forthcoming to talk about any modifications in tools. For them, things have 'remained unchanged'. However, certain evidences of modification of the tools are observed during the study.

One such modification is found in the henhoe. Over time, iron has replaced bamboo and cane in the part, which is used to remove soil debris. Apart from it, rubber and other materials in henhoes are used in certain parts for comfort during work. Such changes in the tool sometimes change their name, as in the case of Lungwa village in Mon district, the name *Gongkongkeu* (henhoe with bamboo strip) changed to *Yangangkeu* (henhoe with iron strip) with the modifications in henhoe. Apparently, these modifications have taken place during the last 20-30 years. On inquiring about the time of change, there was no specific date available. Instead, a broad duration was reported. Similarly, iron wire has replaced cane in *dao* as well. And in case of dibbling sticks, iron-made versions have become visible albeit with limited usage. Prima facie, it is the difference in weight (iron made dibbling sticks become heavier) is responsible for its limited diffusion of iron made dibbling sticks. The reason they gave for replacing cane by iron wire in *dao* is that the latter provide a good grip and makes it easy to use. Interestingly, once again, these newer varieties of tools do not make their earlier versions completely obsolete, as both kinds of dibbling sticks are used in *jhum*. In the same vein, both the henhoes namely *Gongkongkeu* and *Yangangkeu* are used in the *jhum*. A more interesting case is found in the Chenmoho village of Mon district. Here community members use a modified version of an iron made spade to remove soil during cultivation. However, the introduction of the spade has not yet made the use of henhoes obsolete. Normally coexistence of various 'generations' of technology is hardly observed in modern societies contrary to where an innovation often replaces the older technology. From the study, the chapter construes that these innovations, at times, remained confined to specific villages which developed them, suggesting that need for modifications is also, perhaps local, and culture-specific.

In case of tools as well, the name of the innovators could not be ascertained. Although the roles of local blacksmiths are considered important, the credits for such innovations are shared among villagers. In most cases, these innovations are the outcomes of discussions of farmers, blacksmiths and elderly people held in the Village Council meetings. Two aspects are noteworthy: first, the discussions between farmers and others in the society take place without any contract (formal and informal), and secondly, once made, no villagers showed any special interest to attach his or her name to the innovations. Conventionally, a belief in the common property system is attributed for such an attitude. The chapter argues that such absence of portraying the self is a reflection of the belief in spirits, where spirits, and not the physically present human beings, are supposed to be the real drivers of social processes. In Hindu philosophy indeed, falling on the soul is believed to lessen the ego of the self, something contrary to the emphasis on 'self' given by St. Augustine in creating human civilisations mentioned earlier.[25]

VI. Conclusion

A belief in the cyclical or spiral notion of time may, therefore, call for modifications in innovation theories. In particular, the relevance of technological obsolescence, clearly identified the date of innovation and the aspects of recognition of innovators may have to be relooked at if one wants to understand the innovation dynamics in non-market societies. A proper analysis of the implication of time belief in social behaviour may also provide a richer understanding of the reasons behind the sustenance of common property systems in these societies. The chapter argues, although in a premature manner, that the belief in the existence of spirits and souls may provide important clues why these societies do not always strive for individual rights in all spheres of their social life, as is commonly understood in modern societies. Needless to mention, however, that any conclusion requires more empirical research on this issue.

REFERENCES

1. Alexander, C., *Notes on the Synthesis of Form*, Cambridge, MA: Harvard University Press, 1964.
2. Ayanga, H., African Cosmologies Past and Present. In Eisen, A. and Laderman, G. (eds.) *Science, Religion and Society*, ME Sharpe, New York, 2007.
3. Besterman, T., The Belief in Re-birth Among the Natives of Africa, *Folklore*, 41(1), 1930, 43-94.
4. Darlong, V.T., *To Jhum Or Not To Jhum—Policy Perspectives on Shifting Cultivation*, Guwahati: The Missing Link, Society for Environment & Communication, 2004.
5. Davies, P., *The Mind of God: The Scientific Basis for a Rational World*. Simon and Schuster, New York, 1992.
6. De Soto, Hernando, *The Mystery of Capital: Why Capitalism Triumphs in the West and Fails Everywhere Else*, New York: Basic Books, 2000.
7. Eliade, M., *Cosmos and History: The Myth of the Eternal Return*, New York: Harper & Brothers, 1954.
8. Elkana, Y., 'A Programmatic Attempt at an Anthropology of Knowledge', in E. Mendelshohn and Elkana, Y. (eds.), *Science and Culture: Anthropological and Historical Studies of the Sciences* Dordrecht, The Netherlands: Reidel, 1981, pp. 1-77.
9. Fisher, R.J., 'Indigenous Systems of Common Property Forest Management in Nepal', Working Paper No. 18, Hawaii: Environment and Policy Institute, East West Centre, Honolulu, 1989, p. 23.
10. Gadgil, M. and Berkes, F., 'Traditional Resource Management Systems', *Resource Management and Optimization*, Vol. 8, 1991, pp. 127-41.
11. Hacking, I., *Representing and Intervening*, Cambridge, Cambridge University Press, 1983.
12. Hagen, E.E., *On the Theory of Social Change: How Economic Growth Begins*, Homewood, The Dorsey Press, 1962.
13. Hagen, E.E., 'How Economic Growth Begins: A Theory of Social Change', *Journal of Social Issues*, Vol. 19 (1), 1963, pp. 20-34.
14. Hardesty, D.L., *Ecological Anthropology*, New York, Wiley, 1977.
15. Hawking, S., *A Brief History of Time – From The Big Bang To Black Holes*, London, Bantam Books, 1988.

16. Kerkhoff, E. and Sharma, E., 'Debating Shifting Cultivation in the Eastern Himalayas: Farmers' Innovations as Lessons for Policy', Kathmandu, Nepal, International Centre for Integrated Mountain Development, 2006.
17. Kirk, G.S., *Myth: Its Meaning and Functions in Ancient and Other Cultures*, Berkeley, University of California Press, 1970.
18. Kluckholn, C. and Kroeber, A.L., *Culture: A Critical Review of Concepts and Definitions*, New York, Vintage Books, 1963.
19. Lall, S., *Learning to Industralise: The Acquisation of Technological Capability in India,* London, Macmillan, 1987.
20. Latour, B., *Science in Action: How to Follow Scientists and Engineers Through Society*, Cambridge, MA, Harvard University Press, 1987.
21. Merton, R.K., 'Science and Technology in a Democratic Order', *Journal of Legal and Political Sociology,* Vol. 1, 1942, pp. 115-26.
22. Mills, J.P., *The Ao Nagas*, London, Oxford University Press, 1973.
23. Offe, J.A., "Smart Guys Plan for the Future!": Cultural Concepts of Time and the Prevention of AIDS in Africa, *Africa Spectrum*, Vol. 36 (1), 2001, pp. 53-72.
24. Ogawa, M., 'Science Education in a MultiScience Perspective', *Science Education,* Vol. 79, 1995, p. 593.
25. Ostrom, E., 'Private and Common Property Rights', in Boudewijn Bouckaert and De Geest Gerrit (eds.), *Encyclopedia of Law and Economics,* Vol. II, Cheltenham, Edward Elgar, 2000, pp. 332-79.
26. Ibid.
27. Raju, C.K., *The Eleven Pictures of Time: The Physics, Philosophy, and Politics of Time Beliefs*, New Delhi, Sage, 2003.
28. Ramakrishnan, P.S. et al. (eds.), *Methodological Issues in Mountain Research: A Socio-ecological Systems Approach,* UNESCO, 2003.
29. Rogers, E., *Diffusion of Innovations*, New York. Cambridge University Press, 1995.
30. Rosenberg, N., *Perspectives on Technology*, New York, Cambridge University Press, 1976.
31. Rosenberg, N., *Inside the Black Box: Technology and Economics*, New York, Cambridge University Press, 1982.
32. Scaglion, R., 'Yam Cycles and Timeless Time in Melanesia', *Ethnology,* Vol. 38 (3), 1999, pp. 211-25.
33. Schumpeter, J.A., *The Theory of Economic Development*, London, Oxford University Press, 1934.
34. Singh, C., *The Naga Society,* New Delhi, Manas Publications, 2008.
35. Snively, G. and Corsiglia, J., 'Discovering Indigenous Science: Implications for Science Education', *Science Education,* Vol. 85, 2001, pp. 6-34.

36. Thomas, M.M., 'Modernization of Society and Struggle for New Cultural Ethos', *Ecumenical Review,* Vol. VII (4), 1969, p. 429.
37. Tiwari, B.K., 'Innovations in Shifting Cultivation, Land Use and Land Cover Change in Higher Elevations of Meghalaya, India', in P.S. Ramakrishnan et al. (eds.), *Methodological Issues In Mountain Research: A Socio-ecological Systems Approach*, UNESCO, 2003.
38. Worster, D., *Nature's Economy*, Cambridge, Cambridge University Press, 1977.
39. Ziman, J., *Public Knowledge*, Cambridge, Cambridge University Press, 1967.

NOTES

1. Rosenberg (1982) quotes Alexis De Tocqeville to explain how a preference for obsolescence shaped the nature of innovative activities in the early days of modern American civilisation.
2. Recently, a literature is flourishing trying to understand the complex relationship between creativity and innovation. In its core, this literature also attempts to show how creativity should be considered as the backbone of any innovative activity.
3. However, offers a more nuanced variation in the notion of time. See Raju (2003) for details.
4. Merton (1942) for his view on "communism" of data sharing in science.
5. Culture here refers to beliefs, preferences, and behaviours, along with the mechanisms that link these traits to one another, of members of a community. These traits give a particular community a unique distinguishable identity. This identity is subject to change, for a culture is a living organism. Through their interactions and their reactions to external influences, the members of a community transform their behaviours and also the underlying beliefs and preferences. See Kluckholn and Kroeber (1963) for further details.
6. Indigenous science includes the knowledge of both indigenous expansionist cultures (e.g. the Aztec, Mayan, and the Mongolian Empires) as well as the home-based knowledge of long-term resident oral resident peoples (i.e. the Inuit, the Aboriginal people of Africa, the Americas, Asia, Australia, Europe, Micronesia, and New Zealand). See Snively and Corsiglia (2001) for further details.
7. If the "community of beings" worldview can be characterised as an "I-thou" relationship between humans and nature, the "domination over nature" worldview is characterised as an "I-it" relationship. In the latter view, nature is viewed as clockwork

and is considered to exist separately from humans. It could be studied by taking it apart and by asking systematic, testable questions. It could be brought under control and made to yield human benefits. See Worster (1977) for details.

8. By contrast, experimentation in modern science is done in controlled set ups, where natural factors are assumed to be of confounding type, and should be controlled for achieving objectivity and universality.
9. In this respect, it draws interesting similarity with the classical motive of scientists, whose goal is often argued to be pure pursuit of knowledge without concern for social or economic well-being.
10. The ILO Convention on Indigenous and Tribal Peoples, 1989 refuted the assumption that Indigenous Knowledge (IK) is confined only to tribal groups or the inhabitants or the rural folks. According to the convention, IK is also found in communities representing rural or urban, settled or nomadic, original settlers or migrants. This important definition has in a way opened the boundaries where more resemblance, if not in structure but in the spirit, can be found between both the sciences.
11. The "travel" takes place through dissemination of training skills, of observers, in laboratory techniques of measurement and observation. See Latour (1987) for further details.
12. To see how beliefs even have shaped the thought processes even of the greatest scientists, refer to Davies (1992) and Raju (2003) for further details.
13. In the theories of religious history, however, expressions like 'creation' are used aplenty. See, for instance, Eliade (1954)
14. This also ensured that the name does not disappear with the death of a person.
15. Kirk (1970), while accepting that some traditional societies have indeed been found to behave in this fashion, raises objections to the attempts to make this phenomenon universal.
16. Planning, as in agricultural practice, was however not ruled out under such a belief system. Such acts to control the future, presumably, refer to the acts directed to control nature. Many of these societies lived in harmony with nature without attempting to control it. (J.A. Offe "Smart Guys Plan for the Future!': Cultural Concepts of Time and the Prevention of AIDS in Africa', *Africa Spectrum*, 36 (1), 2001, pp. 53-72).
17. Davies (1992) however, points out the diversity in this belief among the various sects within Christianity.
18. Ayanga (2007) also reports that all the African societies have

strong interconnections between time and events.

19. This is not unique to these communities. As mentioned above, many tribes in Africa also continued to believe in the concepts of soul and rebirth, despite being influenced by Christianity and Islam for a long time. See Besterman, 1930 and Singh 2008 for further details.
20. J.P. Mills' (1973) book titled *The Ao Nagas* defined *Morung* as 'a school of informal knowledge'.
21. For the young men the *Morungs* were khel or clan-based. In some tribes, a similar framework existed for girls as well (called in Ao dialect as '*Tsuki*'). They met in informal groups under the supervision of a respected senior woman.
22. With modernity, however, the impact of *Morungs* has become limited.
23. As per the 'The Nagaland Village and Area Council Act, 1978, the Council has special powers to maintain law and order and administer justice within the village boundaries in accordance with the customary laws, and usages.
24. Two kinds of innovative behaviour have been conceptualised: (a) local innovations and (b) collaborative innovations. Local innovations are conceived and implemented by the local people. Collaborative innovations, on the other hand, are often conceived and implemented by external agencies and government research institutions. The chapter concentrates on local innovations for the present study.
25. Max Weber has famously emphasised this aspect to explain less drive for entrepreneurship in this society.

13

Environmental Diseases and Medical Reactions in Twentieth Century South India

V. Raj Mahammadh

Introduction

Epidemic diseases are those in which a whole people or community are affected at one time or other. The ancient medical texts like *Charaka Samhita* and *Sushruta Samhita* contain references to the epidemic diseases and their causation.[1] *Navanitakam* and *Astanga Sangraham* by Vagbhata also elaborated on the medical practices, and treatments for various diseases in India.[2] During the medieval period, the court chronicles, travellers' accounts and biographies described the epidemic diseases experienced on a larger social canvas. In the 16th and 17th centuries, India had witnessed epidemic diseases and their devastating effect on the countryside. In the last two decades of the 19th century, a series of discoveries by scientists such as Koch and Pasteur identified germs which are responsible for communicable diseases.[3] Environmental change manifests in a complex web of ecological social factors that finally impact on disease. The scope of this field involves studying the interactions between environment and human health. Human health is widely and dramatically affected by environment. Environment is mediating the diseases. Thus physical, chemical, biological and social factors are causes for environmental diseases such as cholera, plague, smallpox, fevers, malaria, dysentery, and diarrhoea. The scope for the study of these categories of diseases is very vast. I have therefore taken up for our case study, cholera, plague and smallpox analysed their historical trajectories and social impact in the South India and response of the colonial government.

Diseases and Environment: Cholera

There was a close relation between environment and epidemics. The environmental historians like, Ramachandra Guha, David Arnold, Madav Gadgil, Richard Grove, David Hardiman, Mahesh Rangarajan, Sivaramkrishnan and Vandana Shiva have described Indian environment and its relation to human beings.[4] They argued that colonialism as a watershed in the environmental history of India disturbed the state harmony between the communities. In the 19th and 20th centuries, South Indian society engaged with epidemics such as cholera, plague and smallpox. The period witnessed the growth of tropical diseases in the form of epidemics and their effect on millions of population in India. The cholera disease is characterised by the suddenness of its attack and one of the 'classic epidemics' that scourged the world in the first half of the 19th century began in the Bengali basin and spread rapidly across the provinces in India.[5] The cholera transmission is via the anal, oral route and most frequently follows the ingestion of water or food contaminated with cholera stools. The majority of patients infected with 'Vibrio Cholera' showed signs and symptoms of mild enteritis.

Hindu literature referred to cholera in its sporadic and, endemic forms, but European practioners conjectured that the disease caused by the electrical state of the atmosphere is spread through water and air. The *Arogya Prakasika* (Monthly Health Journal) mentioned environmental causes like open baths, washing clothes, cleaning of cows in wells and open places, drinking contaminated and muddy water, etc. These environmental changes encompass social processes such as urbanisation and creation of transportation, infrastructure, as well as ecologic processes such as land and water use, biodiversity loss, and climate change.[6]

India's premier epidemiologist and the Government Chief Adviser, Bryden believed that the disease cholera is transmited through air. William Farr argued that cholera is spread through contaminated drinking water.[7] The colonial officials believed that the cause of cholera was strictly local in origin and produced within the houses and settlements of villages in India, due to the unsanitary practices of local people. The epidemic crossed into Europe by sea and travelling across the globe, due to the fast development of communications and introduction of railways.[8] Ira Klein has pointed to the significance of epidemiological factors: Cholera longevity in water, synergism with malnutrition and its many immune carriers were fundamental to its 19th century proliferation, as were modernisation and environmental change.[9]

South India in the 19th century, particularly during the Guntur Famine in 1833, cholera contributed to the death of two million populations. Between 1869 and 1871, the cholera epidemic caused about one lakh deaths.[10] Hot dry conditions were inimical to the survival of the water-borne cholera bacillus and the consequent deaths, since drought drove villages frequently to wells, tanks and stagnant pools which were contaminated with cholera.[11] By the 1880s, the railways had ensured easy and fast travelling throughout India. On April 12, 1879, cholera appeared among the 3,00,000 pilgrims at the Kumbamela fairs at various places. In 1900, cholera was responsible for one-tenth of the deaths of the total population in India. It affected mainly the lower classes due to the nature of association of the disease with living conditions and connection with poor sanitary system and polluted water supplies.

In the late 19th century, the famines severely affected and destroyed more than one-third of the population. The frequency of famines was due to the failure of monsoons or shortage of rainfall in the Madras Presidency.[12] The number of people who died of cholera during the period 1901 to 1910 were 6,82,299. In 1906-07, the Madras Presidency had recorded 1,42,811 deaths, a ratio of 3.9 per mile. W.R. Macdonald, Health Officer,

Corporation of Madras, explained that the relation between food materials and etiological factors was the basic cause for cholera. The other causes were, the mouldy rice imported from Rangoon and the dirty water from the Red Hills contributed to the spread of epidemics. The total deaths from cholera were 6,36,746 in 1911 to 1921.[13] Achanta Lakshmi Pati observed that the temples and shrines are the main source for the spread of cholera.[14]

A.J.H. Russell emphasised the relationship between cholera and the rainfall during the period from 1902 to 1921. According to him, cholera appeared in great and sudden exacerbations coinciding with the onset of the monsoons. He said that the long period of droughts, constant famines, lack of drinking water and other climate factors such as humidity, temperature and pressure have contributed to the origin and spread of cholera.[15] Michelle Burge McAlpin argued that during, 1896-1920, the rainfall was significantly less and this scantiness of the rainfall had resulted in an unusually large number of crop failures in India. This contributed to high mortality.[16] The total deaths from 1920 to 1929 were 2,99,924 due to famine, the crops failed and agriculture was destroyed particularly in Kalli Kota, Ganjam, Atagad, Chitrapur, Baierani, and Bodo Guda Estates. There was a huge shortage of food grains and drinking water.[17] During this period, the primary school students' strength and trade and commerce came down.[18]

The ecological and cultural practices have also contributed to the spread of epidemic diseases. Pilgrims gathered at festival centres and they bathed and drank the 'holy' water from a temple tank or from the river and also carried it to their homes. Railway stations, temples and festival centres had caused the spread of cholera, for instance, the Panguni festival of Tamils at Palani in 1921, and the river Amravati contributed to spread the disease easily to human beings.[19] The festival at Puri in Orissa was a recognised source of cholera infection for the Ganjam district. In several cases, the disease was traced to pilgrims who returned from Puri.[20]

In the year 1924, there were 51,971 registered deaths, which was the highest recorded due to the failure of monsoon, decline in agricultural operations and crop failures and the onset of severe famine in many districts.[21] The canal drinking water quickly carried cholera in South India. Similarly, the festivals of Karaimadai, Boppukondapuram, Kapidi, and Agni-Nakshatram at Palani were the centres of infection and the disease spread rapidly over a large area, causing over 3,000 deaths within a few weeks. The Trichinopoly and Tanjore districts not having several days pipe water supply, coupled with heavy floods from Bhavani and Cauvery rivers, caused high mortality.[22] The outbreak of the disease was due to waves from the coastal regions.

Dr. C.I. Manikyam of Port Blair mentioned that high population, small houses, slum areas, lack of ventilation, and drinking water, living surrounding by open drainage, lack of bathing and toilets caused the spread of diseases. For instance, there was only one bathroom and one tap for every fifty families in Madras. So, the mortality cases of cholera from 1930-31 to 1939-40 were 1,81,512 in Madras Presidency.[23] T.G. Gopala Krishna Naidu, Assistant District Health Officer, Tanjore says, the use of agricultural muddy water flowing through canals consisted of chemicals, which were used during agricultural operations. In the delta area, people particularly the Harijans and other lower castes used the contaminated canal water for the purpose of bathing, cooking and drinking which resulted in the transmission of the cholera bacillus infecting thousands of people.[24]

There are cases of dissemination of cholera by the pilgrims returning from festivals like the Panguni Uttiram festival at Palni in Madura district, Madeswaram festival in Kollegal Taluk of Coimbatore district, Srisailam festival in Kurnool, Madura Kali Amman festival at Tottiyam and Samayapuram festival in Trichinopoly district. Similarly the Ceded and Krishna districts were also affected by cholera from dominions of the Nizam of Hyderabad.[25] During 1946-47, the administration made provision for protected water supply and also made provision for sanitary control over the production, distribution and sale of food.[26] Thus, the history of cholera reveals a devastating social impact.

Plague in South India

Plague was the most feared epidemic; it disturbed the ordinary life of people and economy of the country.[27] It is a 'deadly contagious disease' spreading rapidly over a wide geographical space. The pestilences, which are in rats, infect the human body and destroy the immunity system. For the first time in modern India, the plague broke out at Bombay in 1896, imported from Hong Kong by steamship. The epidemic appeared among the *Banias* (merchants), who were residing near the docks.[28] In the year 1894, more than one lakh and in 1896, the death toll was thirteen lakh people due to commercial relations with Hong Kong and *Bustees* and the slums of Calcutta proved to be ideal grounds for the fast spread of plague.[29] By 1899, it had appeared in many smaller towns and later spread into the countryside. The major port cities have links with commercial contacts across India. Once plague entered India, the prevailing pathetic sanitary conditions contributed to a large-scale disaster.[30]

Plague sometimes spreads directly as the bacillus was coughed out of diseased lungs and droplets caused infection in its pneumonia form. The common form of transmission of disease through the contaminated food grains, as the 'Black Rats' activity in the stored grains spread the great plague vector. Moreover, the fleas also carried plague bacilli, transmitted from the local black rats that ultimately transferred plague to humans as alternate hosts. The epidemiological connection between cholera and pilgrimage, Vibrio Cholera enters the body through the drinking water and sometimes through contaminated food. One of the principal modes of disease transmission was through the reservoirs and watercourses. The Hindu pilgrimage centres were the rapid communication to industrial, urban and rural areas. The indigenous and Western medicine failed to locate this epidemic in the larger system of public health.

The plague in South India broke out in August 1898 at Guntakal Junction in Ananthapur district of the Madras Presidency. It spread into many districts in South India. The modern transport contributed to the spread of plague.[31] It was reported that the trading classes like *Baniyas*, Marwaris and various travelling communities and traders brought the plague epidemic to South India. The Indian Plague Commission believed that plague was an air-borne contagion transmitted from the travellers to other human beings. The pneumonia plague transmitted directly through the release of the plague victim's sputum into the air, clothing or bedding or by human intake of plague bacilli through breathing or oral contact. From 1901 to 1920, the total deaths of plague was 1,74,192 due to infection from the passengers.[32] The system of issuing passport was used to enforce surveillance of contacts. For instance, at the inspection station of Jalarpet, 120 cases of plague-infected people were removed from trains.[33]

The crowding, bad town planning, poor sanitary arrangements, ill-ventilated houses, the ineffective and incomplete drainage systems failed to provide sanitation in the streets. Waste in the streets becomes 'Poisonous dust'. The inadequate funds and inadequate health management were other reasons for the spread of plague.[34] The unhygienic conditions and poisoned food grain materials were also responsible for the spread of epidemics.[35]

The period from 1917 to 1921, the seasons were unfavourable for agriculture. This created the shortage of food grains. So India imported poor quality of food grains from Burma and Bengal. It was a marked rise of epidemics.[36] The statistical data reveals that the average rainfall was decreased and several reports characterised the period from 1920 to 1947 as 'unhealthy'.[37] During this period, there was a lack of general water supply, protected vaccinations and environmental hygiene in the entire Indian subcontinent. After India's independence, the Indian government strictly implemented anti-plague measures. Consequently, the plague had almost disappeared in the whole of Madras State.[38]

Smallpox in Madras Presidency

The disease has been known from times immemorial. Smallpox is one of the oldest diseases in India, which first appeared in Europe in the 6th century AD, later it spread to America in 1527 through travellers and migrants.[39] European literature did not reflect much on this disease in India, nor did it form part of the 19th century literature on the diseases of warm climates. Smallpox is transmitted from the virus called "Variola". The nature of the disease is an acute contagious viral infection. Those who were severely infected with the symptoms of the disease usually die, while those who escaped death were likely to be disfigured or incapacitated for the rest of their lives.[40] The source of infection is man, spreads from patient with acute infection. The infection spreads by air through suspended droplets. Direct contact, fomites and flies also play their part in its spread. Smallpox virus remains alive for months in scabs.

In South India, the incident of smallpox increases with termination of the monsoon and decreases with onset of the monsoon. It is maximum during the months of January to April and minimum during the months of the monsoon, i.e. July to September. Apart from atmospheric conditions, social and cultural aspects also act favourably for the spread of smallpox virus. Pilgrim centres, popular religious fairs and marriage festivities were the travel points. The social mobility during these activities makes contact easy. During famines, people wander in search of food and often congregate in relief camps and the towns with famine were easy prey for the transmission and spread of smallpox and other diseases. This shows the close relation between the environment and disease.[41]

In 1916-17, the epidemic was present in all the districts and became a 'tropical disease' after the First World War. The disease diverted attention towards its very different cultural context in India.[42] The goddess Mariamma was linked to many diseases. The disease also showed a striking seasonality. The virus was more active and more readily transmissible in dry weather than in the wet season. The spring months were traditionally a time for congregation and travel. During 1920-29, wherein the total mortality for the decade was 1,46,256, when compared to the previous two decades (1900-20), i.e. 4,31,009 in the entire Madras Presidency. Sir George Newman, the Chief Medical Officer has clearly established the fact that 'Alastrim' or as it is sometimes called 'Pseudo-Smallpox' or 'Para-Smallpox' etc., is really a mild form of smallpox was prevalent in South India.[43] The indigenous traditional or folk practitioners did not engage with Western medicine and on the other hand there was discontent over the intervention of other forms of Western medical practices. The Indians perceived vaccination as a cultural intrusion by the foreign rule and the deep-seated fear and suspension contributed to popular opposition and apathy. The state seems to have failed in demonstrating its willingness to provide adequate financial resources and administrative commitment necessary for an effective control of smallpox. In rural areas, the peasants would refuse the operations of vaccination, because of prolonged illness and opposition of local communities. Often the unscientific production of vaccine and the poor preservation and purification of it had caused mortality from various diseases. So, the number of deaths from smallpox in different age groups from 1930 to 1941 was 75,958 and from 1942 to 1947, the total deaths were 1,07,126. The expansion of urbanisation also created drainage problems and polluted the environment. While the social and environment disruption promoted epidemics.[44]

Western Medicine and Colonial Response

The 20th century has seen the extraordinary improvements made in human health care and life expectancy has vastly improved. Moreover, major famines and epidemics mortality have been controlled due to the rapid and dazzling progress made in medical technology such as new medical drugs, investigative techniques and their increasing access to the population on a larger scale. As part of the medical institutional developments, an early hospital was opened by the British at Madras in 1664 and enlarged in 1679 for the treatment of soldiers in the fort. The second hospital at Madras was built in 1679-88 and the third hospital established in 1690 at James Street in the Fort. The Madras General Hospital was set up in 1772. The earliest mofussil hospitals in the Madras Presidency were set up in 1842.[45] In 1761, the Army Medical Department was established in India for providing services to British troops. In 1798, Edward Jenner discovered the cowpox inoculation method for smallpox. A lunatic asylum at Madras was opened in 1794 for mentally ill patients. Many hospitals and dispensaries were established at district headquarters. The establishment of all the medical institutions like State, Railway, Police, Local and Municipal including Aided and Unaided hospitals in Madras Presidency for the year 1901 was 579 hospitals and 637 in 1910. The total number of patients treated from 1900 to 1910 was 5,95,04,521. In 1921 to 1930, all types of hospitals treated 17,03,330 in-patients and 9,87,77,878 out-patients in Madras Presidency.[46] The vaccine operations from 1865 to 1883 was 82,46,952 [47] and 1929-30 were 21,39,321 and 39,93,703 in 1938-39 in Madras Presidency.[48] Over a period of time, Western medicine became more advanced and scientific. It also proclaimed that Western medicine was universally accepted, although a large majority of Indians accepted it with slight passive resistance. Slowly Western medicine gained in prestige and popularity.

The colonial government introduced the inoculation, vaccination methods, and established various hospitals and dispensaries and medical research institutions. In case of smallpox, the introduction of vaccination was enforced. The King Institute of Preventive Medicine, Guindy, and Haffkins Institute, Bombay prepared and supplied the vaccines. In some cases, successful results were obtained from prophylactic vaccine treatment for cholera. Along with vaccination, the government had implemented cheap chlorination and a practical system of sterilisation all over the Madras Presidency. The use of *Permanganate of Potash* provided some protection to the wells. The new equipment with Horrocks Box was supplied to every District Health Officer for the protection of plague.[49]

The doctors initiated measures like Hankinisation of drinking water-supplies and their subsequent protection from contamination, isolation of infected patients, and wider distribution of medicines, etc. In a few cases, Sir Leonard Roger's method of treatment by saline injection was also attempted with good results. The government had taken steps to improve the sanitary condition at the pilgrim centres, supporting pure drinking water and improvement of conservancy especially in the collection and disposal of night soil. Precautions were taken in maintaining food hygiene, medical arrangements and propaganda work at the pilgrim centres.[50] During 1928-1929, the government initiated the study of water supply filter station at Kilpauk and Hydrogenion.[51] The investigation was done in the Cauvery-Mettur Project area. The experimental work was carried out by Colonel Russell, I.M.S., for better vaccines. During the year 1929, the total number of inoculations done were 1,51,000, with the ordinary Anti-Cholera Vaccine (subcutaneous), in addition to farmers, 21,000 persons were protected with Bili-Vaccine. In 1928, action was taken to combat cholera in municipal areas with an insistence on strict implementation of the District Municipal Act and preventive works.[52]

The vaccination was undertaken as a preventive method in non-panchayat areas. The government introduced various 'Honorary Schemes' for the improvement of health.[53] The inoculation programme, introduction of preventive medicines like bacteriophage, initiations in introducing safe drinking water, sanitation, vigil of fairs and '*melas*', etc., have brought down the mortality of population from epidemics.[54] Apart from inoculation, the government sanctioned grants for the improvement of public health through local bodies. In 1937-38, the grant of Rs. 15,80,300, provided under loans and advances of Rs. 5,90,300, and Rs. 4,68,580 were sanctioned for rural health and safe drinking water as well as drainage schemes.[55] A comprehensive scheme of water supply for rural areas in all parts of the Presidency was also prepared in 1937-38, the government allotted a sum of Rs.10,800 through district collectors.[56]

The colonial government established a permanent Public Health Laboratory in the Madras province, and training was given to all rural medical practitioners. The strength of health staff was increased in epidemic areas.[57] The government had done 17,12,084 anti-cholera inoculations in 1937. The Madras

Public Health Act of 1939 was extended to non-municipal areas.[58] As a result, the mortality came down to the lowest on record in 1939-40 compared to the past 58 years record.[59] The colonial government increased public expenditure on setting up of a few laboratories in different parts of the country, for instance a Central Research Institute at Kasauli was established for the production of vaccine and sera.[60]

The government imposed several restrictions on issuing passports for travelling on accepted routes only. The military also participated in health campaigns. It reduced the transmission of diseases such as cholera and plague.[61] During 1917-21, the number of rats caught and destroyed was 46,985, making a total of 26,23,486 since the beginning of the operations in July 1898. The fumigation experiments in Cumbum Valley achieved good results in case of plague, so it was extended to the rural parts of Bellary and other districts.[62] In 1938, only a single death from plague was registered in Bellary district, and this has synchronised with the fall in the rat population in five villages due to gas fumigation. But in areas where gas fumigation was not taken up, the incidence of plague mortality was reported. As a result, several villages were fumigated with cynogas and special attention was paid to the bionomics of fleas and the destruction of rats and fleas in thatched roofs. In other parts of the Presidency, vigorous preventive measures including inoculation, evacuation, sun disinfection and rat-destruction kept the epidemic under control.[63]

Dr. Chitre initiated experiments to test immunity to plague in rats from different regions. An accurately measured test dose of 'B-Pestis' was used for this experiment. This investigation had shown that the percentage of deaths from plague had been decreased.[64] The total of 84,243 anti-plague inoculations was performed during 1935-36. Cynogas fumigation of rat burrows was carried out extensively, with great success and encouraged local bodies to adopt this method strictly.[65]

A new scheme was also sanctioned for starting a temporary hospital in the Cumbum Valley for experimenting with the use of the anti-plague serum of the Haffkine Institute, Bombay, in treating the cases of plague infection.[66] To control the spread of plague, the Government of Madras has taken up the 'Fumigated with Cynogas Scheme' in several parts of the Presidency. As a result, in 1939, the mortality from plague was recorded the lowest ever since 1898. There were 324 deaths during the year and only five municipalities were affected with a total death roll of seven. The remarkable reduction in the incidence of disease could be ascribed to the cynogas fumigation method.[67]

The practice of inoculation against smallpox was practised in India since ancient times. In 1731, Coult has given an account of this inoculation and called it '*Tikah*'. It was also practised in the Madras Presidency where Mariamma replaced Sitala as the goddess of smallpox. The introduction of Jennerian vaccination in India in 1802 was a landmark in the history of smallpox measures. Though, the colonial state did not invest enough resources in evolving a system of preventive and disease management and therefore the vaccination in Bengal, Bombay and Madras Presidencies turned out to be a slow and prolonged process. The system of vaccination providing temporary relief from various diseases became an active system of prevention in the 20th century. The government adopted several policies, for instance, the establishment of the Vaccine Institute at Belgaum in 1907, which manufactured two hundred thousand doses of calf vaccine by 1911; the King Institute of Preventive Medicine, Guindy supplied vaccine, but that was not sufficient due to the prevalence of many diseases, and lack of facilities for the preservation of lymph.[68]

After 1925, the extension of compulsory vaccination throughout the Madras Presidency and the enforcement of the smallpox rules and regulations were strictly implemented. The government appointed sufficient staff for the maintenance of correct records.[69] As a result, the mortality from smallpox after 1934 was in decline due to the intensive vaccination and re-vaccination campaigns carried out in the epidemic areas. Similarly continuous propaganda work was done and informed the public in matters pertaining to the prevention of the diseases.[70]

Re-vaccination was carried out from time to time with as

much care, promptness and attention, as are bestowed in the case of infantile and primary vaccination. Infantile vaccination was followed by re-vaccination before school age and again between ten and twenty years of age.[71] In 1944, the total number of vaccinations was 8.03 (4.64) millions which was a record number, showing an increase of over three millions under re-vaccinations. In the rural areas the peasants would refuse the operations of vaccination, because of prolonged illness and opposition of local communities. But the health propaganda methods created more awareness on health-related issues. Natural causes like shortage of rains, famines, floods, hail storms and crop diseases, were largely responsible for heavy toll of human life.[72]

The Western medicine and public health policies were introduced for the sole benefit of European civilians and the military needs in the beginning, later it extended to the Indian public, for instance, inoculations, the vaccination, the hospitals and dispensaries brought about a change in its policy in the early 20th century. The indigenous traditional practitioners did not engage with Western medicine and on the other hand there was discontent over the intervention of other forms of Western medical practices. The lack of funds, administrative causes and environmental conditions did not support to eradicate the diseases permanently. In the 20th century there appears to be a marked shift in the preparation of their responsibility or duty to provide medical and health facilities to the whole country. The characterising of the 20th century in colonial India as an '*Age of Epidemic Diseases*' may not be an exaggeration, as the overall history demonstrates a half-hearted attempt by the colonial state in intervening and controlling the epidemic diseases. The colonial states had a negative impact on the system of public health, as the state failed to see the larger causative factors.

REFERENCES

1. Mridula Ramana, *Western Medicine and Public Health in Colonial Bombay, 1845-1895*, Orient Longman, New Delhi, 2002, p. 125.

2. O.P. Jaggi, *Western Medicine in India: Epidemics and Other Tropical Diseases*, Vol. XII, Atma Ram & Sons, Delhi, 1981.
3. Monica Das Gupta, 'Public Health in India: Dangerous Neglect', *EPW*, Vol. 40, No. 49, 2005, p. 5160.
4. David Arnold and Ramachandra Guha (eds.), *Nature, Culture, Imperialism: Essays on the Environmental History of South Asia*, OUP, Dehli, 1996, pp. 1-20.
5. Kevin M. Cahill, *Tropical Diseases: A Hand Book for Practitioners*, Octopus Books Limited, London, 1975, pp. 136-137.
6. *The Arogya Prakasika*, (1920-25 file), pp. 583-584.
7. David Arnold, 'Cholera and Colonialism in British India', *Past and Present*, No. 110-113, 1986, p. 124.
8. Sheldon Watts, 'History of Medicine: Michael Furnell's Crusade Against the Local Influences Theory of Cholera,' *Journal of Ethics*, Vol. II, July 2009, pp. 541-543.
9. Ira Klein, 'Imperialism, Ecology and Disease: Cholera in India, 1850-1950', *IESHR*, No. 4, 1994, p. 497.
10. *Report of the Census of the Madras Presidency 1871*, Government Press, Madras, 1784, p. 2.
11. *Annual Report of the Sanitary Commissioner for Madras, 1877 and 1880*, Government Press, Madras, pp. 12-16; and *The Review of the Madras Famine, 1876-1878*, Government Press, Madras, 1881, p. 125.
12. *Indian Famine Charitable Relief Fund*, Madras Branch, December 21, 1897, Madras, pp.1-24; *Madras Provincial Committee: Report on the Operations of the Executive Committee*, Madras, 1897.
13. *Various Reports on the Administration of the Madras Presidency for the Years of 1901 to 1910*, Government Press, Madras.
14. Achanta Lakshmi Pathi, *Autobiography*, 1973, pp. 137-138.
15. A.J.H. Russell, *A Statistical Approach to the Epidemiology of Cholera in Madras Presidency, Proceedings of the National Academy of Sciences of the United States of America*, Vol. II, No. 10, October 15, 1925, pp. 653-657.
16. Michelle Burge McAlpin, 'Death, Famine and Risk: The Changing Impact of Failures in Western India 1870-1920,' *The Journal of Economic History*, Vol. 39, 1979, pp. 145-157.
17. *Andhra Patrika*, February 15, 1921.
18. *Andhra Patrika*, January 21-22, 1921.
19. G.O. No. 764, P.H., June 1, 1922, pp. 1-7.
20. *The Sixtieth Annual Report of the Director of Public Health and the Thirty-Fourth Annual Report of the Sanitary Engineer, Madras, 1923*, Government Press, Madras, 1924, pp. 14-16.

21. *Sixty-First Annual Report of the Director of Public Health, Madras, 1924*, Government Press, Madras, 1925, pp. 12-16.
22. G.O. No. 1039 P.H. June 22, 1926, p. 1.
23. *Annual Report of the Director of Public Health, Madras for 1938*, Government Press, Madras, 1939, p. 11.
24. *The Arogya Prakasika*, September 1936, pp. 91-93.
25. *Annual Report of the Director of Public Health for 1937*, Government Press, Madras, 1938, pp. 10-11.
26 O.P. Jaggi, *Western Medicine in India: Public Health and its Administration*, Atma Ram & Sons, Delhi, 1979, pp. 136-142.
27. Ira Klein, 'Plague Policy and Popular Unrest in British India', *Modern Asian Studies*, Vol. 22, 1998, p. 724.
28. O.P. Jaggi, *Western Medicine in India: Epidemics and Other Tropical Diseases*, Vol. 12, Atma Ram & Sons, Delhi, 1979, p. 91.
29. G.C. Cook, 'Plague: Past and Future Implications for India', *The Journal of the Society of Public Health*, Vol. 109, 1995, p. 7.
30. David Arnold (ed.), *Imperial Medicine and Indigenous Societies*, OUP, 1989, Delhi, p. 149.
31. Ira Klein, op. cit., pp. 737-44.
32. *The Arogya Prakasika*, May 1929, p. 15.
33. *The Thirty-Eighth Annual Report of the Sanitary Commissioner, Madras, 1901*, Judicial and Administration Statistics of British India, XIII, Vital Statistics, p. 217.
34. *Report of the Madras Drainage Committee*, Government of Madras, 1913, pp. 15-19.
35. *The Proceedings of the Second all India Sanitary Conference held at Madras from November 11 to 16, 1912*, Vol. II, *Hygiene*, Government Central Branch Press, Simla, 1913, pp. 290-96.
36. *Report on the Administration of the Madras Presidency for the Year 1919-1920*, Government Press, Madras, 1921, pp. 11, 92.
37. *The Sixty-First Annual Report of the Director of Public Health*, Government Press Madras, 1924, pp. 17-19.
38. *Madras Administration Report 1952-53*, Part I, Government Press, Madras, 1954, p. 43.
39. *The Andhra Vaidya Patrika*, 1932, pp. 6-8.
40. David Arnold, *Colonizing the Body*, pp. 116-133.
41. David Arnold (ed.), *Imperial Medicine and Indigenous Societies*, OUP, Delhi, 1989, pp. 46-48.
42. David Arnold, *Colonizing the Body*, pp. 133-134.
43. David Arnold, *Imperial Medicine and Indigenous Societies*, pp. 46-48.
44. *Madras Administration Report 1939-40*, Part II, Government Press, Madras, 1940, pp. 79-86.

45. *The Madras Year Book 1923 With an Official, Commercial and General Directory of the Madras Presidency*, First Issue, Government Press, Madras, 1923, p.134
46. *Annual Returns of the Civil Hospitals and Dispensaries in the Madras Presidency for Subsequent Years from 1900 to 1930*, Government Press, Madras.
47. C.D. Maclean, *The Manual of the Administration of the Madras Presidency*, Vol. I, Asian Educational Service, New Delhi, 1987, p. 516.
48. *Annual Report of the Director of Public Health, Madras, for 1938*, Government Press, Madras, 1939, p. 34.
49. G.O. No. 1951, P.H., September 21, 1925, p. 1.
50. G.O. No. 312, P.H., February 9, 1928, pp. 1-3.
51. G.O. No: 244, P.H., January 25, 1929, pp. 1-2.
52. G.O. No. 1604, P.H., August 9, 1928, pp. 1-6.
53. V.R. Muraleedharan, 'Professionalizing Medical Practice in Colonial South India,' *EPW*, Vol. 27, January 25, 1992, pp. 27-30.
54. *Andhra Patrika*, May 9, 1935, p. 5.
55. G.O. No. 2825, October 28, 1937, pp. 1-3 (Education and Public Health Department).
56. G.O. No. 3216, November 24, 1937, pp. 1-3 (Education and Public Health Department).
57. *Annual Report of the Director of Public Health, Madras for 1938*, Government Press, Madras, 1939, pp. 11-12.
58. *Annual Report of the Director of Public Health for 1937*, Government Press, Madras, 1938, pp. 10-11.
59. G.O. No. 581, February 17, 1942, pp. 1-3.
60. Anil Kumar, *Medicine and the Raj*, pp. 203-204.
61. *Madras Plague Proceedings*, 1905 and Ira Klein, op. cit., p. 746.
62. *Report on the Administration of the Madras Presidency for the Year 1933-34*, Government Press, Madras, 1935, p. 157.
63. *Report on the Administration of the Madras Presidency for the Year 1934-35*, Government Press, Madras, 1936, p. 170.
64. *Annual Report of the Public Health Commissioner with the Government of India for 1934*, Vol. I, with Appendices, Government of India, New Delhi, 1936, p. 197.
65. *Madras Administration Report 1935-36*, Part II, Government Press, Madras, 1937, pp. 173-174.
66. G.O. No. 2916 (Public Health), August 16, 1939, p. 5.
67. *Madras Administration Report 1939-40*, Part II, Government Press, Madras, 1939, pp. 79-80.
68. David Arnold (ed.), *Imperial Medicine and Indigenous Societies*,

pp. 52-62 and 155.

69. *Report on Vaccination in the Madras Presidency for the Triennium Ending 1925-1926*, Government Press, Madras, 1926, pp. 1-12.
70. G.O. No. 2717, P.H., October 28, 1930.
71. *Annual Report of the Director of Public Health Madras for 1938*, Government Press, Madras, 1939, pp. 13-14.
72. *Madras Administration Report 1944-45*, Part II, Government Press, Madras, 1946, pp. 117-121.

14

Malaria and Ecology in Northeast India: A Review

Nitish Mondal

Introduction

Malaria is one of the foremost public health issues which impose a great threat on humanity. It is estimated that a total of half the world's populations (3.4 billion people), residing in 104 tropical and subtropical countries are considered to be at major risk of malaria endemic[1] of which a total of 2.57 billion individuals are at risk for *Plasmodium falciparum* (*P. falciparum*) and 2.5 billion cases were caused due to *P. vivax*.[2] Out of which the vast majority of cases have been reported from Africa (85.5%), followed by Southeast Asia (10.0%) and the Eastern Mediterranean Regions (4.0%). The Southeast Asia region contributed a total of 2.50 million reported cases to the global burden, where India alone contributed 76% of the total cases of malaria.[3, 4] The prevalence of malaria is one of the common parasitic infections in India, causes insurmountable problems in many parts of the country.[5] According to the National Vector Borne Disease Control Programme (NVBDC) survey, around 1.50 million cases of malaria are reported from India. Annually, the total mortality caused by malaria was recorded to be 30,014 to 48,660 cases in India. Generally, a total of four species of the *Plasmodium* parasite such as *P. falciparum*, *P. vivax*, *P. malariae* and *P. ovale* cause malaria. Severe malaria cases have been associated with *P. falciparum* which causes the highest morbidity and mortality in India. According to the NVBDC Programme, the total number of 2,79,381 million malaria cases reported in

2011 and 6,43,496 million of them were caused by *P. falciparum*.

The proportion of *P. falciparum* and *P. vivax* varies in various parts of India. The trend and prevalence of positive cases and malaria caused due to *P. falciparum* in India is shown in Figure 1. Historically, the *P. vivax* has been found to be the major malaria causing species in India, but over the past several years the *P. vivax* infections have been significantly decreased, and the ratio of *P. falciparum* versus *P. vivax* malaria (i.e. 0.41, in 1985), gradually increasing (i.e. 0.60 by 1995), and reached 1.01 by 2010.[6,7] Moreover, the recent studies have clearly suggested that the incidence of malaria is between 9 to 50 times greater than actual reported cases, and with an approximately 13-times underestimation of malaria-related mortalities and morbidities in the populations in India.[8]

Occurrences of Malaria

The prevalence of malaria cases are reported throughout the year in India. The expansive geographic distribution and diverse climates provides the ideal environments for the development and sustaining malaria vectors and parasites in India.[5,9] Seasonal variations of malaria prevalence was also reported, where during the monsoon season malaria cases were found to be greater reported as compared to the winter season. During the rainy season more breeding grounds are created and the environmental factors like rainfall directly or indirectly affect the abundance of breeding sites and also the physiology of the vectors.[10] Malaria parasites cease to develop in the mosquito when the temperature is below 16°C-30°C represents an optimal range for most malaria vectors. Humidity over 60% is optimal and within limits the longevity of adult vectors increases with the relative humidity of the air. The transmission is seasonal with increased intensity related to rain and the region is highly receptive to malaria transmission owing to excessive and prolonged rainfall (2–3 metres) promoting vector breeding and longevity due to high humidity (60–90%) and warmer climates (22–33°C) for most of the year. Both *P. falciparum* and *P. vivax* occur in abundance, but *P. falciparum* (the killer parasite) accounts for more than 60% of cases.[10,11] the disease outbreaks characterised by enhanced morbidity are annual events that take a heavy toll on human lives amidst public chaos and panic and the transmission of the malaria pathogen is persistent and is estimated to be low to moderate, maintained mostly by *Anopheles minimus (An. minimus)*, and the other vectors are *An. dirus* and *An. Fluviatilis.*[10,12] The malaria transmission is persistent in the north-eastern region of India and high incidences have been recorded during the months of May to September.[10] The acceleration in the malaria prevalence during this period is due to a sharp increase of the potential malaria vector (i.e. A. minimus) in the region.[10]

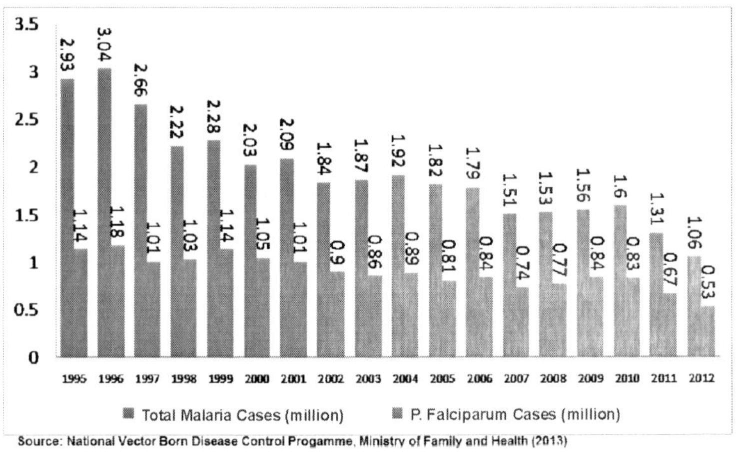

Figure 1: Epidemiological Indicators for Malaria Prevalence in India

The present situation of malaria in India is best described as a malaria endemic country with >95% of the populations at risk of malaria. Reported cases of malaria varies from 1.8 to 2.0 million (1.2 million in 2006) and 1,000 deaths per year. The World Health Organisation (WHO SEARO) estimates that a total of 15 million cases and 19,500 deaths, whereas WHO has estimated a total of 70 million malaria cases.[1] The proportion of *P. vivax* and *P. falciparum* is found to be almost equal but it varies greatly from region to region and seasonally. *P. falciparum* is a killer parasite and it has become resistant to chloroquine with reports of resistance to other anti-malarial drugs. *P. vivax* is sensitive to chloroquine but in the last decade resistance to chloroquine has been reported from a few places in the country.[13] The total number of cases and the percentage of the *P. falciparum* are rising as a result of fall in *P. vivax* in India. Therefore, the prevalence and transmission of malaria in the north-eastern states of India are a daunting epidemiological challenge as its distributions are heterogeneous and intensity are governed by several climatic, physiological and socio-economic risk factors. Therefore, these regions provide the ideal ecological conditions for malaria transmission with undulating uplands intersected by the forested hills, rivers and widely practised 'Jhum' (slash and burn) cultivation land. The area is generally characterised by tropical, humid climate conditions and heavy rainfall during May to September with an average annual rainfall under the influence of the southwest monsoon.[11] Moreover, given its geographical contours and existence of international boundaries the north-eastern states are more vulnerable to high malaria transmissions and the migration of people across the border have led to persistence of malaria in villages near the border. Therefore, this chapter evaluates the existence of heterogeneity, variability, mortality and morbidities and transmission of malaria risks in the diverse ecological niches of northeast India. The scope and challenges in the improvement of several coping strategies, accessibility to health services, improved surveillance and forecasting technology capacities in the vulnerable populations have also been evaluated and argued in relation to malaria prevalence.

Burden of Malaria in Different States of India

India is a tropical country having distinct geo-climatic regions, rich bio-diversity and being the second largest populous country has many of the epidemics which severely affect the public health conditions and causes an enormous economic burden. Malaria being one such vector-born disease its transmission varies with geographic distributions, as the diversity and distribution of Anopheline and Plasmodium species varies significantly across the regions,[14] and the high transmission regions are chiefly distributed in parts of Odisha, Jharkhand, Chhattisgarh, Maharashtra, Madhya Pradesh, West Bengal and Uttar Pradesh. In 2001, India had a population of 1.02 billion with 2.1 million malaria positive cases were with a very high mortality cases.[14] The population of north-eastern states was 39 million, i.e. 3.96% of the country's population. Of the total burden of malaria in India, north-eastern states contribute 10% malaria and 11% *P. falciparum* cases and 20.0% malaria deaths. In the north-eastern region malaria vectors are *An. minimus* (perennial species), *An. baimaii* (monsoon species), and *An. fluviatilis* (winter species). These mosquito species are highly efficient in the transmission of malaria.[12,15] Northeast India has a high risk area for the occurrence of malaria transmission due to several ecological paradigms like tribal malaria, forest malaria and project malaria. The prevalence and the caused mortality of malaria in the north-eastern states are described in Figure 2.

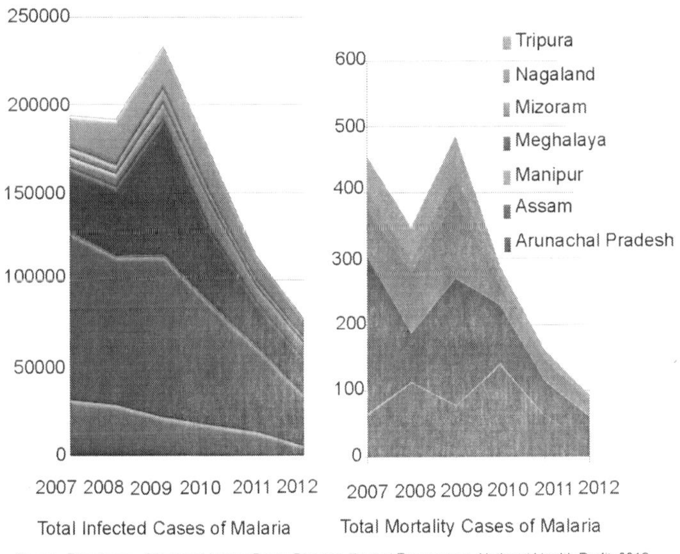

Figure 2: Prevalence of Total Number of Malaria Prevalence and Morality Cases in Northeast India

Malaria transmission in the north-eastern states of India is a daunting epidemiological challenge as its distributions are heterogeneous and intensity is governed by many climatic, environmental and physiological risk factors.[10,16] The *P. vivax* is found to be the major malaria parasite in the Indian subcontinent contributing to the majority of cases.[13] However in the northeast region, the situation is different where a total of 60.0% malaria cases are caused by *P. falciparum.*[17,18] The major vector species include *An. dirus, An. minimus* and *An. fluviatilis* considered to be the prominent vectors responsible for transmission of the disease in these states of north-east India.[19,20] The malaria transmission is perennial and focal outbreaks are common due to the favourable environment to the vectors' survival and proliferation throughout the year.[9.18,19] The north-eastern states of India, the existing literature generally suggested to be the prevalence of malaria has been largely restricted to the population living in poverty, poor socio-economic and nutritionally vulnerable segments.[20,21] A very high prevalence was observed in all the tea estates indicates that the parasitic load is significantly greater and malaria transmission continuous without interruptions. Therefore, the people basically engaged in socio-economically deprived regions that contribute to most malaria cases every year could be given a significant priority in order to strengthen the control programmes in the region.[21]

Age and Sex Specific Prevalence of Malaria Prevalence

The prevalence studies were conducted to identify the malaria disease outbreaks and/or epidemic investigations in India. There is very limited information on the age, sex and population specific seasonal variation on the prevalence of malaria in different paradigms in the country. Several studies have reported that tribal populations are found to be more vulnerable in malaria prevalence in India.[22,23] The greater malaria exposures were reported among the tribal populations residing in the forest ecological niches.[23,24] The individuals or populations working in the tea garden regions in the north-eastern Indian states were found to have significantly greater risk factors to suffer from malaria.[10,12] The comparison of the populations suggested that the prevalence of malaria was found to be relatively lower among non-tribal than tribal populations in north-east India.[25,26] Poor socio-economic conditions and socio-cultural factors play an important role in maintaining a high degree of malaria transmissions.[24,25] However, increasing socio-economic status has shown decreasing prevalence of malaria transmission in Indian populations.[27] The burden is generally significantly higher in males than females in all age groups. Several studies have shown that children in the states including Assam and Arunachal Pradesh are found to have greater prevalence of malaria than adults. There was no sex-specific reservation, and both sexes are significantly equally affected by the malaria infections. Several research studies have already reported similar findings in populations.[6,10] The males have generally more risk of acquiring the malaria infection due to maximum outdoor activities.[18] The prevalence of malaria has shown a significant reduction in the north-eastern states, where less than 20.0% of malaria endemic communities are reported to be asymptomatic cases.[27,28] Apparently, inadequate interventions against the parasite reservoir in the communities facilitate the year-round malaria transmission and the associated risks are assessed to be much greater in vector dense areas in northeast India.[25]

Effect of Environment on Malaria Prevalence

It is estimated that over a total of 650 million people depended on climate-sensitive sectors, livelihood and over 973 million people are exposed to several vector-borne malaria parasite diseases in India.[29] The projection of climatic factors indicates a wider exposure to malaria for the Indian population in the near future.[29,30] The climate change has surfaced as a new threat and poses a major challenge for ongoing efforts to contain vector-borne diseases in India.[18,31] The current trend suggested that the seasonal occurrence of malarial vectors in north-east India, were mostly abundant during the monsoon season.[5,10] Moreover, the seasonal abundance pattern of the malarial vector was found to vary in the forests in relation to different habitats.[9,10] The daily temperature and relative humidity model analysis showed that Orissa, West Bengal and southern parts of Assam will still remain malaria prone and the transmission windows will open up in Himachal Pradesh and the north-eastern states.[18,31] An alarming rate of deforestation has been reported in north-eastern states in India.[31] Furthermore, almost half of the populations are reported to be at risk of the malaria prevalence which resides in forest ecological niches and provides hot beds of malaria transmissions.[9,32] The dense forests areas often lack infrastructure and residents of tribal populations with distinct genetic traits, socio-cultural beliefs and practices are affected by the transmission dynamics of malaria.[9] There was higher seasonality of concentration of malaria transmission in the forest areas than non-forest regions as reported in north-eastern states (e.g. Assam).[32]

The Problem of Insecticide Resistant Vectors

Malaria epidemics have become a common public health problem and caused more devastation. The recent past decades have encountered several endemic in Indian populations. The development of insecticide resistance in malaria vectors has been a major problem for achieving effective vector control.[33] The major vector of malaria *An. culicifacies* responsible for generating 65.0% malaria cases has developed resistance to dichloro-diphenyl-trichloroethane (DDT) and Malathion.[34] Synthetic pyrethroids are being sprayed to control the emerging epidemics. Multiple insecticide resistant mosquito strains have emerged so that malaria control is attainable partially, if at all. Malaria returns year after year requiring spraying, but due to limited resources spraying is carried out in 10.0% endemic population. Malaria vectors are susceptible to DDT, Malathion and Synthetic Pyrethroids but because of the exophilic and or exophagic vectors behaviour they avoid resting on the sprayed walls, and thus avoid the killing action of insecticides. Several studies have also reported recent information on the levels of resistance to DDT and insecticides (e.g. dieldrin, deltamethrin in mosquito populations of north-eastern India.[34,35] The

Anopheles sp is found to be resistant to DDT and dieldrin and susceptible to malathion and synthetic pyrethorides in most parts of India.[36,37] Differences in insecticide resistance status were also observed between insecticides (e.g. DDT) and malaria cause vector species of Assam.[24,38] The DDT resistant types of vectors were also reported from the Garo hills of Meghalaya.[39]

The Burden of Drug Resistant Malaria

The current trends have suggested that the emergence and widespread of malaria parasites which are resistant to several available anti-malarial drugs are, therefore, considered to be a major cause for concern in the populations. The recent reports have suggested that the anti-malarial drug resistance of *P. falciparum* in India has historically travelled from the north-eastern region of India along the Myanmar border.[11] It is evident that in 1973, the chloroquine resistance in *P. falciparum* was first reported from Manjha in Karbi Anglong district,[40] and then several incidents were reported from Nowgaon district in 1974 in the north-eastern state of Assam, India.[41] More cases were then identified in next 3 to 4 years from the several districts of Assam, Arunachal Pradesh, Mizoram and Nagaland.[18,42,43] Although, the resistance to chloroquine is present in the entire country the problem is more pronounced in areas with intense P. *falciparum* transmission like the north-eastern states and Orissa where there is intermixing of population like project areas including construction sites and several urban, suburban habitats and along international borders. In most of the studies, only late treatment failure to chloroquine has been observed probably because of semi-immune nature of the population. Although the available data on sulfadoxine pyrimethamine resistance is limited and it appears that the efficacy of this drug is within acceptable limits except in limited areas like the Indo-Myanmar border in Arunachal Pradesh and some parts of Assam.[44,45] and Tripura.[18] The situation is further complicated by a high proportion of *P. falciparum* (more than 60.0% cases), a killer parasite that has become multi-drug resistant.[19,46]

Problems in Malaria Control

Malaria transmission is found to be a dynamic process and it involves several inter-related determinant factors, from unmanageable natural environmental conditions to several man-made disturbances to nature.[9] Several material and non-material factors such as unusual climatic conditions, inadequate surveillance, unsatisfactory laboratory services and inadequate indoor residual insecticide spray were instrumental for the outbreaks in the north-eastern regions.[47,48] The prevalence of malaria as well as mosquito densities in different clusters of the malaria affected villages was inversely related to the distance from the forest areas in north-east India.[9,48] It is generally accepted that the abundance of forests generally serve as hotbeds of malaria transmission. Therefore they provide conditions such as forest ecological niches, temperature, rainfall and humidity conditions that are found to be conducive to distribution, transmission and the survival of the malaria vectors in tropical and sub-tropical regions.[9] Similarly, the variation season and types of malaria vectors (e.g. terrestrial and forest) also creates major difficulties in the malaria control. The insufficient efforts to detect cases early and institute treatment in the malaria affected areas are the possible reasons for the occurrences of greater prevalence and increase prevalence of mortality and morbidity of malaria in the north-eastern region.[49] Although, several studies have shown that there is abundance and wide prevalence of positive vectors species and they were found to have the insecticides (e.g. DDT) resistance types in north-east India.[37,39,40] Studies have reported that there is a significant occurrence of mono and multi-drug resistant malaria parasites causes and increases the mortality and morbidity of malaria in the north-eastern states of India.[18,42,46] The incidence showed a very high proportion of DDT and malathion resistant variety of vectors.[50] The international borders encourage cross-border malaria transmissions.[10,49] The environmental conditions of the north-eastern states are found to be highly receptive for malaria transmissions.[10] Owing to the diverse geo-physical conditions, the north-eastern regions of India have varied ecological diversities, inaccessible areas, where vector control measures as well early treatment and diagnosis facilities are difficult to assess and implement, as a manifestation, the malaria control remains a challenge in these areas.[11] The administrative and socio-economic problems are also hampering the successful malaria control in the north-eastern states of India.[49]

Knowledge, Coping Strategies, Accessibility to Health Services

The knowledge regarding transmissions of malaria, self-prevention and treatment seeking behaviours are still found unsatisfactory among the tribal and non-tribal communities in India.[24,26,27,51] However, the comparison studies have clearly shown that the tribal populations residing in the urban habitats are found to have better knowledge regarding diagnosis of malaria transmission and prevention of mosquito breeding than their rural counterparts.[26,27] Sharma et al.[52] reported that sex (e.g. female), illiteracy and tribal population were more likely to have been associated with wrong beliefs about fatality of malaria. Several researchers have already reported that a sizable proportion of the populations still had misconceptions and hence appropriate communication strategies should be developed.[52,53] However, the tribal population adherence to anti-malarial medications is found to be significantly poor, inadequate prevention, with low-density and inconsistent use of preventive measures were also reported.[54] The community level study has clearly shown that knowledge, literacy, ethnic (e.g. tribal) and gender (e.g. male) have a significant effect to suffer from malaria in Assam[27] and Tripura[22] of the north-eastern states of India. However, the poor knowledge about the new strategies of insecticide treated bed nets are also significantly absent among the populations residing in the malaria risks areas in India.[52]

The research findings have clearly shown that the proper knowledge about the malaria transmission has reduced the vector breading in the population.[10,49] The innovative approaches for promoting the use of insecticide treated nets and long lasting insecticide treated bed nets strengthen effective implementation of new policies.[55] The researchers have already proposed that the supervision and monitoring will be strengthened by deployment of Malarial Technical Supervisors and Vector Borne Diseases consultants at district level of the malaria prone areas of India.[55] Proper water management has been found to be associated with the lower malaria occurrence (e.g. improved drainage system, filling and levelling sites with stagnant water).[49] Proper environment modifications have shown the significant decrease in the prevalence of vector-borne diseases in India.[24,49] Proper access of appropriate healthcare facilities, early detection of parasite and awareness towards the malaria infection by intervention programmes targeted against the spread of malaria, careful search for malarial parasites and urgent supply of anti-malarial drug should be undertaken.[49] There is a need for new indoor residual insecticides which has longer residual life or complete coverage of population with long lasting insecticide treated nets for effective vector control.[28,37] The improving community-level knowledge about malaria using culturally-appropriate healthcare education materials; making traditional healers partners in malaria control; promoting within-village rapid diagnosis and treatment facilities will be helpful to reduce the prevalence of malaria.[55] Proper implementation of healthcare facilities, knowledge, awareness and treatment related to malaria transmission should be implemented at the community level.[49] The active participation of the individual and the community level is also warranted to reduce the malaria prevalence across the nation. The environment modifications are essential in order to reduce the malaria transmission and vector prevalence.[28,49] The use of appropriate and effective insecticides and insect repellents should be ensured for the protection of vector-borne diseases. The effective environment management plays a crucial role in malaria control and more research to identify specific environmental management measures for reduction of vector or vector-people contact is suggested. It has been recommended to develop environmental control strategies as a long-term strategy to reduce the malaria prevalence and transmission intensity which in turn would place less reliance on the heavy use of anti-malarials and insecticides and then to assess reduction in clinical malaria.

Conclusion

Malaria is generally well-known for its debilitating and impoverishing consequences and, therefore, estimation of the true burden and controls are essential to addressing these issues with the final aim to improve the human resource.[4] This review paper provides the evidence based on trends in the prevalence of malaria risks in Indian populations in general and north-eastern state in particular and argues that more systematic, timely, and empirically-based approaches are urgently needed to track the rapidly evolving landscape of the variability and transmission of malaria. The present paper has also highlighted that despite comprehensive malaria control programmes, the reduction rate, intervention and control of such malaria prevalence were found to be significantly unsatisfactory and inadequate in Indian regions, Moreover, the targeted interventions are basically needed to reduce the overall malaria disease burden and vector activities in the malaria affected areas in India. These are hyper-endemic malaria prevalence and transmission rates are comparable to those found in many regions of the globe. Therefore, an individual and community based malaria protection measures, development of appropriate knowledge and awareness at individual and community level will certainly reduce the malaria prevalence and transmission, could be very important and effective measure to improve the overall conditions in the highly endemic areas. A multidisciplinary approach that integrates clinical and field studies with advanced laboratory, molecular, and genomic methods will provide a powerful combination for malaria control and prevention in India.

REFERENCES

1. World Health Organisation (WHO), *World Malaria Report: 2013*, Switzerland: World Health Organisation, 2013, pp. 1–199.

2. Gething, P.W., et al., 'A long neglected world malaria map: Plasmodium vivax endemicity in 2010', PLoS Negl Trop Dis, Vol. 6, No. 9,e1814, 2012, [doi: 10.1371/journal.pntd.0001814].
3. Snow, R.W., et al., 'The global distribution of clinical episodes of Plasmodium falci-parum malaria' *Nature,* Vol. 434, No. 3, 2005, pp. 214–217.
4. Kumar A, et al., 'Burden of Malaria in India: Retrospective and Prospective View' *American Journal of Tropical and Medical Hygiene,* Vol. 77, No. 6, 2007, pp. 69–78.
5. Das, A., et al., 'Malaria in India: The Centre for the Study of Complex Malaria in India' *Acta Tropica,* Vol. 121, No. 3, 2012, pp. 267-73.
6. Singh, N., Kataria, O., and Singh, M.P., 'The Changing Dynamics of Plasmodium Vivax and P. falciparum in Central India: Trends Over a 27-Year Period (1975–2002)' *Vector Borne Zoonotic Disease,* Vol. 4, No. 3, 2004, pp. 239–248.
7. Singh, N., et al., 'Changing Scenario of Malaria in Central India: The Replacement of Plasmodium vivax by Plasmodium falciparum (1986–2000)' *Tropical Medicine and International Health,* Vol. 9, No. 3, 2004, p. 364–71.
8. Dhingra, N., et al., 'Adult and Child Malaria Mortality in India' *Lancet,* Vol. 376, No. 9754, 2010, pp. 1768–74.
9. Kar, N.P., et al., 'A Review of Malaria Transmission Dynamics in Forest Ecosystems' *Parasite and Vectors,* Vol. 9, No. 6, 2014, p. 265. doi: 10.1186/1756-3305-7-265.
10. Dev, V., et al., 'Physiographic and Entomologic Risk Factors of Malaria in Assam, India', *American Journal of Tropical and Medical Hygiene,* Vol. 71, No. 4, 2004, pp. 451-456.
11. Mishra N., et al., 'Declining Efficacy of Artesunate Plus Sulphadoxine-pyrimethamine in Northeastern India', *Malaria Journal,* Vol. 22, No. 1, 2014, p. 13, 284 [doi: 10.1186/1475-2875-13-284].
12. Dev, V., Hira, C.R., and Rajkhowa, M.K. 'Malaria Attributable Morbidity in Assam, Northeastern India', *Annals of Tropical Medicine and Parasitology,* Vol. 95, No. 8, 2001, pp. 789–796.
13. Dua, V.K., Kar, P.K., and Sharma, V.P. 'Chloroquine Resistant Plasmodium vivax Malaria in India', *Tropical Medicine and International Health,* Vol. 1, No. 6, 1996, pp. 816-819.
14. Acharya, A.R., et al., 'Trend of Malaria Incidence in the State of Karnataka, India for 2001 to 2011', *Archives of Applied Science Research,* Vol. 5, No. 3, 2013, pp. 104–111.

15. Dev V., 'Malaria Survey in Tarajulie Tea Estate and Adjoining Hamlets in Sonitpur District, Assam', *Indian Journal of Malariology*, Vol. 33, No. 1, 1996, pp. 21–29.
16. Dutta, J., et al., 'Malaria—Resurgence and Problems', *Indian Journal and Community Medicine*, Vol. 29, No. 1, 2004, pp. 171–172.
17. Mohapatra, P.K., et al., 'Detection and Molecular Confirmation of a focus of Plasmodium Malariae in Arunachal Pradesh, India', *Indian Journal of Medical Research*, Vol. 128, No. 1, 2008, pp. 52-56.
18. Dhiman, S., et al., 'Malaria Epidemiology along Indo-Bangladesh Border in Tripura State, India.' *Southeast Asian Journal of Tropical Medicine and Public Health*, Vol. 41, No. 6, 2010, pp. 1279–89.
19. Dev, V., Bhattacharyya, P.C., and Talukdar, R. 'Transmission of Malaria and its Control in the Northeastern Region of India', *Journal Association of Physician India*, Vol. 51, No. 11 , 2003, pp. 1073–76.
20. Rabha, B., et al., 'A Cross Sectional Investigation of Malaria epidemiology Among Seven Tea Estates in Assam, India', *Journal of Parasitic Diseases*, Vol. 36, No. 1, 2012, pp. 1-6.
21. Kumar, S. and Debbarma, A. 'Predictors of Knowledge Towards Malaria of Rural Tribal Communities in Dhalai District of Tripura, India', *Mymensingh Medical Journal*, Vol. 22, No. 4, 2013, pp. 825-832.
22. Garg, B.S., 'Epidemiological Situation of Malaria in South East Asia with Focus on India', *Indian Journal of Clinical Biochemistry*, Vol. 12, No. 1, 1997, pp. 44-48.
23. Dev, V., Dash, A.P., and Khound, K., 'High Risk Areas of Malaria and Prioritizing Interventions in Assam', *Current Sciences*, Vol. 90, No. 1, 2006, pp. 32-36.
24. Sharma, S.K., Pradhan, P., and Padhi, D.M., 'Socio-economic Factors Associated with Malaria in a Tribal Area of Orissa, India' *Indian Journal of Public Health*, Vol. 45, No. 3, 2001, pp. 93-98.
25. Singh, T.G., Singh, R.K., and Singh, E.Y. 'A Study of Knowledge About Malaria and Treatment Seeking Behaviour in Two Tribal Communities of Manipur' *Indian Journal of Public Health*, Vol. 47, No. 2, 2003, pp. 61-65.
26. Dev, V. and Phookan, S. 'Malaria Prevalence in Tea Estates of Brahmaputra Valley of Assam, India', *Journal of Parasite Dissease*, Vol. 20, No. 2, 1996, pp. 189–192.
27. Shiv, Lal., and Sonal, G.S., and Phukan, P.K. 'Status of Malaria in India', *Indian Academy of Clinical.Medicine*, Vol. 5, No. 1, 2000, pp. 19-23.

28. Gogoi, S.C., et al., 'Susceptibility of Plasmodium falciparum to chloroquine in Tea Garden Tribes of Assam, India', *'Southeast Asian Journal of Tropical Medicine and Public Health,* Vol. 26, No. 2, 1995, pp. 228–230.
29. Garg, A., et al., 'Development, Malaria and Adaptation to Climate Change: A Case Study from India', *Environment Management,* Vol. 43, No. 5, 2009, pp. 779-789.
30. Dhiman, R.C., 'Emerging Vector-borne Zoonoses: Eco-epidemiology and Public Health Implications in India', *Front Public Health,* Vol. 30, No. 2, 2014, p. 168.
31. Saxena, R., et al., 'Impact of Deforestation on Known Malaria Vectors in Sonitpur District of Assam, India', *Journal of Vector Borne Disease,* Vol. 51, No. 3, 2014, pp. 211-215.
32. Nath, D.C., and Mwchahary, D.D. 'Association Between Climatic Variables and Malaria Incidence: A Study in Kokrajhar District of Assam, India' *Global Journal of Health Science,* Vol. 5, No. 1, 2012, pp. 90-106.
33. Sharma, S.K., et al., 'Impact of Changing Over of Insecticide from Synthetic Pyrethroids to DDT for Indoor Residual Spray in a Malaria Endemic Area of Orissa, India', *Indian Journal of Medical Research,* Vol. 135, No. 3, 2012, pp. 382-388.
34. Sarkar, M., et al., 'Insecticide Resistance and Detoxifying Enzyme Activity in the Principal Bancroftian Filariasis Vector, Culex Quinquefasciatus, in Northeastern India', *Medical Vector and Entomology,* Vol. 23, No. 2, 2009, pp. 122-131.
35. Kumar, K., et al., 'Multiple Insecticide Resistance/Susceptibility Status of Culex Quinquefasciatus, Principal Vector of Bancroftian Filariasis from Filaria Endemic Areas of Northern India' *Asian Pacific Journal of Tropical Medical,* Vol. 4, No. 6, 2011, pp. 426-429.
36. Singh, R.K., et al., 'Bionomics and Vectorial Capacity of Anopheles Annularis with Special Reference to India: A Review', *Journal of Community Diseases,* Vol. 45, No. 1-2, 2013, pp. 1-16.
37. Gopalakrishnan, R., Baruah, I., and Veer, V. 'Monitoring of Malaria, Japanese Encephalitis and Filariasis Vectors', *Medical Journal of Armed Forces of India,* Vol. 70, No. 2, 2014, pp. 129-133.
38. Dhiman, S., et al., 'DDT and Deltamethrin Resistance Status of Known Japanese Encephalitis Vectors in Assam, India', *Indian Journal of Medical Research,* Vol. 138, No. 6, 2013, pp. 988-994.
39. Dev, V., Sangma, B.M., and Dash, A.P. 'Persistent Transmission of Malaria in Garo Hills of Meghalaya Bordering Bangladesh, North-east India' *Malaria Journal,* Vol. 9, No. 1, 2010, p. 263.
40. Sehgal, P.N., et al. 'Resistance to Chloroquine in Falciparum

Malaria in Assam State India' *Journal of Communicable Diseases*, Vol. 5, No. 2, 1973, pp. 175–180.

41. Arora, U., et al., 'Emergence of Drug Resistance in India' *Journal of Indian Medical Association*, Vol. 106, No. 10, 2008, pp. 678-681.
42. Baruah, I., Talukdar, P.K., and Das, S.C., 'The Drug Sensitivities of Plasmodium falciparum in the Sonitpur District, Assam, India' *Southeast Asian Journal of Tropical Medicine and Public Health*, Vol. 36, No. 3, 2005, pp. 587-590.
43. Goswami, D., et al., 'Chemotherapy and Drug Resistance Status of Malaria Parasite in northeast India', *Asian Pacific Journal of Tropical Medical*, Vol. 6, No. 7, 2013, pp. 583-588.
44. Ahmed, A., et al., 'Prevalence of Mutations Associated with Higher Levels of Sulfadoxine-pyrimethamine Resistance in Plasmodium Falciparum Isolates from Car Nicobar Island and Assam, India' *Antimicrobal Agents Chemotherapy*, Vol, 50, No. 11, 2006, pp. 3934-3938.
45. Mohapatra, P.K., et al., 'Evaluation of Chloroquine (CQ) and Sulphadoxine/pyrimethamine (SP) Therapy in Uncomplicated Falciparum Malaria in Indo-Myanmar Border Areas', *Tropical Medicine and International Health*, Vol. 10, No. 5, 2005, pp. 478-483.
46. Dua, V.K., Kar, P.K., and Sharma, V.P. 'Chloroquine Resistant Plasmodium Vivax Malaria in India' *Tropical Medicine and International Health*, Vol. 1, No. 6, 1996, pp. 816-819.
47. Prakash, A., et al., 'Malaria Control in a Forest Camp in an Oil Exploration Area of Upper Assam' *National Medical Journal of India*, Vol. 16, No. 3, 2003, pp. 135-138.
48. Prasad, H., 'Evaluation of Malaria Control Programme in Three Selected Districts of Assam, India' *Journal of Vector Borne Disease*, Vol. 46, No. 4, 2009, pp. 280-287.
49. Mahapatra, P., and Chalapati Rao, P.V., 'Cause of Death Reporting Systems in India: A Performance Analysis' *National Medical Journal of India*, Vol. 14, No. 3, 2001, pp. 154-162.
50. Sharma, V.P., 'Re-emergence of Malaria in India', *Indian Journal of Medical Research*, Vol. 103, No. 1, 1996, pp. 26-45.
51. Dambhare, D.G., Nimgade, S.D., and Dudhe, J.Y. 2012. 'Knowledge, Attitude and Practice of Malaria Transmission and its Prevention Among the School Going Adolescents in Wardha District, Central India', *Global Journal of Health Science*, Vol. 4, No. 4, 2012, pp. 76-82.
52. Sharma, A.K., Bhasin, S., and Chaturvedi, S., 'Predictors of Knowledge About Malaria in India', *Journal of Vector Borne Disease*,

Vol. 44, No. 3, 2007, pp. 189-197.

53. Vijayakumar, K.N., et al., 'Knowledge, Attitude and Practice on Malaria: A Study in a Tribal Belt of Orissa State, India with Reference to Use of Long Lasting Treated Mosquito Nets' *Acta Tropical,* Vol. 112, No. 2, 2009, pp. 137-142.
54. Sundararajan, R., et al. 'Barriers to Malaria Control Among Marginalized Tribal Communities: A Qualitative Study', *PLoS One,* Vol. 8, No. 1, 2013, p. e81966 [doi: 10.1371/journal.pone.0081966].
55. Dasgupta, T., et al. 'Exploiting Structural Analysis, in Silico Screening, and Serendipity to Identify Novel Inhibitors of Drug-Resistant Falciparum Malaria', *ACS Chemical Biology,* Vol. 4, No. 1, 2009, pp. 29-40.

List of Contributors

1. **Vulli Dhanaraju,** Assistant Professor, Department of History, Assam University (Central University), Diphu Campus, Assam.
2. **Manash Mazumdar,** Assistant Professor, Department of History, Lumding College, Assam.
3. **Nandini Sinha Kapur**, Eminent Historian and Director, School of Interdisciplinary and Trans-disciplinary Studies, Indira Gandhi National Open University (IGNOU), New Delhi.
4. **Hashik N.K.,** Assistant Professor, Department of Cultural Studies, Tezpur University, Assam.
5. **Samuel Berthet**, Professor, Department of Sociology, School of Humanities and Social Sciences, Shiv Nadar University, Noida.
6. **Geetashree Singh,** Post Doctoral Scholar, Department of History, Assam University, Silchar, Assam.
7. **Dinjangam Riamei,** Doctoral Scholar, Department of History, Department of History, Assam University, Silchar, Assam.
8. **Pradip Chattopadhyay,** Professor, Department of History, University of Burdwan, West Bengal.
9. **Reep Pandi Lepcha,** Research Fellow under the Ryorchi Sasakawa Young Leaders Fellowship Fund (SYLFF), Department of English, Jadavpur University, Kolkata, West Bengal.
10. **Resenmenla Longchar,** Assistant Professor, Department of History, ICFAI University, Nagaland.

11. **Ngamjahao Kipgen,** Assistant Professor, Department of Humanities and Social Sciences, Indian Institute of Technology (IIT), Guwahati, Assam.
12. **Abhinandan Saikia,** Assistant Professor, Tata Institute of Social Sciences (TISS), Guwahati Campus, Assam.
13. **V. Raj Mahammadh,** Assistant Professor and Head, Department of History, Government Degree and PG College, Kadiri, Anantapuram, Andhra Pradesh.
14. **Nitish Mondal,** Assistant Professor, Department of Anthropology, Assam University, Diphu Campus, Assam.

Index